BTEC Tech Award

# CHILD DEVELOPMENT

Student Book

Second Edition

Hayley Marshall-Gowen

Diane Walker-Cairns

Heather Higgins

Published by Pearson Education Limited, 80 Strand, London, WC2R 0RL.

www.pearsonschoolsandfecolleges.co.uk

Copies of official specifications for all Pearson qualifications may be found on the website: qualifications.pearson.com

Text © Pearson Education Limited 2022
Editorial by QBS Learning
Typeset by QBS Learning
Original illustrations © Pearson Education Limited 2022

First published 2019
Second edition published 2022

23
10 9 8 7 6 5 4

**British Library Cataloguing in Publication Data**
A catalogue record for this book is available from the British Library

ISBN 978 1 292 44459 8

**Acknowledgements**
The publisher would like to thank the following for their kind permission to reproduce their photographs:

(Key: b-bottom; c-centre; l-left; r-right; t-top)

**Cover**: Sturti/E+/Getty Images

**Component 1: 123RF:** Mario Ondris p.4, Andrei Afanasiev p.27(tl), Zoya Fedorova p.36, Jasmin Merdan p.51; **Alamy Stock Photo:** Sanjeevi v p.27(tr), Steve Prezant/Image Source p.27(bl), Chuck Franklin p.27(br), Amelia Ayaoge p.41; **Imagestate:** John Fox collection p.37; **Pearson Education Ltd:** Jules Selmes p.8(tr) and 21, Roddy Paine p.10; **Shutterstock:** 2xSamara.com p.3, Natee K Jindakum p.5, Zulufoto p.8(tl), Marlon Lopez MMG1 Design p.8(bl), Tom Wang p.8(br), Eurobanks p.12, Antonio Guillem p.23, Zyn Chakrapong p.26, Nikodash p.38(b), Wavebreakmedia p.38(t), Donot6 Studio p.39, Yuliya Evstratenko p.44, ArtOfPhotos p.46, Olga Enger p.49, FamVeld p.53, Shutterstock p.30, p.42 and p.54.

**Component 2: 123RF:** Rawpixel/123RF p.64, Wong sze yuen/123RF p.98; **Getty Images:** SolStock/E+/Getty Images p.69, Jupiterimages/Stockbyte/Getty Images p.117; **Pearson Education Ltd:** Roddy Paine/Pearson Education Ltd p.62, Jules Selmes/Pearson Education Ltd P.63, P.65, P.78, p.84, 85, 88, 90, 102(l), 105, 107, 108 & 112, Rob Judges/Pearson Education Ltd p.102(r), Lord and Leverett/Pearson Education Ltd p.114(t); **Shutterstock:** KK Tan/Shutterstock p.61, DenisProduction.com/Shutterstock p.66, Seeme/Shutterstock p.70, Anneka/Shutterstock p.76, George Filyagin/Shutterstock p.80, Chonrawit boonprakob/Shutterstock p.81, Yulya Shilova/Shutterstock p.82, Eric Broder Van Dyke/Shutterstock p.86, DGLimages/Shutterstock p.92, Artem Efimov/Shutterstock p.95, Zurijeta/Shutterstock p.96, Karen H. Ilagan/Shutterstock p.110, Kelly MacDonald/Shutterstock p.113, Cristina Annibali/Shutterstock p.114(b).

**Component 3: 123RF:** Alona Stepaniuk/123RF p.147(tc), Klavdiia Prokusheva/123RF p.147(tr), Wavebreak Media Ltd /123RF p.170; **Alamy Stock Photo:** Carolyn Jenkins/Alamy Stock Photo p.147(bl), CBsigns/Alamy Stock Photo p.147(bc), Zefrog/Alamy Stock Photo p.147(br), MediaWorldImages/Alamy Stock Photo p.159, ZUMA Press, Inc/Alamy Stock Photo p.181; **Agefotostock:** Brand X Pictures/SuperStock/Agefotostock p.187; **BTHA:** Lion Mark, used with permission from British Toy and Hobby Association p.147(tl); **Getty Images:** Jasmin Merdan/Moment/Getty Images P.178; **Pearson Education Ltd:** Jules Selmes/Pearson Education Ltd p.156, 171, 172 & 177, Studio 8/Pearson Education Ltd p.157; **Shutterstock:** Jaren Jai Wicklund/Shutterstock p.121, Kamira/Shutterstock p.122, Jaimie Duplass/Shutterstock p.123, Thomas M Perkins/Shutterstock p.125, Melpomene/Shutterstock p.127, Wavebreakmedia/Shutterstock p.128, Rob Hainer/Shutterstock p.131, MIA Studio/Shutterstock p.132, Unguryanu/Shutterstock p.133, Stockyimages/Shutterstock p.134, Ann in the uk/Shutterstock p.137, Antos777/Shutterstock p.138(l), Steve Heap/Shutterstock p.138(r), Gundam_Ai/Shutterstock p.142, New Africa/Shutterstock p.144, Nolte Lourens/Shutterstock p.145, Ucchie79/Shutterstock p.148, Milatas/Shutterstock p.149, Champion studio/Shutterstock p.150, Africa Studio/Shutterstock p.153, PhotoMavenStock/Shutterstock p.155, Oleg Mikhaylov/Shutterstock p.165(t), Vladvm/Shutterstock p.165(b), Stephen Denness/Shutterstock p.174(l), Lori Martin/Shutterstock p.174(c), Glenda/Shutterstock p.174(r), Robert Kneschke/Shutterstock p.176, Photka/Shutterstock p.182, Thomas M Perkins/Shutterstock p.185.

All other images © Pearson Education

**Websites**
Pearson Education Limited is not responsible for the content of any external internet sites. It is essential for teachers to preview each website before using it in class so as to ensure that the URL is still accurate, relevant and appropriate. We suggest that teachers bookmark useful websites and consider enabling learners to access them through the school/college intranet.

**Notes from the publisher**
Pearson has robust editorial processes, including answer and fact checks, to ensure the accuracy of the content in this publication, and every effort is made to ensure this publication is free of errors. We are, however, only human, and occasionally errors do occur. Pearson is not liable for any misunderstandings that arise as a result of errors in this publication, but it is our priority to ensure that the content is accurate. If you spot an error, please do contact us at resourcescorrections@pearson.com so we can make sure it is corrected.

# Contents

# CONTENTS

# About this book

This book is designed to support you when you are taking a BTEC Tech Award in Child Development.

## About your BTEC Tech Award

Congratulations on choosing a BTEC Tech Award in Child Development. This exciting and challenging course will introduce you to the early years sector. The early years sector focuses on the learning, development and care of children from birth to 5 years. In the UK, there are approximately 2 million childcare places for children aged under 5 and many different types of early years settings, ranging from childminders and nannies to nurseries, crèches and pre-schools. Knowledge of child development is also important in a variety of healthcare roles, such as paediatricians, psychologists, occupational therapists, and speech and language therapists.

## How you will be assessed

You will be assessed in two different ways. Components 1 and 2 are assessed through internal assessment. This means that you will be given an assignment brief that has been produced by Pearson and you will be given a deadline for completing it. The assignment will cover what you have been learning about and will be an opportunity to apply your knowledge and skills. Your teacher will mark and moderate your assignment and award you with a grade. Your third assessment (for Component 3) will be an external assessment. This will be an exam that is set and marked by Pearson. You will have a set time in which to complete this exam. The assessment will be an opportunity to bring together what you have learnt in Components 1 and 2.

## About the authors

**Hayley Marshall-Gowen** worked in the early years sector before becoming a lecturer in further education. She went on to become Head of Childcare at a secondary school and has also been an examiner for childcare qualifications. She now works in regulation and inspection. Hayley has written several books and teaching resources, and enjoys seeing students develop into confident practitioners.

**Diane Walker-Cairns** has been working with young people for over 15 years. She began volunteering with young offenders, offering support and guidance with a view to getting them back into education to improve their outcomes. She qualified as a teacher two years ago and has since taught health and social care, child development, psychology and sociology, successfully increasing knowledge and skills to support all in their future career pathway.

**Heather Higgins** is a qualified nurse with several years' experience of supporting children and babies with a variety of medical conditions. She has also worked with children under 5 who have additional needs, including those who have experienced accidental and intentional trauma.

While her own children were young, Heather worked as a registered childminder and volunteered in playgroups and summer play schemes. Heather has a BA (Hons) in Applied Social Studies, a PGCE and an MEd in Human Relations. She taught Child Care and Health and Social Care up to Higher National Level and is now the Pearson Senior Standards Verifier for Health and Social Care. Heather is also a volunteer childcare worker at her local church, supporting a play and learning programme for children 0–5 years from a variety of home backgrounds.

# How to use this book

The book has been designed in a way that will help you to easily navigate through your course. Each component of the course is covered in a separate chapter that makes clear what you are learning and how this will contribute to your assessment. There are opportunities for you to test your understanding of key areas, as well as activities that will challenge and extend your knowledge and skills. You will get the most from this book if you use each feature as part of your study. The different features will also help you develop the skills that will be important in completing your assignments as well as preparing you for your external assessment.

## Features of the book

This book is designed in spreads, which means that each pair of facing pages represents a topic of learning. Each spread is about 1 hour of lesson time. Your teacher may ask you to work through a spread during a lesson or in your own time. Each spread contains a number of features that will help you to check what you are learning and offer opportunities to practise new skills.

**Getting started** A short activity or discussion that will introduce you to what you will be covering in the lesson.

**Activity** These will help you learn about the topic. You may be asked to work in pairs, groups or on your own.

**Best practice** Hints and tips to embed good or best practice in a real-world or workplace context, to add a workplace dimension and make learning relevant to practice.

**Did you know?** These include interesting facts that relate to what you're learning about.

**Link it up** This indicates where what you're learning about is covered in another part of the course.

**Key terms** Important words or terms are defined.

**Check my learning** This is an opportunity to check back over what you have learnt. It may be a discussion or homework activity.

At the end of each learning outcome there is a section that outlines how you will be assessed and provides opportunities for you to build skills for assessment.

**Assessment Activity** This is a practice assessment that reflects the style and approach of an assignment brief. In Component 3, tasks in the assessment activity features will be similar to those you should expect in your external assessment.

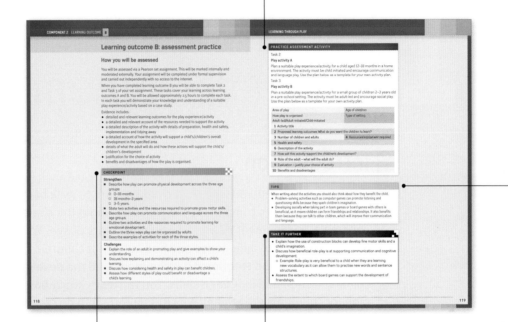

**Tip** A hint or tip that will help you with your assessment.

**Checkpoint** This feature is designed to allow you to assess your learning. The 'strengthen' question helps you to check your knowledge and understanding of what you have been studying, while the 'challenge' questions are an opportunity to extend your learning.

**Take it further** This provides suggestions for what you can do to further the work you've done in the practice assessment.

# 01 Children's Growth and Development

## Introduction

Have you ever wondered why most children learn to walk before they learn to talk? In this component you will learn about the characteristics of children's development between birth and 5 years of age. You will learn about development milestones and find out about children's physical, cognitive, social and emotional development, and the development of their communication and language skills. You will learn about how professionals monitor children's growth and why it is important to do so. You will also explore the factors that can influence a child's rate of growth and development.

You will examine how physical influences, such as ill health and diet, can affect children's development. You will learn about how environment, such as poor housing, can have long-term effects on children's growth and development. Lastly, you will investigate how social and financial factors, such as the provision of early education, can influence children's development.

## LEARNING OUTCOMES

In this component you will:

| | |
|---|---|
| A | understand the principles of growth and development |
| B | understand how factors impact on children's overall development. |

# Growth

## KEY TERM

**Growth** an increase in size and mass.

- The newborn skull has two small areas where the bones have not fused, called fontanelles. These gaps usually close at around 6 months of age.

## DID YOU KNOW?

Young babies' skulls are so soft that their heads can become misshapen if they always lie in the same way in their cot or in a car seat. This is known as 'flat head syndrome'.

## KEY TERMS

**Proportion** the extent of something considered in comparison to something else.

**Consistent** remaining the same over time.

**Circumference** the distance around something, in this case, the baby's head.

There is a wide range of 'normal' when it comes to growth. A person's size, shape and weight depend on multiple factors.

You might be the same age as your classmates, but have you noticed that your heights vary greatly?

## Changes to physical size

**Growth** is an increase in size and mass. It is something that can be measured. The body of a newborn is very different to that of an adult. The head is disproportionately large in size compared to the rest of its body. This is because it contains a brain that by time the baby is 9 months old is already half the size of a full-grown adult's brain. Newborns have just enough strength and control over their muscles to move their head from side to side. However, they are unable to hold up their own head, so an adult must support their head when holding them.

### Bone changes

Babies have more bones than adults. They are born with approximately 300 bones, whereas adults have just 206. Their bodies need to be soft and flexible to withstand being squeezed down the birth canal during birth. As they grow, their bones harden and some small segments of bone fuse together to make larger bones.

Children grow rapidly from birth to the age of 5. The areas of the body that grow most quickly in young children are the skeleton, the muscles and the brain. Children increase in weight and height and the circumference of their head gets bigger.

Table 1.1 gives some comparisons of growth between a newborn and a 5-year-old.

 Table 1.1: Comparisons of growth between a newborn and a 5-year-old

| Newborn | 5-year-old |
| --- | --- |
| Large head in comparison to body | Head more in **proportion** to body |
| Weak muscles unable to lift own head | Able to co-ordinate movements and use muscles |
| Length around 50 cm | Height around 113 cm |
| Weight around 3.4 kg | Weight around 20.4 kg |

## How growth is measured and recorded

Measuring children's growth is important to check their growth is **consistent** and they are developing as expected. However, it is also important that health professionals monitor children's all-round health. This helps to identify any possible concerns early on and make sure that support can be given to the child as soon as possible if needed.

Growth is measured in several ways:
- weighing the child
- measuring length and then height (once the child can stand up)
- measuring head **circumference**.

These measurements are carried out as soon as babies are born, and repeated at regular intervals until the health professionals are satisfied that the child is growing well. They can assess this by using a developmental chart (or centile chart). This is a graph where health professionals can mark children's development (height and weight) on a line that plots the growth pattern that is expected. If the marks they make over time do not follow the line, the child's growth is not following an expected pattern. For example, this might be because they are not gaining weight.

A child's centile charts are found in the Personal Child Health Record (PCHR), or Red Book. This is where all the information about a child's growth and development is stored. Unlike other health records, parents and carers own their child's Red Book. This means they can share the information with any new professionals the child needs to see, such as consultants at a hospital. Parents and carers often like to keep their own growth records, such as by measuring a child's height against a door frame.

**ACTIVITY**

Using the internet, research centile charts. What information do they show?

Do you still own your 'Red Book'?

## The 2-year-old's check

One way health professionals check children's development is to offer a health check for all children aged around 2 years. Often, the health visiting team will start to review a child's development at home, as this helps the parent or carer and child feel more comfortable. They will provide parents with an Ages and Stages Questionnaire or ASQ-3. Usually the health visitor will then regularly visit the child or might invite them to the local clinic. The 2-year-old's check also helps parents and carers to look after children's health at home. Figure 1.1 illustrates the different areas covered in the 2-year-old's health check.

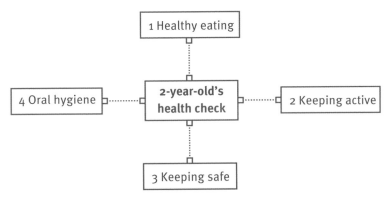

◧ It is important to brush babies' teeth as soon as they grow in at between six months to a year.

◧ Figure 1.1: The 2-year-old's health check.

## The National Child Measurement Programme (NCMP)

This is a national programme to measure the height and weight of children aged 4 to 5 years old in the reception year at school. It tells a national picture of levels of early childhood obesity by calculating a body mass index centile.

To work out body mass index, or BMI, you calculate weight in kilograms divided by the square of height in metres. This helps to work out how much fat an individual has.

The information obtained through the NCMP is used to help plan for services and support to help target the underlying reasons for obesity – for example, by helping families to understand the importance of a balanced diet. It can also help with planning facilities and services, such as leisure centres and support groups.

# Roles and responsibilities of individuals involved in measuring and monitoring growth

**GETTING STARTED**

Identify three reasons why growth might be measured in children and give the reasons for this.

It is essential for doctors and healthcare professionals, such as health visitors, to measure a child's growth. This helps them to make sure that the child is developing well, and to identify any possible signs of ill health or disability. It will also show whether the child's growth is consistent with the expected patterns.

## Health professionals

A midwife looks after women before their baby is born, during birth and immediately after birth.

Midwives need to know the size of the baby prior to birth. A radiographer will do an **ultrasound scan**. This is used to measure the size of unborn babies.

It is important for midwives to measure the growth of the unborn baby for the following reasons:

- Babies that appear small for their **gestation** might have an underlying medical condition.
- A large baby might need assistance to be born, such as by **caesarean section**.
- A large baby might be an indication that the mother has diabetes.
- Some disabilities might present in differences in size.

At birth, the medical team will measure the babies' growth. This is to confirm that their growth is as expected. Health visitors or general practitioners (GPs) will then check these measurements regularly to make sure the child is growing well. They will use the centile chart in the Red Book to record this information.

## Social care workers

Sometimes a social worker or family support worker might need to review and monitor a child's growth. This might be because there are concerns about the parent or carer's ability to meet the basic needs of the child. An example might be where a parent has **neglected** their child. Social workers might monitor the growth of a child if there is a concern about the child's health or the family are having extra support.

## Early years educators

Early years educators do not formally measure children's growth. However, a childminder, nursery manager or the child's key person might observe that a child has lost weight when they are caring for them. This could indicate that there is a problem. It could be that the parents are neglectful, abusive or finding it difficult to afford to feed their child. It could be that the child has an illness.

Early years educators might also notice if a child had gained weight. They might be able to offer the family advice on healthy eating and encourage the child to be more active to help them to develop a healthy lifestyle.

## Parents and carers

Parents and carers want to be assured that their child is growing well. They will probably not formally measure their children's growth. However, they might notice their child is getting bigger in size and is growing out of their clothes. This is a good way for parents to be certain that their child is getting enough nourishment. Parents might observe children's growth when they look longer in their cot, for example, or, once they are walking, if they have to start to duck when walking underneath the dinner table.

**KEY TERMS**

**Ultrasound scan** a high-frequency sound wave that creates an image on a screen of inside the body.

**Gestation** the period of time during which the baby develops in the womb.

**Caesarean section** birth through an incision made in the abdomen.

**Neglect** the failure to care for a child properly.

**BEST PRACTICE**

Health visitors must try to maintain good relationships with parents and families to ensure they are effectively supporting them and their babies.

**LINK IT UP**

You can find out more about the effects of poverty and low income on pages 54–55.

# Importance of measuring growth

Measuring growth is important to tell parents and carers that their child is growing well. By using charts and expected patterns, professionals are able to identify any issues at an early stage. Table 1.2 outlines some possible growth concerns. Steady weight gain is usually a sign that children are healthy.

☐ **Table 1.2: Growth concerns and reasons**

| Growth concern | Possible reason for concern |
|---|---|
| Newborn is smaller than expected | The baby might be premature or has not received sufficient nutrients in the womb. |
| Baby is not gaining weight | The child is not getting enough milk. This could be due to issues with breastfeeding or bottle feeding. |
| Baby fails to gain weight over time | There could be an underlying medical condition or illness. It could be that parents are not meeting the child's needs, or the child is a victim of neglect. |
| Child is gaining weight too quickly | The child might have an unhealthy diet or is not getting enough exercise. |

## Summary of growth

There are different expectations for children's growth at different ages that are shown on the centile charts for weight and height. By the time babies are around 4 months old, they have usually doubled their birth weight. At around 6 to 9 months, babies will gain weight rapidly and might have a rounded appearance. This is completely normal. By 1–2 years of age, children will become mobile. As they are more active, their weight gain will slow down.

Unless there is a concern about children's weight or height, from the age of 2 years children will probably not be measured by professionals. However, professionals might want to continue to monitor a child's weight and height if the child is overweight. This is because being overweight can have a significant impact on children's health and wellbeing and make them prone to illness. Professionals can help to advise parents and carers about children's diet and physical activity.

Children who are underweight might need to have health checks to make sure that they do not have a medical condition. If there is no medical condition, parents and carers might need advice about healthy eating and support to ensure that their child can put on weight.

**LINK IT UP**

You can find out more about childhood obesity and nutrition on pages 39–40.

**CHECK MY LEARNING**

Under each heading, complete a brief description of how and why each person might monitor children's growth.

1 Health visitors
2 Social workers
3 Early years educators
4 Parents

**ACTIVITY**

Look at the following case study.

*When Arun was weighed at birth, he was smaller than expected.*

*At 6 months old, the health visitor noticed that Arun was not following the expected line for his birth weight and weighed less than at his 4-month-old health check.*

1 What might the health visitor expect to see when she plots Arun's growth on a development chart?

2 Why do you think the GP might be concerned about the health visitor's findings in relation to Arun's growth?

Evaluate what could be the reason for Arun's pattern of growth.

# The principles of development

How do you know everything you know today?

You have seen, heard, watched and understood. Over time, you have mastered new skills and learned new things. This is how you have developed.

Although everyone develops at a different rate, generally, **development** follows a pattern or a consistent sequence as shown in the following pictures.

◘ Although children develop at different rates, it would be unlikely that a child could write their name before they learned to walk.

## Milestones

A child's ability to learn new things is dependent on many different factors. Some children pick up new skills quickly while others might need to practise something new several times before they can accomplish it. But even though children develop at different rates, the stages they go through usually follow the same sequence or pattern. For ease, professionals tend to separate children's development into different areas so it can be identified and assessed more easily. These are often separated into stages according to the age at which they are most likely to happen. These are called **milestones**.

### Developmental milestones

As with growth, there is a wide range of what is considered to be 'normal' development. Developmental milestones (also called developmental norms) are worked out by studying groups of children. The study will take into account all children's significant development and then find an **average** (usually the **mean**). Why do you think some children might have a slower rate of development than others?

◘ Table 1.3: An example of how developmental milestones could be worked out

| How developmental milestones are worked out |
|---|
| Twenty children are studied to see when they take their first steps.<br>• One child takes their first steps at the age of 9 months.<br>• Three children take their first steps at 11 months.<br>• Six children take their first steps at 12 months.<br>• Six children take their first steps at 14 months.<br>• Three children take their first steps at 18 months.<br>• One child takes their first steps at 20 months.<br>By calculating the mean, we learn that the average age for children to take their first steps in this study is 14 months. However, anywhere between 9 months and 20 months would be considered 'normal'. |

## Who uses developmental milestones?

Young children's development is generally formally measured by early years professionals (such as nursery staff and childminders). This is because they are responsible for supporting children's learning and need to see whether children are making good progress. They might review children's development by observing them. They will then use developmental milestones, such as the Department for Education's version, which is called Early Years Outcomes. This enables them to see whether children's development is progressing as they would expect.

### ACTIVITY

Look at the case study below.

*Ella is 8 months old. She was born full term and is making good progress. She can now sit up by herself and is starting to reach for objects.*

Carry out some research to find out what Ella's next developmental milestones are likely to be.

### BEST PRACTICE

Developmental milestones are tracked against Early Years Outcomes by early years educators. The key person for a child must keep organised records of that child's developmental progress.

## Holistic development

Children's development is **holistic** in the sense that it rarely occurs in one area alone. Even something that appears straightforward, such as walking, still requires development in other areas. Children will not walk unless they have the desire to. If a child is encouraged to walk and praised for trying, they may persevere in order to please their parent or carer. This is a good example of where physical and emotional development are linked.

### KEY TERM

**Holistic** made up of parts that are interconnected.

## Summary of growth and development

- There is a wide range of what is considered to be normal growth and development.
- Development is holistic; developing in one area supports progress in other areas of development.
- Growth and development are measured to ensure that children make good progress.
- A child's growth and development does not usually follow a rigid pattern, but by having expected patterns, professionals can quickly identify any potential issues.

### CHECK MY LEARNING

Design a poster or information leaflet about development milestones.

You need to include the following information.

1 How development milestones can be used to help measure children's progress.

2 Why one person might use development milestones.

# Development across ages of birth to 18 months: physical development

**GETTING STARTED**

Work in a small group to make a list of all the things that a newborn baby can do.

Discuss what parents or carers must do for a newborn baby in the first hours of its life.

**KEY TERMS**

**Full term** a baby that is born at or around 40 weeks of pregnancy.

**Primitive** belonging to an earlier stage of historical development. Primitive reflexes are possibly left-over skills needed before humans evolved.

◘ It is helpful to think about young children's physical development as top to toe. Physical development generally starts with gaining control of the head and moves down the body to the toes and walking.

Have you ever thought about what a newborn baby can do?

Newborn humans appear pretty helpless. They need someone to meet all of their basic needs in order to survive. However, despite this apparent vulnerability, newborn babies are born with an impressive set of skills.

## Infant or primitive reflexes

Babies born on or around **full term** have **primitive** reflexes. These reflexes are apparent immediately after they are born. Midwives or doctors check the reflexes to confirm that the baby is well and their central nervous system is working. It is thought that these reflexes originate from a time when humans were much less evolved and so these reflexes helped the baby to survive in the early stages of life. Primative reflexes generally disappear around the age of 2 to 6 months, when babies make more deliberate actions and movements.

Table 1.4 shows what amazing reflexes a newborn baby is born with.

◘ Table 1.4: Newborn babies' amazing reflexes and the reasons these reflexes exist

| Reflex | Description | Possible reason for reflex |
|---|---|---|
| Sucking reflex | The newborn will automatically suck on anything that touches the roof of their mouth, such as a nipple or teat of a bottle. | This is a survival instinct so that the baby can feed as soon as they are born. |
| Startle reflex (also known as Moro reflex) | If the baby's head is suddenly moved or they hear a loud noise, they fling their arms and legs in the air and make a grasping movement. Often, they will cry straight afterwards. | Mothers often carry their newborns around. If the baby is slipping from their grasp, this response might alert the new mother that she is about to drop the baby. |
| Walking or stepping reflex | If babies' feet come into contact with a flat surface, they will make stepping motions as if walking. | It could be that, when being carried around by their mothers, the baby would be able to hold on and move its body as the mother moved across the ground, helping it to stay clinging on to her. |
| Rooting reflex | When a finger, breast or teat is brushed across the baby's cheek, they will turn their head towards it. | This is another survival instinct. It means that the baby can find the nipple or teat to attach for feeding. |
| Grasp reflex (also known as palmar grasp reflex) | If a finger is placed in the palm of a baby's hand, they will close their fingers tightly around it. So strong is their grasp that they can support their own body weight for a few seconds if gently lifted while over a soft surface. | It is likely that this is again a reflex that enabled babies to tightly grip onto their mothers while being carried. |

## Control over the body

Physical development usually happens in sequence as children's muscles start to strengthen and develop. But all children develop at different rates and in different ways and there is no fixed developmental time-frame for children. Table 1.5 provides more information about the development of 'motor skills'.

■ **Table 1.5: Gross and fine motor skills**

| Gross motor skills | |
|---|---|
| **Head control** | |
| Newborn | The baby's head falls backwards and so an adult must support it when holding the baby. |
| 3 months | The baby now has better control of the muscles in their neck and can hold their head upright for several minutes. |
| 6 months | The baby can now hold their head up fully and turn their head confidently. |
| **Sitting up** | |
| Newborn | If held in a sitting position, the baby will slump forward. |
| 3 months | The baby can sit in a seating position if supported by a seat, parent or carer holding them. |
| 6 to 9 months | The baby will now start to sit up by themselves but will still fall backwards or forwards when they become tired, so needs careful watching. |
| 12 months | The baby will be able to pull themselves to sitting from lying down, or sit down from standing. |
| **Prone position (lying on stomach)** | |
| Newborn | The baby lies on their tummy with their legs and arms drawn into their body. |
| 3 months | The baby can lift their head, and sometimes shoulders, off the floor. |
| 4 to 6 months | The baby will start to roll over or turn. |
| 6 to 9 months | The baby might now be starting to push themselves onto their knees and will start to crawl. |
| 12 to 15 months | Children can get themselves up and down from a lying position. |
| **Walking** | |
| Newborn | The baby has sagging knees and cannot support their own weight. |
| 3 to 6 months | The baby will start to bounce and bear weight when supported by an adult. |
| 9 months | The baby might stand for a few moments when holding on to furniture or someone's hand. |
| 12 to 15 months | The child will be able to walk holding on an adult's hand for balance. After building confidence, children will start to take their first few steps alone, or they might start walking confidently. |
| Fine motor skills | |
| **Using hands** | |
| Newborn | The baby will clench fingers around anything placed in their palm. |
| 3 months | The baby will watch their own hands and fingers as they move them. |
| 6 months | If they see a toy, the baby will now start to reach for it and can hold toys in their hand, letting go and dropping the toy frequently. |
| 9 months | Now the baby can hold toys and pass them from one hand to another, dropping them less often. |
| 12 months | The child will now start to use their forefinger and thumb to pick up tiny objects. They can feed themselves with their fingers and usually find their mouth. |
| 15 months | The child can now grasp a crayon in the fist, although they might swap hands. They can make scribbles on paper. They can now start to hold and drink from an open cup but will spill the drink often. |

## Freedom to move

It is essential that babies and young children have the opportunity to move and stretch their muscles. If babies spend too much time restricted in seats or chairs, they are not able to practise kicking and stretching their arms and legs, which is essential for the healthy development of their muscles.

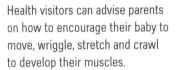

**BEST PRACTICE**

Health visitors can advise parents on how to encourage their baby to move, wriggle, stretch and crawl to develop their muscles.

**ACTIVITY**

Create a presentation to share with your class. You need to demonstrate your knowledge of physical development.

Physical development involves the big muscles in the body (gross motor skills) and the smaller muscles in the hands (fine motor skills). For a baby aged 0–18 months, suggest:

- one suitable activity or toy that will support their fine motor skills
- one suitable activity or toy that will support their gross motor skills.

Suggest how the toys might help to promote the baby's physical development.

**CHECK MY LEARNING**

Write a sequence of physical development for a newborn baby up to the age of 18 months.

You could choose to divide this into gross motor skills and fine motor skills.

# Development across ages of birth to 18 months: communication and language development

■ Parents and carers are often very excited the first time their baby smiles at them.

There are three parts to communication and language development: speaking, listening and understanding. These three areas encompass the development of speech sounds and language, learning to pay attention, and social skills.

## Crying

The main way that young babies communicate with others is by crying. This tells those around them that they need something and expect to have their needs met. Some babies cry a lot. This can be stressful for new parents and carers as they try to work out how they can stop their baby from crying so much.

Reasons why babies cry might be because:

- they are hungry
- they are cold or too hot
- they have a pain (this could be caused by wind)
- they are uncomfortable
- something has startled them.

## First communication

Young babies need to hear lots of language to learn how to talk. Until they learn to talk, babies become experts at using body language to make themselves understood and for social interaction. Around the age of 6 to 8 weeks, babies start to smile. This is a clever way of building bonds with those around them. This is because we find a baby's smiling face irresistible and cannot help smiling back. Therefore, the baby quickly realises that smiling gets them attention.

## Crying less and making more sounds

By around 3 months old, babies cry less. This is because they have learned that someone is always going to be there to feed them to stop them feeling hungry and cuddle them to make them feel safe. Babies will also be starting to make other noises, such as soft cooing, and starting to practise other sounds. They might shout or squeal. Babies sometimes surprise themselves with the noises that they can make. Table 1.6 lists some of the common sounds that babies make. They will also now start to turn their head to listen to a familiar voice.

At around 6 months old, babies will start '**babbling**', which is the precursor to talking and then eventually holding a conversation. It is around this age that babies might start to laugh and giggle spontaneously. Sometimes, this is in response to someone making them laugh and other times because they find something mundane hilarious, such as wind blowing in their face.

By 9 months old, babies will start more advanced, tuneful babbling. Although these are usually streams of sounds the baby has put together as they move their tongue and lips, parents and carers recognise them as early attempts at real words. As a result, they praise the baby and respond, which encourages the baby to make the sounds again.

◻ Table 1.6: Common word sounds that babies make

| Sounds baby make | How the sound is made |
| --- | --- |
| Bababa | This sound is made by opening and closing the lips. |
| Dadada | This sound is made by putting the tongue on the roof of the mouth behind the top gums or teeth. |

## Starting to use words

At around 12 months old, children cry much less and usually only for a reason that their parent or carer understands. They are now much more skilled in communicating. Now, children might be using individual words. These might be real words, such as 'more', or made-up words that carry meaning, for example, 'bot' meaning 'bottle'.

By this age, children might start to point at things that they want. Eventually, they might combine pointing with a word, such as 'that'. They realise that this is more likely to make their parent or carer get what they want or tell them what it is. At around a year old, children will start to copy what they hear, especially if the words they hear sound familiar to them. So they might be able to adapt the word 'that' and say 'cat', for example, when they see their pet. Once they can hear words and put them into context, such as saying 'cat' when their pet walks into the room, children can begin to understand much more of the world around them.

Around this time, parents and carers might start giving children simple two-word instructions or questions, such as 'where's cat?'. The child can now combine their understanding, their body language and their early speech to respond. They can point at the cat and say 'cat', recognising what was asked and being able to respond in a way that their parent or carer can understand. This shows their growing ability to listen, understand and speak.

By 15 months old, children's vocabulary is expanding at a phenomenal rate and, like a sponge, the more they hear the more they absorb. Now, they can name familiar things and people.

**ACTIVITY**

Choose one or more of the children from the list below. Suggest an activity you could do with the child to help to encourage their communication and language development.

*Evana is 8 weeks old. She is now in a routine of sleeping and feeding and has short periods of around ten minutes where she is alert and likes to look around her.*

*Taneeshiya is 8 months old. She is making lots of noises and giggles when her parents hide their faces with their hands.*

*Hubert is 17 months old. He can repeat short words and can say the names of his favourite toys.*

**CHECK MY LEARNING**

Write a timeline of communication and language development for birth to 18 months old.

# Development across ages of birth to 18 months: cognitive and intellectual development

### GETTING STARTED

Solve this simple problem.

Unscramble these letters to spell a word.

Tompenvedel

What skills did you use? How did you go about it? How long did it take?

### KEY TERM

**Cognitive development** improving your information processing, memory and problem solving.

**Perseverance** continued effort and determination, despite difficulty.

### BEST PRACTICE

Health visitors can recommend baby sensory classes, which use lights, bubbles and soft scarves that can stimulate the development of the senses. This stimulation can also be done at home.

### DID YOU KNOW?

Traditional nursery rhymes can help children to learn about complicated ideas.

Think about the traditional rhymes 'Old MacDonald had a Farm' and 'The Wheels on the Bus'.

'Old MacDonald' teaches children about animal noises and what animals live on farms, and helps them to improve their memory.

'The Wheels on the Bus' helps children to learn that wheels turn, doors open and close, and wipers go back and forward. These are complicated ideas for young children.

Babies very quickly learn new skills and make sense of the world. They learn through watching and copying. Children need to process information they learn. They also need to remember what they have learned. Young children have a phenomenal capacity to remember new things. Like a computer, children use their memory to solve problems. For example, they might know that their dog is called Ben but will have to learn that 'Ben' does not mean dog. They need to learn that other dogs have different names. People might also be called Ben and they are not dogs. This sounds obvious, but for young children, they need to unravel and understand these highly complicated ideas.

## Problem-solving skills

Intellectual or **cognitive development** has nothing to do with being a genius or how many questions you can answer. It is about how you approach a problem and try to solve it, and what you do if you cannot solve the problem. Concentration and **perseverance** are all part of intellectual and cognitive development. Young children need to have a desire to try, try and try again. They need to face problems they cannot solve and be challenged. If, after trying to walk for the first time, a baby fell over and gave up, they would never learn to walk.

## Development of the senses

Babies discover the world using all their senses (see Table 1.7). Everything they encounter stimulates them and they start to learn about the world. Obviously, this can be dangerous, which is why parents and carers have to supervise children closely.

 Table 1.7: Development of the senses

| Touch | Babies respond positively to gentle touch. It stimulates them and makes them feel safe. However, they have a low tolerance for some sensations, such as having an uncomfortable seam on their clothing. Young children want to touch everything, even if it is something prickly, hot or sharp. |
|---|---|
| Taste | Babies enjoy the sweetness of the taste of milk. As they develop, they will explore everything with their mouths. This is because they have more nerve endings there than any other part of their body. This can be dangerous because of the risk of choking or eating something that is toxic. |
| Hearing | Babies need to hear language to be able to talk and communicate. Too much noise can upset babies. |
| Vision | A newborn baby can only see objects close up and only in black and white. Eyesight develops rapidly over the following months – developing full colour and distance vision by 3 years. |
| Smell | It is thought that before babies develop good eyesight, they rely on the smell of people who are familiar to them to recognise them. This might be why babies have a stronger sense of smell than adults. |

## Recognition of self

One of the most sophisticated and complicated ideas that a child has to discover is that they exist and are a separate, individual person. They must learn this before they can start to understand about how they impact on the world, such as how they can cause others to feel by their actions. They need to know they have a name and to understand that when someone uses that name, they are talking to them. Babies tend to smile at themselves in the mirror from around 9 months old. By a year old, children generally know their own name and will respond when called.

### The mirror test

One way that **psychologists** have explored this aspect of development is through 'The Mirror Test', developed by Gordon Gallup Jr. This is also sometimes known as the 'Rouge Test'. Without the child realising, a small red dot or lipstick mark is placed on their forehead. Then the child is placed in front of a mirror.

- At 6–12 months old, the baby will gaze at themselves in the mirror for a few seconds and then smile in a friendly way as though they are meeting another baby.
- At 13–24 months old, the baby will see themselves and see the dot on their head. They will point at the dot in the mirror, seeming not to recognise that the other child is themselves.
- At 20–24 months old, the baby will approach the mirror, see the dot and rub their head to remove it.

Psychologists believe that, until the child tries to rub the dot on their own head, they are not aware of the concept that the image in the mirror is themselves.

## Attention span

By 3 months old, babies are starting to concentrate for very short periods of time. This is because they are more wakeful between feeds and sleep. They will watch what is happening around them and begin to anticipate what might happen next in their routine. By six months, babies are starting to concentrate and will focus their attention on familiar people and objects. They now know the different pitches and tone in people's voices and will respond accordingly. For example, children will be frightened and shy away from a raised voice.

Babies might spend their longest periods of attention on food when they are **weaning**. Parents and carers usually start weaning their baby between 6 and 9 months of age. Babies will enjoy exploring objects with their mouth and trying different tastes as they start eating solid food. Feeding themselves and exploring food is important for babies' development and concentration.

## Learning through playing

Playing is essential to babies' learning. It helps them to process information, remember things and solve simple problems.

Around the age of 9 months old, babies will enjoy social play. They particularly enjoy dropping toys on purpose and games of peek-a-boo, and they love listening to adults singing songs and rhymes. This helps with their communication and language development and teaches them about being sociable. Rhymes can help children to learn more about the world, especially if they include actions.

Babies watch and copy adults and the things they see around them. For example, at around 1 year old, children start to realise that they can wave to say hello and goodbye. If they wave, usually someone will wave back. Babies enjoy copying actions, whether this is the actions to songs or clapping their hands when they have done something they are proud of. They might even copy when playing peek-a-boo with an adult and hide their face behind their hands. Copying is one of the many ways that children start to learn to do things themselves.

# Development across ages of birth to 18 months: social development

Children need to develop secure, positive relationships with others. Babies love to be around other people. They learn about people and from people, and it stimulates them to talk and think. Socialisation is essential to their learning. The first social experiences babies will have are with their parents, carers and siblings. They might also spend time with grandparents and other family or friends. Later, they will have secondary socialisation with people outside of their families.

## Forming relationships

In the first few weeks of life, babies care very little about who meets their needs for feeding, changing their nappy and keeping them warm. Although they might recognise familiar voices from the womb, all they care about is that their needs are being met.

As babies get a little older, around 3 months of age, they will start to prefer the familiarity of their parents and carers. They enjoy being held and will study faces closely. At this age, babies will instinctively prefer to look at a happy, smiling face. They are quick to smile at anyone who is smiling at them and will usually be happy to be passed around the family for a cuddle.

Early socialisation is very important: it helps babies to start to work out the world. The more positive social experiences young babies have, the more relaxed and sociable they are likely to be as they grow older.

During the COVID-19 pandemic, babies and young children missed out on important social contact outside their immediate families because of lockdowns and the need for social distancing. Some nurseries, pre-schools and childminders noticed that children were starting in their early years setting with a delay in their social development because of this. As a result, practitioners needed to support children as they learned how to interact with other people for the first time.

## Fear of strangers

Before we evolved into the sophisticated, social human beings we are today, we needed to have **innate** skills to help keep us alive and safe. Around 6 months of age, babies will be able to identify the difference between people they know and people they do not know. By 9 months old, babies will start to vocalise this and might start to cry if a stranger talks to them or wants to pick them up. This can be quite embarrassing or upsetting for parents and carers, especially if the 'stranger' is a friend or member of the family. During this time, babies need reassurance and comfort from their parents or carers.

Fear of strangers is an important stage in children's development and does not mean that the baby is antisocial or dislikes the stranger. In time, as children grow, they will start to enjoy the company of new people, and parents and carers will need to teach children that they should not talk to strangers unless they tell them it is safe to do so.

## Playing with others

Play is vital to babies' and children's development. Even from a young age, babies need to have time to play, because this is when they learn about how to interact with others. Around 9 to 12 months old, children love games that involve a sense of surprise. This is because they enjoy the suspense of knowing that something is going to happen, and they can barely contain their excitement.

Examples of games that involve suspense:
- peek-a-boo (the parent or carer hides their face and then quickly moves their hands away, saying 'peek-a-boo!')
- hide the toy (the parent or carer hides a toy underneath a blanket or behind their back and then quickly exposes it).

Children enjoy playing with their parents and carers but are even more fascinated by watching other children play. Until around the age of 2 years, children may play by themselves. However, from around 15 months old, children will enjoy being around other children of different ages. This is why it is important for parents and carers to take children to places where they can enjoy playing alongside others. Table 1.8 describes some of these places

**BEST PRACTICE**

Health visitors should provide leaflets or other resources to new parents and carers to help them find out about local authority baby services, such as soft play or stay-and-play sessions to help babies start to socialise.

**Table 1.8: Ways that parents and carers can help children to socialise**

| Places where babies can socialise | How it helps their social development |
| --- | --- |
| Toddler groups | This is a great way for children to learn about sharing and turn taking and to watch what others can do. |
| Supermarkets | Babies will smile at strangers and enjoy the response they receive. |
| Playgrounds | Babies enjoy watching others and will show excitement at others' enjoyment. |
| Libraries | Hearing stories and other people's voices will intrigue babies, who will be fascinated by them. |

**ACTIVITY**

Many parents and carers introduce children to technology from a young age. For example, it is common for children under the age of 2 years to spend time looking at media on tablets and electronic devices. This is commonly called 'screen time'.

Research and develop a guide for parents and carers to explain the positives and negatives of introducing young children to technology. Find out whether there is any evidence that excessive screen time is damaging to a child's social development.

**CHECK MY LEARNING**

Design a web page or magazine article which identifies what parents and carers can expect for children's social development from birth to 18 months old.

# Development across ages of birth to 18 months: emotional development

## GETTING STARTED

It is important that adults help babies to develop emotionally.

Working in a small group, write down as many different emotions as you can think of.

Chose four emotions and identify what might trigger this emotion in a baby under 18 months old.

## DID YOU KNOW?

John Bowlby was the first researcher to develop the theory that children need to form relationships with a small number of adult carers. He studied babies and found out that they form very close attachments with their parents and carers. This attachment helps babies to learn to trust adults, be sociable and become emotionally secure.

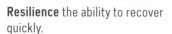

## KEY TERM

**Resilience** the ability to recover quickly.

## LINK IT UP

You can find out more about fear of strangers on page 16.

Babies need to develop their emotional **resilience**. Very young babies can only express themselves through crying. As children become older they cry less, as they find other ways to express themselves and explain their feelings. Babies need to become independent and want to do things for themselves. Parents and carers must do everything for newborn babies. Slowly, children need to learn how to feed themselves, dress themselves and use the bathroom. An adult must teach children these skills. However, it is just as important that adults teach young children to understand their emotions. Children need to learn about who they can trust and develop relationships with a wide range of people as they grow older.

## Development of bonds and trust

It is important for babies to form attachments to a small number of adults. Attachment is a two-way process between the adult and the baby. The adult needs to bond with the baby too. If babies experience poor attachment, it can have a damaging effect on their ability to form relationships for the rest of their life.

Signs that a baby is developing attachment to their parents and carers:
- The baby will turn their head in the direction of their parent or carer.
- The baby will smile and giggle when they see their parent or carer.
- The baby will stop crying and settle when they are held by their parent or carer.
- At around 3 months old, the baby will begin to show pleasure at their care routines, for example, moving their arms and legs when they see the bottle or breast at feeding time.

## Developing preferences

Around 6 months old, babies will start to show that they prefer to be around people that they know. They might demonstrate this by raising their arms to be picked up, turning away from people who they do not know or crying when they see a stranger. Around this age, babies will start to learn about emotions through their interactions with other people. They will visibly startle and might cry when they hear a raised voice, as they recognise this is something to be concerned about. They are starting to understand the pitch and tone of their parents' or carers' voices and much prefer it when people use sing-song or soft voices.

## Separation anxiety

Around 9 to 12 months, babies start to develop such strong attachments to their parent or main carer that they become anxious and distressed when they leave. Around this age, babies are also becoming more wary of strangers. It is very important that everyone caring for babies around this age recognises separation anxiety and how it can affect babies and young children. If babies attend a nursery or pre-school, they must be assigned a 'key person'. This is a person who will develop a close relationship with the child and their family and provide individual care for them. This means that the baby can develop a strong relationship with the same familiar person when they are apart from their main parent or carer.

## Being curious

At about 12 months old, all of children's learning starts to come together. This leads to them starting to take a keen interest in the world around them. Children are usually mobile by a year old, either by crawling or walking. This means they can follow their curiosity and explore the world around them. This might be studying a tiny ant crawling across the garden path or banging on the window as they watch the rain falling. Everything that children encounter fascinates them.

At around a year old, children start to take an interest in toys, such as teddy bears, musical toys, building bricks and push-along toys. However, it isn't just toys that capture children's imagination, and they are just as happy playing with household and natural objects (see Figure 1.2).

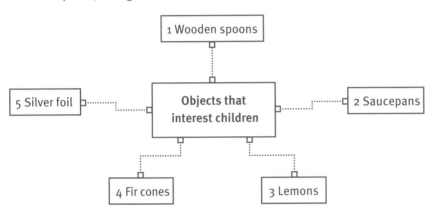

Figure 1.2: Children do not need lots of expensive toys.

## Asserting their feelings

At around 15 to 18 months old, children will start to experience new, strong emotions. They will not know what these emotions are, but they can be powerful and confusing. Children will want to become independent and assert themselves. One of the first ways that they do this is by refusing to co-operate with their parents and carers. As they begin to become independent, they start to think for themselves. This can be challenging for parents and carers.

Some of the ways that children might show their independence are by:
- refusing to get dressed
- wanting to carry things that are big or heavy
- not co-operating at mealtimes and insisting on feeding themselves
- wanting to put their own or other people's shoes on.

## Jealousy

At around 15 to 18 months, children might experience jealousy for the first time. This is usually prompted by their parent or carer giving attention to another child or a new sibling. Children do not understand that they feel jealous but will be unhappy at seeing their parent or carer show affection for someone else.

Children's expressions of jealousy are shown by:
- reacting strongly, crying or screaming
- trying to push the baby or child out of the way
- stamping their foot or throwing things
- hurting themselves, such as by throwing themselves on the floor.

**ACTIVITY**

*Dorota is 10 months old and starting nursery for the first time. Her mother is anxious about leaving her.*

Imagine that you are going to be the key person looking after Dorota. How might you help her to settle at the nursery? What emotions do you think Dorota might experience and how might she show these?

Finally, what do you think Dorota might want to play with?

You could write a plan, put your responses in a table or use a mind map.

**CHECK MY LEARNING**

Identify four things you have learned about children's emotional development. Put these into a mind map or chart. You might want to use this to help you to find out more by doing some further research about each area.

# Development across ages of 18 months to three years: physical development

From 18 months, a child becomes mobile and more independent and starts to understand more about the world around them, soaking up every experience on offer. Children develop physically in two ways: they develop locomotion (the ability to move from one place to another) and hand–eye co-ordination.

## Moving confidently and keeping safe

Previously, as babies, children's movements were unco-ordinated and accidental. As they become older, children start to find out what their bodies can do. However, as they increase in skill, they face greater risks.

By 18 months, most children are walking confidently and with co-ordination. They walk steadily and without support. Initially, they may still spread their arms out wide for balance and will often bump down on their bottoms to stop. As they become more co-ordinated and controlled, they are able to stop safely. By the age of 2 years, children will be able to run, usually managing to avoid obstacles. However, they are very prone to accidents, as they are eager to get from one place to another at speed.

Next comes climbing. Young children love to practise climbing up stairs, and this can be dangerous. Children will first place one foot on a stair and then bring the other foot to meet it. This is a good technique but requires balance because, for a moment, they will be standing on one leg. When this happens they are at risk of falling backwards, so it is important for an adult to accompany them and hold their hand. At 2 years old, they will be able to climb the stairs using one foot on each step. By 2 years and 6 months, children will have gained in confidence using the stairs if they use them regularly, and they might jump off the bottom stair, landing safely on two feet.

Table 1.9 shows some of the many ways that children can strengthen their balance, co-ordination and control.

◻ **Table 1.9: Activities that help children to strengthen their balance, co-ordination and control**

| Physical activity | Age | Benefits |
|---|---|---|
| Riding a balance bike | Around 18 months to 2 years | This helps children to strengthen the muscles in their back and legs. They will also be balancing when they lift their legs off the floor. |
| Sit-and-ride toys | Around 18 months to 2 years | Unlike the balance bike, these usually have four wheels and are stable. Children need to propel themselves along using their legs. This strengthens the muscles in their thighs and calves. |
| Throwing and catching a ball | Around 2 years | The child needs to use hand–eye co-ordination, and the activity strengthens the muscles in their arms. As they increase in ability, their throws and catches become more accurate and successful. |
| Kicking a ball into a goal | Around 2 years and 6 months | At first, children will lack power and precision in their kick. The ball will not travel far and probably will not reach the goal. As they increase the strength of their leg muscles, they will kick with more power and have more accuracy. |

◘ If an adult throws a ball towards a child, they will often grasp too late as their brain is not yet sending quick enough messages from their eyes to their hands.

## Developing hand–eye co-ordination

An essential part of children successfully gaining control over their physical skills is developing their hand–eye co-ordination. It is difficult to catch a ball or write your name with your eyes closed. This is because your eye follows the ball or the pencil and tells your hands where they need to be. Young children take some time to develop their hand–eye co-ordination. This means their actions are not always co-ordinated.

## The early stages of writing

At around 2 years old, some children will start to prefer to use one hand more than the other, although they might still swap over. Adults will probably first notice this when children are starting to hold chunky pencils and crayons. They will grip the crayon with their whole hand and with quick movements make marks on the paper. As children practise the marks they can make, they will often draw in circular movements and draw vertical lines. These are the very first attempts at writing, and eventually these marks will become letters. To help children with their hand–eye control and early writing, adults can start to draw lines and patterns that children can copy. Eventually, children will be able to copy their own name.

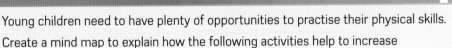

**ACTIVITY**

Young children need to have plenty of opportunities to practise their physical skills.

Create a mind map to explain how the following activities help to increase children's physical skills:
- playing at soft play areas
- dressing a doll
- chalking on a board.

When you have finished, you could suggest an outdoor activity that might help children to develop their physical skills.

**CHECK MY LEARNING** ■ ■

List five physical skills that you would expect a 3-year-old to be able to demonstrate without help.

# Development across ages of 18 months to 3 years: cognitive and communication development

## Cognitive and intellectual development

Children between 18 months and 3 years old are beginning to increase their interest and attention span. They are continually thinking, and at around 2 years old they start to develop their own fascinations and will respond enthusiastically to familiar items or characters. One way to develop children's intellectual learning is through books.

### Development of information processing

Reading to children and helping them to develop an interest in and enjoyment of books helps to boost their intellectual and cognitive development. Listening to someone read not only helps to promote children's speech and language, it unlocks their imagination and helps them to experience different emotions. Young children will often be able to retell a story from memory. This can make it appear that they can read much earlier than they actually can. This is because children can become so excited and interested in characters that they will know a story off by heart. Repetition is important for children's learning and they show delight in repeating songs and rhymes they know.

The little mouse felt sad, where was his mummy?

'Hooray', said the little mouse. His Mummy wasn't missing after all and he felt happy.

▢ Stories help children to think and develop empathy. What emotions do you think the book here might provoke in children?

### Learning through play

Play is hard work for children. It helps them to find out about the world around them and make sense of things that they do not yet understand.

At around 18 months old, children will love to help adults around the home. They are highly curious and want to find out about everything they encounter. Young children like to be included in daily routines and chores, such as sorting washing, sweeping the floor and tidying away their toys. They will have a developing memory and will know where things belong and can return toys to their box, for example. At around the age of 2 years, children will want to do more than help adults: they will want to *be* them. They will start to use their imagination and take part in **role-play**.

At 18 months old, children might know their name and will point out body parts and features on their face if prompted. They will also be curious about others and might want to touch people's faces as they explore other people's features too. By 2 years and 6 months, many children will know their own full names and the names of others and objects. Their play starts to develop rapidly, and they can start to act out things that are highly complicated. For example, they might decide they are the 'doctor' and want to perform examinations on any willing adults.

## Communication and language development

### Development of speech sounds and language skills

At around 18 months, parents and carers will notice words among the babbling. At first, this is likely to be naming people and things. At this early stage, children have no concept of the uniqueness of words. This can lead them to think that all women are called 'Mummy'. They might recognise the noise a dog makes and call all dogs 'woof'. The way that adults respond to these early uses of language determines how quickly children use and repeat language. As they begin to understand the power and purpose of language, children copy everything they hear and their vocabulary rapidly develops.

The more adults talk to children, the more words they learn and the more quickly they talk themselves. Adults will notice that children will often pick up words that adults say in a different pitch or tone. So, they might say 'bye-bye' because we tend to say this in a sing-song voice and accompany it with the action of waving. Young children recognise this different tone and the action and will copy.

### Listening and attention skills

Communicating successfully requires children to listen and pay attention. Young children find this difficult and it is a skill they need to learn.

### Formation of sentences

At around 2 years old, children know around 50 words and might put two or three words together to make a sentence, such as 'Daddy car gone'. These sentences do not always make sense but, as children develop and the more words they learn, the longer the sentences they use.

Children's speech starts to develop rapidly. By 2 years and 6 months, children will have broadened their vocabulary. This means that they will now know around 200 words and can use most of these in context. Their sentences will be short and might miss out some words or not be quite correct. For example: 'When I goded to the zoo, I sawed a giraffe'

The child is becoming aware of the importance of tense and knows that going to the zoo happened in the past. However, they do not know how to use the word 'went' and instead they try to use the word they know: 'go'. They also might now know how to use the word 'saw' and think it needs changing. Although this isn't correct grammar, the child can make themselves understood and these small errors will soon be corrected as the child hears more and more language.

**BEST PRACTICE**

Parents and carers can repeat back a child's sentence to them, correcting any mistakes. This helps them learn the language without being told explicitly that they made an error.

**DID YOU KNOW?**

It is not uncommon for young children to develop a stammer. This is thought to be because they are learning so quickly that their brains are working faster than their ability to talk, meaning they stumble over words. This is usually a temporary phase.

**CHECK MY LEARNING**

Link up the themes of children's cognitive and intellectual development. Explain how reading to young children can help to promote: curiosity, make-believe; naming objects and people. With a partner, identify three stages of children's communication and language development between 18 months and 3 years.

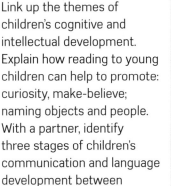

**ACTIVITY**

Look at the following case study and respond to the questions. Make notes and discuss with a partner.

*Amira is almost 2 years old. She is just starting to copy what she hears. She will say familiar words, such as 'daddy' and 'more'. Amira loves music and playing with toy animals.*

1  What do you think Amira's next milestones in talking will be?

2  Give two ways that her carers might be able to encourage her development.

# Development across ages of 18 months to 3 years: social and emotional development

**GETTING STARTED**

In a small group discuss why you think children can benefit from attending some form of early years care.

**KEY TERMS**

**Egocentric** Thinking only of yourself and not the feelings or wishes of others.

**Early years settings** Childcare provided by a childminder, nursery, pre-school or creche.

**BEST PRACTICE**

Childminders should be encouraged to take children to play centres to socialise with other children of their age. Specific sessions for childminders are available at some play centres.

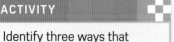

**ACTIVITY**

Identify three ways that adults can encourage children to play together, sharing and taking turns.

## Social development

Between the ages of 18 months and 3 years, children make important steps in their social development. This is because it is often around this age that children start to spend more time away from their parents and carers. Children might start nursery or pre-school or attend a childminder's care at around the age of 2 years old. For the first time, they might need to meet people and work out relationships by themselves.

### Development of secure, positive relationships with others

Young children are **egocentric** and think everything in life revolves around them. This leads them to act impulsively based on their own desires. Parents and carers need to make children aware that others have desires as well. For example, a child might take something and say 'mine'. Sometimes, no amount of encouragement from adults can help the child to understand that just saying 'mine' does not mean that it belongs to them. However, around 18 months, children understand 'you', 'my' and 'mine'.

### Being independent

As children start to attend **early years settings** and spend time away from their main carer, they need to learn to become independent. Around the age of 2 years, children will start to take responsibility for dressing themselves. They might be able to slip on their shoes or put on their coat but will probably still need adult help to do them up. Adults can help children to become independent by not doing things for them once they start to be able to do them themselves. This can be difficult, because children will not be skilled and might make mistakes or take longer to do things.

When children are around 2 years and 6 months, they will be able to feed themselves with a spoon and fork. Some children, if they have had opportunity to practise, might even be able to use a safety knife to cut their food. Children will get messy and spill their drinks, but letting them try helps them to become confident and independent.

### Toilet training

Making the transition from nappies to using the potty or toilet is a big milestone for children and parents.

For children to become toilet trained, they must first recognise the sensation of predicting a bowel or bladder movement. Then they need to link these feelings to suitable words, e.g. 'wee' and 'poo'. Then they need to be able to get to the potty or the toilet and undress in time.

### Development of friendships

When children start pre-school or nursery they will meet other children. Developing friendships is difficult for young children. This is because, at this age, young children think of themselves more than others. They might not want to share or take turns. However, children quickly enjoy playing with others and they learn important social skills that help them to become well-adjusted adults.

# Emotional development

Children need to learn about the emotions that they experience to be able to understand and control them. This happens around the same time that children are starting to develop their sense of identity and wanting to be more independent. Children need to develop trust for others and become emotionally resilient.

## Knowing how others feel

Young children do not have **empathy** for others – they must learn this. Ways of helping young children to develop empathy include:

- showing concern for them when they are tired, hurt or upset
- pretending with dolls and soft toys, cuddling them and treating them gently
- showing children how to handle pets with care and concern
- reminding them to be gentle when playing with others.

While children's empathy is still developing, they cannot put themselves into other people's shoes. It is usual for young children to be impatient and demanding. At around 2 years of age, children will find it very difficult to wait and will expect their parent or carer to meet their needs immediately. Their behaviour might seem very unreasonable.

## Tantrums

Young children do not have the vocabulary or experience to describe how they are feeling. Sometimes their emotions can become so strong that they do not know how to deal with them. Around 18 months old, children will have mood swings and will switch between wanting to do everything for themselves and wanting someone to do everything for them. This can lead to them starting to become overwhelmed and they will cry.

At around the age of 2, some children can have what is sometimes called 'temper tantrums'. They feel cross and angry, often without really knowing why. This can lead to them displaying the way they feel by lying on the floor, shouting, crying or refusing to co-operate. This is a normal stage of development that will decrease as children's ability to recognise and understand their feelings increases.

By the age of 2 years and 6 months, children start to cope better with their emotions. They have more language to explain their needs or wants and be understood.

Parents and carers can help children when they are having a tantrum by:
- staying calm
- ignoring the behaviour
- distracting the child with a toy
- praising the child when they stop the tantrum and have calmed down.

How parents and carers can reduce the likelihood of children having a tantrum:
- Show the child empathy, e.g. by saying they can see the child is feeling upset.
- Distract the child before the tantrum starts by doing something different.
- Give the child a chance to make choices and do things for themselves.
- Explain the reasons for rules and boundaries.
- Give children some responsibility and things they can do to feel more grown up.

■ Table 1.10: Behaviour displayed by young children as they start to play and learn as part of a group

| Type of behaviour | Reason for behaviour |
| --- | --- |
| Hoarding toys | If children are used to having all their toys to themselves, sharing them can be difficult. Also, some children might feel that the toys are far better than the ones they have at home and want to play with everything at once. |
| Snatching | Children might assume that all the toys and equipment belong to them, just like the ones at home. |
| Hitting | If children do not have good communication skills they might be unable to resolve arguments by talking about it and so they lash out. |
| Biting | This could be because children are still exploring the world using their mouths and do not appreciate that it causes others pain. |

**KEY TERM**

**Empathy** – being able to understand the feelings of others.

**ACTIVITY**

New parents have written in to a magazine with their parenting dilemmas. Give some advice about how they can deal with each situation.

*I am a mother of an 18-month-old child. She just seemed to change overnight. First she wants me to put her shoes on, then she shouts at me because she wants to put them on herself. I have no idea what is happening.*

*My son is 2 years old and has such temper tantrums. I do not know why. I am embarrassed to take him out.*

**CHECK MY LEARNING**

Create a mind map of the different types of emotional behaviour children might show between the ages of 18 months and 2 years and 6 months. Include suggestions of how an adult can help to support children with their emotions.

# Development across ages of 3 to 5 years: physical development

Children become increasingly confident, sociable and capable as they leave babyhood behind and start to prepare for going to school. What skills do you think are most important for young children to learn before they start school?

## Locomotion and balance

By the age of 3 to 5 years, children are developing their locomotion and refining their balance. They no longer need to walk with their arms outstretched to balance and their movements are deliberate and purposeful. They are able to run, climb and balance skilfully. However, children around this age lack spatial awareness. Their co-ordination is not fully developed, so they might have frequent trips, bumps and falls as they play (see Table 1.11).

▣ As children grow they need further ways to test out their abilities and challenge what they can do. Playgrounds offer opportunities for developing balance and locomotion.

▣ Table 1.11: Activities that help children to strengthen their balance, co-ordination and control

| Age | Children can | Games to play |
|---|---|---|
| 3 years | Use the whole of their foot to balance and go up on tip-toes | 'What's the time, Mr Wolf?'<br>Children tip-toe behind the 'wolf', creeping up until the 'wolf' turns around and runs after them. |
| | Ride a tricycle using the pedal | Roads and traffics lights.<br>Children follow a road chalked on the path and need to stop when the adult shouts red, get ready when the adult shouts amber and go when the adult shouts green. |
| | Throw, catch and kick a ball | Football.<br>The child tries to kick the ball into a net and the adult tries to catch the ball. |
| 4 years | Run at speed | Running races.<br>Children run between two points to see who is fastest. Obstacles can be added, such as a tunnel to wriggle through. |
| | Balance along a line drawn on the floor | Crocodile soup.<br>The children need to walk around a chalked circle on the floor. If they fall off the line, they fall in the soup and get eaten by crocodile. Adults can make it more difficult by asking children to hop, change direction, close their eyes or jump. |

| Age | Children can | Games to play |
|---|---|---|
| 5 years | Climb confidently | Provide children with a slide so they become used to climbing the steps before sliding. The adult can take children to parks and try out bigger slides. |
| | Skip and hop | Adults can increase children's skills by teaching them to skip in different ways, first without a rope, then with a rope. As they become better at jumping to skip, the adult can encourage them to hop on alternate feet over the rope. |
| | Increase control when playing with a ball | Piggy in the middle. Three children stand in a row. The children at the end need to try to throw the ball over the child in the middle. If the child in the middle catches it, the person who threw it takes a turn in the middle. |

**ACTIVITY**

Investigate what play provision is available for children locally. Is there a range of play equipment for young children to be able to develop their physical skills?

1 Complete a study into the benefits of your local park for developing children's physical skills.

2 Recommend some changes that might improve the play provision.

**BEST PRACTICE**

Nurseries and pre-schools should regularly restock items such as crayons and pencils to ensure children have access to toys that can help them develop their fine motor skills.

## Holding small tools, such as pencils

Children are in control of their fine motor skills. They can use scissors and have greater control over the movement of their fingers. It is essential that children practise their fine motor skills, as they are needed for writing, cutting and typing on computers.

1 Fisted grip

2 Digital grip

## Writing

Children cannot just pick up a pencil and write. There are various stages they go through before they learn to hold a pencil and have full control over it. Pencil grip is important because it affects the fluency of writing and legibility of the child's handwriting. By the age of 4 years, children can hold a pencil like an adult and copy letters. They have good pencil control by the age of 5.

3 Tripod grip

4 Dynamic tripod

■ **Tripod grip means that only small movements of the wrist are needed when writing. This means that children can write sentences without getting aching wrists.**

**CHECK MY LEARNING**

Review the types of physical development below and give an explanation of each:
• locomotion
• balance
• hand–eye co-ordination
• dynamic tripod grip.

# Development across ages of 3 to 5 years: cognitive and communication development

## Cognitive and intellectual development

Between the ages of 3 and 5 years, children gain a wide range of knowledge. They have begun to understand words and their meaning and have become aware of numbers.

### Development of information processing

By now, children can hold a pencil and make marks, although they might not grip it correctly. They know that print carries meaning because they enjoy books and they might be starting to recognise their own written name. There are many ways that adults can help to increase children's interest in reading and writing (see Table 1.12).

◻ Table 1.12: Ways that adults can encourage early reading and writing

| Activities to encourage early reading | Activities to encourage early writing |
|---|---|
| • Singing songs and rhymes<br>• Reading stories together<br>• Looking at pictures and photographs<br>• Role playing stories and characters<br>• Having name cards or placemats<br>• Displaying pictures with words<br>• Practising sounds of letters, such as 'sssssnake'<br>• Looking at different types of books | • Having lots of different materials to draw and write with<br>• Threading beads onto a string, playing with dough and using scissors to strengthen finger muscles<br>• Finger painting |

### Concentration

As children become more inquisitive and learn more quickly, their attention span increases. This means that they spend longer periods of time concentrating on activities. By the time they are 5 years old and ready to start school, children will usually concentrate for long enough to complete a simple task, such as writing their name or completing a simple sum.

### Memory

From 3 years old, children develop long-term memories and are able to recall information to apply later. For example, they remember sounds that letters make to help them to read or recall a past event to solve a problem.

Children have a superb memory and are now learning so much so quickly that at times their memory becomes jumbled. They might, for example, not quite remember what is real and what is not. Children might retell parts of a story or television programme but think that it happened to them. Some children develop an incredible ability to remember things that interest them, such as the names of dinosaurs or makes of cars.

By 4 years old, young children can often count up to ten. However, this does not mean that they know about numbers or mathematics. Learning about even basic mathematics is a complicated process. It involves knowing that numbers exist, that a numeral represents a number. Then children need to understand how many make up that numeral. They need to understand numbers come in order, starting at zero, and that combining or removing numbers creates new numbers. By 4 years old, children use this knowledge and can start to do simple sums.

## Making sense of new things

Children start to put what they have learned into context. At around 3 years old, children will have a concept of time and know that there is a past, a present and future. This helps them to put their life in order. Ordering and sorting ideas and concepts helps children to make sense of the huge amount of new information they encounter each day.

## Problem-solving skills

Around 3 years old, children will start to sort, match and order items. They do this with exceptional skill when they have a particular interest. For example, children that are interested in dinosaurs will be able to quickly identify toy dinosaurs and will instantly recognise that toy farm animals are not dinosaurs.

# Communication and language development

Children are now becoming much more confident and vocal. They will use language to share ideas, ask questions and build relationships. By 3 years old, many children have clear speech and their **vocabulary** is expanding rapidly. Like adults, all children enjoy using language to communicate and build relationships with others. They learn quickly that others will react to what they say, and this gives them power.

Around the age of 3 years, children have clear speech, can use personal pronouns and plurals correctly, and can listen to stories and understand most instructions. By asking questions, children learn that they can find out things. They will start to ask 'why' in response to what adults say. Sometimes, adults will not have the answer to this.

Children around the age of 4 begin to understand that what they say will have an effect on others. They might tell their grandparents they love them and know this makes them happy. They might say sorry after they doing something they shouldn't have done, because they know that parents and carers will forgive them.

As children's speech and language becomes more sophisticated, they are able to talk about the past and the future and they will also learn about humour and will start to tell jokes. At the age of 4, most of children's jokes revolve around what amuses them, such as toilet humour. If they make others laugh or cause outrage, they have achieved what they set out to do.

Around the age of 5, when children start to make connections with others outside of their immediate family, they might start to learn new things about people and gain new ideas. Their speech will be fluent and grammatically correct, with a wide range of vocabulary, and they will enjoy telling stories to people they know. These might be accounts of things that they have experienced and places they have visited, or they might be made-up stories. Children also enjoy hearing other people talk. They might stop what they are doing, stare and give their full attention as they listen intently. They are also now able to understand complex instructions.

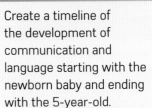

**LINK IT UP**

Children are becoming more confident and interested in writing. On page 21 we looked at children's early attempts at writing.

**ACTIVITY**

Create a timeline of the development of communication and language starting with the newborn baby and ending with the 5-year-old.

You might choose to do this using a computer or present your work in a table or as a collage.

**KEY TERM**

**Vocabulary** The range of words a person knows.

**BEST PRACTICE**

The key person for each child will assess their language level and if any issues are spotted they should talk to a parent or carer about how to support their needs.

**CHECK MY LEARNING**

Children who have a speech and language delay often have a delay in their social development too.

Discuss several ways that children use communication to build social relationships.

# Development across ages of 3 to 5 years: social and emotional development

◘ Young children rarely see differences and enjoy playing all together.

## Social development

When children play they are starting to understand the world around them, solve problems and learn about how to get along with others. Children's play happens in stages and this helps friendships to form.

### Development of secure, positive relationships with others

Children are now starting to feel confident and secure enough to separate from their parents and spend periods of time away from them. Around this time, other people, such as teachers, start to influence the way that they think. Young children will often enjoy playing at being teachers. This helps them to work out these new relationships.

Learning to be sociable and get along with others can be difficult for children because they are still learning that other people have feelings and emotions. They may act impulsively at times as they do what they want. Adults need to help children to be sociable, for example through the games they play with them (see Table 1.13).

◘ Table 1.13: Games that help children to become sociable

| Age of child | Games and activities | How it helps children to be sociable |
|---|---|---|
| 3 years | Completing a jigsaw puzzle together | When children work with another person to complete a task, they learn to co-operate. By completing a jigsaw puzzle with another person, the child will learn about turn taking and sharing. |
| 4 years | Show and tell | In groups, such as school and nursery, show and tell is an important way for children to find out about each other. Children will have something they want to show and talk about. This gives them a sense of independence. Others need to listen. This helps children to be sensitive towards others. |
| 5 years | Hide and seek | As children get older, they can learn to play games that have rules. Hide and seek requires children to use different skills, such as counting, patience and the self-restraint not to look if they are the seeker. The hider needs to keep still and remain hidden. |

### Accepting others

Children are curious about the world they live in and the people who live it. Unlike some adults, children are very accepting of each other and their differences. Between 3 and 5 years old, children have little regard for gender, ethnicity, race or ability. Just being the same age is enough for children to consider someone their friend. By the age of 5, children will start to find characteristics about others that they like or are similar to their own. They begin to choose their own friends. Children might enjoy making each other laugh and they begin to develop a sense of humour. Finding the same things funny can help to strengthen a friendship.

# Emotional development

Emotional development helps children to become resilient and confident and to trust others. Children need to have trust in others in order to form friendships, seek out comfort when feeling ill, upset or needing reassurance, and behave in a way that is socially acceptable.

## Development of bonds and trust

As children become able to talk and express themselves more easily, temper tantrums become less frequent. They will also start to express their close bonds with people who are important to them.

Here are some ways that they might show this:

- drawing pictures for their family
- holding hands
- telling family members that they love them
- wanting to copy them.

These behaviours show that children are happy and confident and trust the people who care for them.

## Increase in independence

Becoming more confident and self-assured will enable children of about 4 years old to be able to carry out tasks and skills independently. Skills that show independence include:

- using the toilet
- brushing their teeth
- using a fork to eat
- washing and drying hands and face
- putting on their own shoes.

## Developing emotional resilience

Young children need positive relationships, praise and encouragement in order to build their self-esteem and ultimately their emotional resilience (see Table 1.14).

☐ **Table 1.14: How to tell if a young child has low or high self-esteem**

| Evidence of high self-esteem | Evidence of low self-esteem |
|---|---|
| • Willingness to take part | • Unable to play |
| • Ability to make friends | • Poor concentration |
| • Ability to recover quickly after failure | • Emotional outbursts |
| • Stable emotions | • Disappointment in effort and work |
| • Pride in achievements and efforts | • Inability to get along with others |

Adults can promote children's self-esteem by:

- having realistic expectations
- praising children when they achieve something
- encouraging and not criticising
- joining in with children's play
- listening to what children say
- being respectful of children's ideas, views and efforts.

## Bounce-back ability

Children need to be confident and able to get along with their peers. They need to share resources and ideas to become effective learners at school and for the rest of their lives. Young children will not always be able to agree, and there will be disputes that adults will have to help resolve. But by developing emotionally, children will learn to resolve conflict themselves and bounce back quickly from disappointments and move forward feeling positive.

## BEST PRACTICE

Nurseries and pre-schools can create a 'learning journey' book for each child and include photos of their family to help develop emotional bonds by talking about a child's special people.

## ACTIVITY

Becoming independent is vital for children's development.

Design a product or resource that parents and carers can use to help children aged 3 to 5 to become more independent.

For example, some toothbrushes have timers to help children to know how long they need to brush their teeth for. So you could design a similar product, or a resource such as an information leaflet.

## LINK IT UP

You can find out more about temper tantrums on page 24.

## CHECK MY LEARNING

Give one way that children aged 3 years might demonstrate they are able to wait to have their needs met.

Explain how children can develop emotional resilience.

Describe what is meant by 'bounce-back ability'.

# Summary of development across the ages

|  | 0–18 months | 18 months–3 years | 3–5 years |
|---|---|---|---|
| **Physical development** | A baby is born with infant reflexes in order to help them to survive.<br><br>By 3 months old, these reflexes disappear and babies make purposeful movements, such as moving their head and watching their fingers.<br><br>As the babies grow, they start to develop in strength. By 6 months old, most babies can sit up with support, and roll. By 9 months, they might be crawling and passing toys between their hands.<br><br>At around 12 months old, babies will start to walk with support and can start to feed themselves finger foods.<br><br>At 15 months old, most children can walk by themselves and will hold things, such as a crayon, purposefully. | At 18 months, children move confidently, walking steadily and stopping. They will begin to climb stairs and ride on balance bikes and sit-and-ride toys.<br><br>By 2 years old, children can run at speed and safely. They will throw and catch a ball and will draw circles and lines using a crayon.<br>At 2 years and 6 months, children can jump from a step, kick a large ball and start to copy lines when drawing. | At around 3 years old, children can balance on one foot, ride a tricycle using the pedals, and hold a pencil between their thumb and finger. They might be able to make jagged cuts in a piece of paper using scissors.<br><br>By 4 years old, children run, avoiding obstacles. They have good balance and can draw a recognisable person as they will now hold a pencil more like an adult.<br>At 5 years old, children can run, hop, skip and play ball games. They now have good control when writing and drawing. |
| **Cognitive and intellectual development** | At birth, babies' senses are developing.<br><br>By 3 months, they have more alert, wakeful periods and will recognise familiar routines, such as feed times.<br><br>Between 6 and 9 months, babies will recognise familiar objects and people and respond to familiar voices. They will explore objects with their mouth and look for objects that have fallen out of sight.<br><br>By 12 months old, children know their own name and will look when called. They will copy adults, such as clapping hands. | At 18 months old, children can point to their body parts and are becoming more curious.<br><br>By 2 years old, children recognise pictures in books and enjoy simple make-believe games, such as role-play.<br><br>Around 2 years and 6 months, children will be starting to become aware of their name. They will start to name familiar people and objects. | By 3 years, children are becoming more aware of colours and can sort and order by category, such as when they play with shape sorters.<br><br>At around 4 years old, children can count to 10 and will sing songs and nursery rhymes. They will be able to solve simple problems, such as puzzles.<br><br>By 5 years old, children have progressed from counting to doing simple mathematical sums. They are also starting to become more competent in reading and writing. |
| **Communication and language development** | Babies cry when they are newborn as this is the only way that they can communicate.<br><br>At around 6 weeks old, babies will start to smile.<br><br>At around 6 months old, babies start babble. They laugh and giggle and make sounds to attract attention.<br><br>By 12 months old, children are using single words and pointing to explain what they want. They can understand very simple instructions.<br><br>At 15 months old, children can name familiar people and objects. | At 18 months old, children will say a few words, such as 'mummy' or 'daddy'. They will understand more of what is said to them and repeat words they hear.<br><br>By 2 years old, children will be using around 50 words. They might even be joining words together. They enjoy listening to stories.<br><br>At around 2 years and 6 months, children will now know about 200 words and be learning more each day. They will use some simple sentences. | At 3 years old, children speak clearly and use correct sentences. They understand simple stories and enjoy listening to stories.<br><br>By 4 years old, children talk about past events and things they will do in the future. They enjoy making people laugh by telling them jokes. They ask questions and listen intently to the response.<br><br>At 5 years old, children speak fluently. They have a vast vocabulary and understand far more complicated instructions. |

| | 0–18 months | 18 months–3 years | 3–5 years |
|---|---|---|---|
| Social development | At 3 months old, babies respond to being giving attention and might smile. By 6 months babies start to recognise familiar people and might be wary of strangers.<br><br>By 9 months old, babies might cry at the sight of people they do not know.<br><br>Around 12 months old, children like to play simple games, such as peek-a-boo.<br><br>At 15 months old, children like watching others socialising and other children playing. | By 18 months old, children start to understand terms such as, 'you', 'my' and 'mine'. They will enjoy copying their parents and carers.<br><br>By 2 years old, children can dress and undress, with some help. They are beginning to learn about toilet training as they become more independent.<br><br>At 2 years and 6 months old, children can use a spoon to feed themselves. They will start to play with other children but will find sharing and taking turns difficult. | At around 3 years old, children will start to play with others and will be able to take turns.<br><br>At 4 years old, children are aware of others and are starting to become sensitive to their feelings. Their independence increases and they develop a sense of humour as they start to find things funny.<br><br>By 5 years old, children chose friends based on characteristics they like. They know there are rules and can usually follow them. They enjoy team games and have a desire to win. |
| Emotional development | Newborn babies will cry for attention but start to settle quickly. They will turn their head and smile as they build a bond with their parents and carers.<br><br>At around 6 months old, babies prefer to be with their familiar parent and carer. They recognise the different emotions people show in their faces and prefer to look at a happy face.<br><br>Between 9 months old and a year, babies become cautious of strangers and want to be with their parent and carer. They are starting to explore the world around them and enjoy looking at toys and objects.<br><br>At 15 months old, children are less dependent on their parent and carer but might become jealous if their parent or carer gives attention to others. | At 18 months old, children find it hard to regulate their emotions and vary between wanting to be independent and wanting adults to do things for them. They are starting to learn about other's emotions.<br><br>At 2 years old, children will probably be having tantrums as they struggle to cope with strong emotions. They are demanding and cannot wait for attention.<br><br>By 2 years and 6 months, children will start to cope better with their emotions and develop an awareness of their own identity. They might start to test boundaries and deliberately not do as they are told. | The 3-year-old is more patient and can wait for their needs to be met. They co-operate with others, such as helping to tidy up. They are now much better at explaining how they are feeling.<br><br>At 4 years old, children are confident and able to do things for themselves, such as feed themselves and get dressed. They will still look for adults for comfort if they are hurt or upset.<br><br>Children at 5 years old begin to form close friendships and are becoming able to recover from disappointments and upset. They know most social rules but might want adults to help them to resolve arguments and disagreements. |

# Learning outcome A: assessment practice

## How you will be assessed

You will be assessed via a Pearson set assignment. This will be marked internally and moderated externally. Your assignment will be completed under formal supervision and carried out independently with no access to the internet.

When you have completed Component 1, your teacher will give you an assignment to complete. It will include three tasks. The first task relates to learning outcome A. For Task 1, you will demonstrate your knowledge and understanding of the principles of growth and development. You will be allowed approximately 1 hour to complete the task.

Evidence includes:

- all expected milestones
- a detailed and relevant account of how to measure a child's growth
- a detailed account of the role and responsibilities of individuals involved in the care of the child
- a well-developed reasoning showing the importance of measuring and monitoring a child's growth.

### CHECKPOINT

#### Strengthen

- State how children's growth and development are measured using growth charts and developmental milestones.
- State the five different areas of development.
- Give examples of children's growth and development in each of the five areas from birth to 5 years.

#### Challenge

- State how growth is measured in individual children.
- Explain how milestones in development are determined.
- Assess which toys can help children with their fine motor skills.
- Discuss which games and activities can help children develop their social skills.

### ASSESSMENT ACTIVITY | LEARNING OUTCOME | A

To complete this task you must work individually.

Kojo is 18 months old. Produce a booklet on Kojo's expected growth and development. You can use the Summary of development across the ages on pages 32–33 to help you.

Your booklet must include:

Part 1 – Development

- the expected milestones for his stage of cognitive development

Part 2 – Growth

- how his growth would be measured and recorded
- what the role and responsibilities are of individuals involved in measuring and monitoring his growth
- why it is important to measure his growth

## TIPS

The grading criteria for Learning Outcome A use different command verbs, such as **assess**, **complete**, **discuss**, **explain**, **match**, **state** and words asking you to make a choice, such as **which**.

It helps to know what the words **assess, discuss, explain** and **state** mean. This will help you to respond fully.

Imagine you are being asked the same questions about something very simple, such as the pen that you are writing with.

**State** simply, this means what is it? *It is a pen.* Or to expand, *it is a black pen.*

**Explain** what the pen looks like. *The pen is a black ball point pen with transparent casing. It has a lid to prevent leakages, however the pen has started to leak so this is not effective. It has half the ink missing.*

**Discuss** what the pen is, its different aspects. *It is an ink pen that is used for people to write on paper. It writes in black ink which is dry to the touch but smudges if you run your hand over it. This pen is also leaking, which means it might leave a mess on the page.*

**Assess** how good the pen is at its job using relevant information to make a conclusion. *The pen writes in black ink and the ink has lasted well as the pen is three years old. It is comfortable to hold because it is narrow. The pen was relatively cheap, so it is good value for money. However, the pen ink smudges slightly and has started to leak so it is no longer effective to use.*

## TAKE IT FURTHER

**Discuss** the role of two professionals who are responsible for measuring children's growth and development of a newborn baby.

*For example, when the baby is born, they will be checked by a midwife or paediatrician to review the infant reflexes. For example, they will check that that the baby can grasp, suck and startle. If the midwife or paediatrician does not find these reflexes, the medical professionals might conclude that the child was born prematurely, is unwell or perhaps has a disability. If they didn't make these checks, this might lead to the baby becoming ill and not receiving suitable medical attention.*

**Assess** how children, families and wider society benefit from monitoring children's growth.

## TIPS

Remember that children's development usually happens in order, so when you think about an aspect of development, such as children's physical development, start at the beginning.

Babies cannot walk before they can sit up and they cannot run before they can walk. This will help you to think about the sequence of development.

# Physical factors that impact on children's overall development: during pregnancy

In a group, create a mind map of the reasons why it is important to look after health and wellbeing in pregnancy.

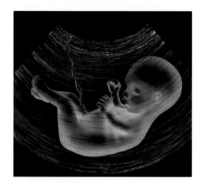

■ Before birth the baby's future is being determined. There have been advances in detecting abnormalities early on in pregnancy. Why do you think some people are unhappy about this?

**DID YOU KNOW?**

It is difficult for medical professionals to know how much alcohol is safe to drink in pregnancy. For this reason, it is advised that alcohol is avoided in pregnancy.

**KEY TERMS**

**Foetus** means offspring and is what a human baby in the womb is called after 8 weeks.

**Spina bifida** is caused when the spine and spinal cord of a baby in the womb fail to develop properly.

**Placenta** a circular organ in the uterus of a pregnant woman that nourishes and maintains the foetus through the umbilical cord.

How well a child will grow and develop can be determined early on, even before they are born. This is because some health factors begin during pregnancy. You might know of some life choices that can harm an unborn child and so should be avoided in pregnancy. How well a child grows and develops depends on different factors. Physical factors, such as the parents' genetics and what a child eats; environmental factors, such as where a child lives; and socio-economic factors, such as their social group, relationships and education, can all affect a child's growth and development.

**ACTIVITY**

Select one inherited condition and investigate how it might impact on a child's growth and their physical, intellectual, emotional and social development.

Produce a table to present your findings.

## Maternal nutrition and exercise

Parents cannot change their genes or prevent genetic abnormalities. However, they can take action to make sure that they are healthily during pregnancy.

During pregnancy, a healthy diet helps to provide a **foetus** with all the nutrients that it needs to grow and develop. Lacking vitamins and minerals can lead to the foetus not developing correctly. It is recommended a folic acid supplement is taken during pregnancy to reduce the risk of **spina bifida**. Some foods are best avoided during pregnancy, such as soft unpasteurised cheeses and pâté. They are thought to be linked to an increased risk of miscarriage or premature birth. Babies that are born prematurely are at a higher risk of some health conditions, such as cerebral palsy, vision problems and learning disabilities.

It is not a good idea to suddenly take up strenuous exercise while pregnant. However, regular, gentle exercise, such as swimming and walking, can help with fitness in pregnancy. Being physically fit and active can help to maintain healthy weight gain and prepare the mother for labour. Being overweight in pregnancy increases the risk of miscarriage, gestational diabetes and high blood pressure. Having high blood pressure in pregnancy can lead to the baby needing to be born early.

## Effects of parental drug or substance abuse

Taking drugs and other harmful substances, such as alcohol, during pregnancy is never good for health. It also poses a risk to the unborn baby. Babies that are exposed to toxic substances can be born with deformities. This is because drugs and alcohol are toxic and affect the foetus at the early stages of development. Later on in pregnancy, the unborn baby is exposed to harmful substances as they pass through the **placenta**. This can lead to premature birth, death, being born suffering from withdrawal from drugs and learning disabilities.

Drinking too much alcohol in pregnancy can lead to foetal alcohol syndrome. This is where alcohol passes through the placenta and can damage cells in the brain, spinal cord and other parts of the baby's body. This causes the child to be born with physical and mental disabilities.

## Premature birth

The average length of pregnancy is 40 weeks. Not all babies will arrive on time. Some will arrive later or be 'overdue' and some will arrive a couple of weeks early. Babies that are born before 37 weeks are considered to be **premature**.

This can have an effect on a baby's development (see Table 1.15).

◻ Table 1.15: Growth of premature babies between 24 and 36 weeks

| Number of weeks of pregnancy | Growth of the premature baby |
|---|---|
| 24 weeks | • The baby is covered in fine hair called lanugo.<br>• They have not developed fat so cannot keep warm.<br>• Their eyes are still fused shut and eyebrows and eyelashes haven't developed.<br>• Skin is delicate and thin.<br>• All internal organs are under-developed. |
| 26 weeks | • Lungs are under-developed and babies cannot breathe for themselves.<br>• At this age, their skin has become slightly thicker and they have fingerprints. |
| 30 weeks | • Vital organs are developed, but babies at 30 weeks will usually still require help with breathing.<br>• Babies at this age have a weak sucking reflex, but can digest milk.<br>• They might be physically small and have a large head and small body. |
| 34 weeks | • The bones are now fully formed, but the lungs are not yet fully developed.<br>• Babies can now suck, but get tired very easily so they cannot take in enough nourishment. |
| 36 weeks | • Babies still do not have enough fat to keep themselves warm and their lungs are still not fully formed, but babies born at 36 weeks look more like full-term babies. |

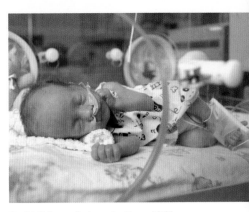

◻ At 24 weeks' gestation, 40% of babies will survive. Just two weeks later at 26 weeks, around 77% of babies will survive.

**KEY TERM**

**Premature** born before the expected date of arrival. Medically, this is before 37 weeks of pregnancy.

### How prematurity affects development

Being born prematurely can sometimes have an effect on children's development; this might include the following:

- Poor muscle tone: can mean that the child takes slightly longer to crawl or walk.
- Smaller in height and weight than peers: can mean children are 'babied' by other children the same age or adults have lower expectations because they perceive them as being younger.
- Delay in meeting developmental milestones: can mean that children need extra help to catch up with their peers.
- Hearing difficulty: can delay speech and can mean that children are less able to make relationships with others.
- Sight problems: can delay development and can mean that children need extra care to keep them safe.
- Cerebral palsy: can cause muscle weakness or, in more serious cases, can mean that children need lifelong special care.
- Learning difficulties: can lead to children not being able to develop at the same rate as their peers.
- More likely to have attention deficit hyperactivity disorder (ADHD): can lead to social difficulties.

**DID YOU KNOW?**

Albert Einstein, Isaac Newton and Charles Darwin were all born prematurely.

**CHECK MY LEARNING**

Write three pieces of advice for a parent-to-be about the benefits of a healthy lifestyle during pregnancy for the healthy growth and development of the baby.

Have a discussion on your table about possible reasons why a foetus's growth may be delayed in the womb.

# Physical factors that impact on children's overall development: disabilities and health status

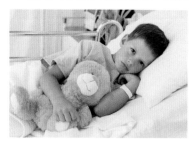

▣ **Children with chronic ill health often spend time in hospital. How do you think professionals support children to reduce the impact of illness on development?**

▣ **Asthma is a common condition that can be very serious.**

As children grow older, different physical factors may affect their ability to grow and develop. They may have additional needs or a disability or they may have chronic or acute illnesses.

## Disabilities and additional needs

Some children will have a disability or additional need that is present from birth. Table 1.16 shows some of these and how they may affect development.

▣ **Table 1.16: Disabilities that can be present from birth**

| Type of disability | Explanation | How it might affect development |
|---|---|---|
| Hearing impairment | A hearing impairment can be genetic, or it could be due to a complication from infection in pregnancy or a complication at birth. | Hearing screening tests can identify if a baby has any hearing difficulties, as this can cause a delay in speech and communication. |
| Visual impairment | Visual impairment can vary from having the ability to see shapes and colours to blindness. Some children are unable to see some colours; this is called colour blindness. There are different reasons why children might have visual impairment: it could be caused by illness or infection or because of damage to the eye or the part of the brain that is responsible for vision. | Visual impairment can make it difficult for children to walk without support to avoid tripping and falling. A child with visual impairment might find it more difficult to develop social relationships early on because they cannot see people's faces. |
| Cerebral palsy | This term covers a range of disorders that affect movement and balance. It can be caused by a bleed on the brain or a reduction in the supply of oxygen to the brain. | Children might experience a delay in meeting their milestones. They might find walking and talking difficult and need speech therapy, physiotherapy or medication. |
| Down's syndrome | This is a genetic disability. Older parents are more likely to have a child born with Down's syndrome. Children who have Down's syndrome have a greater risk of having a **congenital** heart defect. People with Down's syndrome often share physical traits, such as almond-shaped eyes and a flatter bridge of the nose. | Every individual grows at a different rate. However, children with Down's syndrome might have a delay in their learning and be later in hitting their developmental milestones. |

## Health status

Some children live with **chronic** illness. This can have a negative effect on their development and wellbeing. Living with a condition that causes pain and discomfort and requires regular trips to see medical professionals can affect children's resilience and the way that they view themselves. It can also mean that they miss out on time playing with others.

## Eczema

This is a common condition in young children. It is caused when the immune system overreacts to irritants and allergens. Eczema causes patches of dry, cracked, sore skin. It is most common on the hands, face, scalp and elbows and behind the knees. Eczema can be very itchy and this can disrupt children's sleep.

## Asthma

This is a common chronic disease of the airways in the lungs. It causes wheezing, tightness of the chest and coughing. It can, in serious cases, result in death. Most children are able to take medication to keep their asthma under control. Although there is no cure, it can improve with age. Children with asthma might be less able to take part in physical activities due to being out of breath. If asthma is difficult to control, children might spend long periods in hospital and so miss out on mixing with others at nursery or pre-school.

## Repeated short-term illness

Some children might be prone to repeated short-term illness. This can have a negative impact on children's development. Some common short-term illnesses include:

**Colds** can make children tired as they might wake up at night coughing. They might need time off pre-school or nursery and miss out on playing with their friends.

**Ear infections** can be a sign of an underlying condition such as glue ear. This can cause pain and discomfort and hearing loss. This can delay children's development of speech and language.

**Vomiting and diarrhoea** can be especially dangerous in babies, as they can quickly become dehydrated. Over time, repeated vomiting and diarrhoea can result in children losing weight and becoming prone to further illness and infection.

## Obesity

Being overweight can cause a multitude of issues for children's health and wellbeing. The main cause of obesity in children is not being active enough and consuming too many calories. Some illnesses and medication can make children more prone to putting on weight. Being overweight can affect children's self-esteem and confidence. The risks of obesity are illustrated in Figure 1.3.

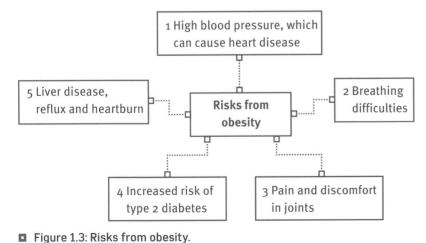

■ Figure 1.3: Risks from obesity.

■ Obesity can cause health problems.

**ACTIVITY**

Choose a health condition to focus on.

Design a poster that alerts others about how the condition can impact on children's growth and development.

For example:

Children who develop asthma might need to spend lots of time in hospital receiving treatment. This means they miss out on interacting with other children their age, which affects their social development. Children might not be able to be as active as they would like due to feeling out of breath. This can lead to children becoming overweight.

**CHECK MY LEARNING**

Explain the difference between chronic and short-term illness.

Assess how each can have a negative impact on children's emotional and social development.

# Physical factors that impact on children's overall development: diet and exercise

**GETTING STARTED**

With a partner discuss one positive of breastfeeding and one positive of bottle feeding.

## A healthy diet

What we eat affects our health positively or negatively. From birth, parents have to make choices about how to feed their children. Research tells us that breastfeeding is best for babies. It helps babies to build an emotional bond with their mother, protects from illness and reduces the likelihood of obesity later, which can impact on physical development and health. Breast milk is packed full of antibodies that can help boost a baby's immune system. However, not all women are able to breastfeed. Babies who are not breastfed are given specially formulated powdered milk.

Everyone needs to eat a balanced diet (see Figure 1.4 and Table 1.17). This is a mixture of carbohydrates, proteins, fats, vitamins and minerals, milk and other dairy. Not eating a good diet can lead to deficiencies that can affect health. Young children need to have a portion size equivalent to the size of the palm of their hand.

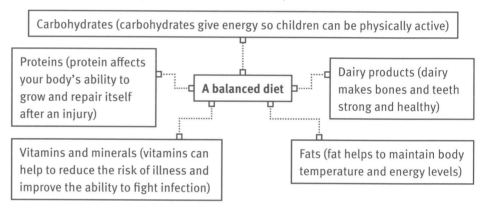

Carbohydrates (carbohydrates give energy so children can be physically active)

Proteins (protein affects your body's ability to grow and repair itself after an injury)

A balanced diet

Dairy products (dairy makes bones and teeth strong and healthy)

Vitamins and minerals (vitamins can help to reduce the risk of illness and improve the ability to fight infection)

Fats (fat helps to maintain body temperature and energy levels)

▢ Figure 1.4: Young children need to eat a balanced diet to be healthy and grow.

▢ Table 1.17: The effects of diet on children's growth and development

| Age | How diet affects children's growth and development |
| --- | --- |
| 0–18 months | Until around 6–9 months, babies need only milk to keep them healthy. As they grow older, milk is not enough. A balanced diet is essential to help a child to grow.<br><br>Lack of essential vitamins and minerals can make babies irritable and less likely to sleep well. Sleep is important for babies because this is when their bodies grow. |
| 18 months–3 years | Children are now much more mobile, so they need the right foods to give them energy. Young children need to eat little and often to help power their bodies. Without suitable foods children will become lethargic (sluggish and tired) and less likely to want to be active and learn. |
| 3–5 years | As children get older they need to have enough food to help them to concentrate and learn. Some food additives and colourings have been found to affect children's concentration and behaviour.<br><br>Food that is high in sugar leads to children gaining weight and having high energy followed by very low energy. This can make them disruptive and behave badly. |

**ACTIVITY**

Write a plan for a healthy breakfast, lunch and dinner for a 4-year-old.

1 Can you identify the different food types in the meals?

2 Describe the benefits of your meals for children's growth and development.

Too much or too little of an individual food group can make children unwell. Not enough vitamins and minerals in their diet can lead to the child's body being slow to heal. Hair and nails might become brittle and they might become constipated. In serious cases, being deficient in vitamin B12 can lead to anaemia. If left untreated, this can cause permanent damage to the body. Eating a balanced diet helps to prevent dietary deficiencies.

## Exercise

It is not just what you eat that affects your health. Exercise is another component of being healthy (see Table 1.18). Children under the age of 5 should be active for at least three hours a day spread out through the day. Children could ride bicycles, play on trampolines, crawl through tunnels or go swimming. Any activity that involves children moving their bodies is exercise. Young children who can walk should be encouraged to walk instead of being strapped into a buggy. This encourages their locomotion, co-ordination and balance. Being an overweight child usually leads to being an overweight adult and that has risks for health, such as diabetes and heart disease.

Children should maintain a healthy weight and take part in as much activity as possible. Being overweight can affect children's self-esteem and confidence. It can lead them to not feeling confident to join in with social activities and this can affect their wellbeing.

◻ Exercise is fun for children and should be part of their daily routine. How can parents and carers encourage children to be active?

◻ Table 1.18: The effects of exercise on children's growth and development

| Age | How exercise affects children's growth and development |
| --- | --- |
| 0–18 months | Babies need to have space to move and stretch their muscles. They need to flex and strengthen the muscles in readiness for crawling and walking.<br>Children at this age have bursts of energy and get tired quickly, so they need to rest and sleep often. |
| 18 months–3 years | As children get older they need to sleep less and can be active for longer. Children need to build up stamina.<br>Without the opportunity to run and enjoy freedom in their movements, they might be delayed in walking and developing their gross motor skills. This can lead to them having more frequent accidents. |
| 3–5 years | Children should be physically active for three hours a day. This is to help reduce the risk of obesity and to make sure that children are healthy and growing well.<br>As children get older a daily routine of exercise and fresh air helps them to concentrate and learn. |

### CHECK MY LEARNING

Plan one hour of activities for a 3-year-old child. It should include a suitable snack halfway through.

Your plan needs to suggest different ways that the child will be physically active and how this might promote their intellectual, emotional and social development.

# Environmental factors that impact on children's overall development: housing

Where a child grows up and those around them can affect their lives. There has been lots of research that suggests that where you grow up and what experiences you have shape your future life. Experiencing **housing needs**, such as not having suitable housing or having to move to temporary accommodation, can be very distressing for children and their families. Some families live in **areas of deprivation**. These are areas where there might be poor-quality housing, overcrowding and high rates of crime.

Why do you think some families might not have a permanent home?

Living in a house that is safe and secure is taken for granted by many people. However, not everyone has the luxury of having a roof over their head. There are many reasons why families find themselves living in poor-quality or temporary housing. Losing your home or living in poor-quality housing is incredibly stressful and can lead to long-term difficulties, such as debt, depression and poor health. This can affect a person's capacity to parent and children's wellbeing (see Table 1.19).

◻ Many people take living in a house that is safe and secure for granted.

Families that live in poverty often face social deprivation; this means not having normal interactions with the rest of society. They are also likely to be deprived of the essentials in life, such as food, clothing, warmth and amenities.

◘ Table 1.19: The effects of housing on children's growth and development

| Age | How housing can affect children's growth and development |
|---|---|
| 0–18 months | Babies who live in cramped housing might not have a peaceful place to sleep. Noise and light disrupt sleep, leaving babies restless, tearful and unhappy. A quiet space can help babies to sleep well.<br>The family might not have room to store suitable equipment for babies, meaning that they might be more at risk of accidents.<br>Having more space can allow babies to move around, especially as they practise crawling and walking. |
| 18 months–3 years | Children that have to move house often might find it difficult to settle. Parental stress at moving frequently might lead to family arguments and children not having attention from parents to help them to learn.<br>A stable family home can help parents to develop relationships within the community that can be good for young children's social development, too. Overcrowded accommodation can mean that there is little space for children's toys to help them to learn. Having their own space can help children to understand about their own belongings and help them to gain a sense of identity. |
| 3–5 years | Children who move house often might miss out on attending pre-school, nursery or school. This means that they do not start to form friendships with others and this can affect their learning.<br>Living in a flat might mean that children do not have access to an outdoor space to play, so they cannot develop their large muscles as well as those with an outdoor space.<br>Having a quiet place to rest and sleep helps children to wake up refreshed and ready to learn. |

## ACTIVITY

Look at the three case studies below.

Draw up a table identifying how you think each might affect children's growth and development.

Case study 1
*Inka is 3 years old and lives with her mum. They are currently living in a hostel which is miles away from family. They hope to be rehomed soon. Inka is frightened as she is often woken up at night by other residents in the hostel.*

Case study 2
*David is 5 years old. His father has lost his job. His mother does not work. His parents cannot afford to pay their mortgage and their house is being repossessed. This will mean that the family will be homeless. David's mother suffers from depression and his father is under a lot of stress.*

Case study 3
*Tomas is 8 months old and his family live on the 18th floor of a block of flats. There is a high level of crime on the estate and Tomas's mother is too frightened to go out without her partner, who works long hours.*

## CHECK MY LEARNING

Give examples of the effects on aspects of a child's growth and development of living in poor housing conditions.

Assess the impact on growth and development of living in poor housing conditions.

# Environmental factors that impact on children's overall development: the home

Everyone has a different home life. Some children have a happier home life than others. For example, sadly, some children suffer from abuse or neglect from their parents or carers. Children's experiences in the home help to shape their behaviour and emotions.

## Stability

All families go through difficulties from time to time. Parenting can be stressful and, at times, adults can find it hard to know how to deal with new situations. Most parents and carers learn from mistakes and do the best that they can to be supportive and caring for their children. Having a **stable** home life is very important for children. It means that they know what to expect, there is a routine that generally meets their needs well and they know they can rely on their family to take good care of them. Table 1.20 gives more detail about this.

☐ Table 1.20: Stability helps children to develop their confidence and sense of security

| Stable support from parents | Unstable support from parents |
|---|---|
| Reliable routine for bedtime and mealtimes. | No routine. Children go to bed very late or have their sleep disrupted. There are no regular mealtimes. Children are often hungry. |
| Sensible, fair rules and expectations for behaviour. | Parents do not put rules in place, so children act in ways that are dangerous to themselves and others. Parents keep changing their expectations, or they are unrealistic, meaning children do not know how to meet expectations. |
| Parents prioritise children and their wellbeing. | Parents act in chaotic and confusing ways for children; for example, they drink too much alcohol and/or use drugs. Parents might invite lots of new people to the home. |
| Children go to pre-school or nursery regularly and parents support their learning. | Children do not attend pre-school or nursery regularly and parents are uninterested in their learning. Children might not have chance to mix with other children of a similar age as parents do not view this as important. |

☐ Child abuse has an immediate and sometimes long-term effect on children. Help is available for anyone who is concerned that they are the victim of abuse or know someone who is being abused. Do you know who you could call if you had a concern about child abuse?

## Contact with extended family

Normal family life includes some arguments, disagreements and stressful periods. Families come under pressure for a variety of reasons. During this time, they often look to the wider family and their friends for support.

Extended family, such as grandparents, aunts and uncles, and cousins, can offer support in stressful times. Children will often enjoy spending their time with family and this can give parents a much-needed break.

According to a recent study, two in five grandparents provides regular care for their grandchildren. This can help parents a great deal and children will benefit from being cared for by someone who loves them.

### Positives of families offering childcare for children

- Children will be familiar with family, so likely to settle and be content.
- Family often provide care for children for free, saving parents potentially hundreds of pounds.
- Parents know that their family are safe and do not need to check they are suitable.

### Negatives of families offering care for children

- Parents and family might clash over behaviour and expectations for children.
- Family might have other responsibilities, meaning that children must fit in to their routine.
- Children might develop very strong attachments to family members, meaning they miss them when they are not in their care.

## Parental conflict

Children who grow up in households where there is constant **conflict**, such as arguing, shouting or physical aggression between adults, are victims of abuse. In the early years, children learn everything they know from the people around them. Therefore, if they see aggression, violence and verbal abuse, they will think that this is a normal way to act. Young children might be woken by arguments at night, so their sleep is disrupted. They might also become anxious and fearful and find it difficult to want to play and learn. Table 1.21 summarises the effects of home life on children.

◻ **Table 1.21: The effects of the home on children's growth and development**

| Age | How the home environment affects growth and development |
|---|---|
| 0–18 months | Babies who suffer abuse will be slow in developing. They might have poor attachments to adults. Babies might cry often. |
| 18 months–3 years | At this age, children might appear withdrawn and unable to play. Suffering abuse and parental conflict might mean that children are nervous and scared. They might show signs of distress, such as rocking or head banging. They might show little interest in playing. |
| 3–5 years | Children that have spent time growing up around violence and abuse often do not know that this behaviour is wrong. This might mean that they act in an aggressive way and find it difficult to get along with other children. Children who have suffered neglect might be behind in their development, might speak less and might appear to have a lack of interest in playing and learning. |

## Parents' mental health

Pregnancy involves lots of changes to hormones and can affect the mother's mood and emotions. This is sometimes called 'baby blues' and is perfectly normal after the baby is born. The mother's hormones will usually return to normal after a few days. However, just like ill health involving any other part of the body, some people experience poor mental health. Some women are already living with mental health problems when they become pregnant and others may experience problems because of hormonal changes during pregnancy. Having mental health problems may result in the mother not seeking care during pregnancy and making poor lifestyle choices.

A new mother can feel overwhelmed and anxious about being responsible for caring for a new life. Without good support, this can lead to poor attachment between mother and baby or the mother having negative thoughts and feeling desperate. Ultimately, this can mean she isn't able to care for herself and her baby or child well.

Mental health problems can be linked to other behaviours that could have a negative effect on children's development. Examples include having a poor diet, poor hygiene, substance abuse, failure to seek medical help for illness, or difficulty in forming relationships, leading to isolation and depression.

Sometimes, a person's emotional state means they are not able to think clearly and make good decisions. If someone has significant mental health issues, they might feel exhausted and unable to cope, meaning that they neglect the needs of their children.

**KEY TERM**

**Conflict** a serious or violent argument

**LINK IT UP**

You can find out more about the benefit of extended families on pages 52–53.

**ACTIVITY**

Look at the case study. What do you think the risks are for Belinda and her unborn baby?

*Belinda has a long history of depression and self-harm. She is now 34 weeks pregnant. Initially, she seemed positive about the pregnancy and attended all of her appointments with her midwife. In the last few weeks Belinda has missed all of her appointments and does not respond to phone calls or letters from the hospital. At her last appointment, she was underweight and looked dishevelled. The midwife was concerned as she had some deep cuts on her arms.*

Why do you think medical professionals might be concerned about Belinda's baby after it is born?

Imagine you are the medical professional. Write a report about why you are worried about Belinda and her unborn baby. Explain why it is important that Belinda has the right help now.

**CHECK MY LEARNING**

Write a description of an 'ideal' home environment for a child. You might want to present this as a storyboard, a mind map or a table.

# Environmental factors that impact on children's overall development: drugs, alcohol and smoking

Alcohol is often portrayed on television and in films as being glamorous and exciting. While drinking alcohol in moderation is not a concern for adults, heavy misuse of alcohol can have a devastating impact on a person's health and wellbeing.

Use of illegal drugs has different potential consequences. Not only will they make the user unwell and unpredictable in their behaviour, they can also lead to criminal activity and possibly imprisonment. Unpredictable and criminal behaviour poses a risk to children. If a parent is imprisoned, this can have financial, social and emotional implications for the family.

Smoking, though legal, has serious risks to health. Children who inhale second-hand smoke are at risk of developing cancer and breathing difficulties. Breathing conditions, such as asthma, are made worse by cigarette smoke.

Mothers are often asked about their alcohol and drug use and whether they smoke during pregnancy. Why do you think doctors might need to know this?

## The effects of alcohol and drugs on children's development

☐ If a parent or carer consumes alcohol there can be a harmful effect on children. Do you think this person would be able to parent well?

There are two types of drugs: prescription medication and illegal drugs. **Prescription drugs** are drugs that have been given to a person by a medical professional. However, if these drugs are not used in the way the medical professional has prescribed, this can be detrimental to health. **Illegal drugs** do not have a medicinal purpose and have not been prescribed by a medical professional.

Consuming alcohol and drugs can have a negative effect on the individual:

- Impaired judgement can lead to parents missing feeds for babies, allowing young children to engage in dangerous behaviours or leaving children with people who are unsuitable to care for them.
- More frequent accidents, such as the parent falling on the child or while carrying them. They might break furniture or equipment, making it dangerous. If the parent drives, children are at serious risk of being in an accident.
- Poor physical and mental health might mean that parents neglect children's basic needs, fail to support their learning and disrupt their ability to make good attachments with other people.
- Confusion and forgetfulness can lead to serious accidents, such as fires, as parents might forget to switch off cookers and equipment. The parent might forget to collect children from nursery or school, meaning the child becomes distressed.
- Erratic and dangerous behaviours can be frightening for children and leave them with low self-esteem. They might also start to copy behaviour, leaving them liable to have accidents.
- Drugs and alcohol are poisonous to young children and, if they are able to get hold of them and consume them, can be fatal.

## Smoking

Smoking cigarettes damages health. Secondary smoke or passive smoking is also damaging to health. Children who breathe in smoke are more at risk of:

- respiratory difficulties
- ear infections
- eye infections
- worsening asthma
- some cancers.

It is illegal to smoke in public places and in 2015 it became illegal in England to smoke in a car with children inside. Smoking increases the risk of sudden infant death syndrome, where babies can die without any identifiable cause, and can also contribute towards the likelihood of children developing glue ear. Glue ear can affect children's hearing and lead to a delay in developing language and communication skills. Children who live in households where parents smoke might be more prone to breathing problems and this can restrict their physical development.

## Parental health

There is lots of help and support for parents and carers who have difficulty with alcohol use, drug use or smoking. Doctors can provide support to help stop smoking, such as nicotine patches, chewing gum and nicotine replacements. Midwives and the National Health Service provide programmes that can help with reducing alcohol consumption. Those who are addicted to drugs can have drug replacement medication and attend programmes to help them to quit drug use.

**ACTIVITY**

Write a report about how a parent's alcoholism or drug taking can make them less able to parent children under 18 months and under 5 years old.

Consider the following areas:

1 meeting children's physical needs

2 meeting children's emotional needs.

**CHECK MY LEARNING**

What are the long-term effects on a child of a parent smoking, consuming an excessive amount of alcohol or using drugs?

# Social factors that impact on children's overall development: discrimination

**GETTING STARTED**

In pairs, explore a popular misconception.

For example, 'All people with blond hair are dumb' → 'Stephen Hawking had blond hair and he was a genius'.

When looking at socio-economic factors we look at the relationship between social and financial factors.

Why do you think that income or lack of it has an impact on children's growth and development?

Discrimination occurs when assumptions are made about a person or group of people and they are treated less favourably as a result. Discrimination can take place for a variety of reasons, such as gender, race, age, social background or ability.

## Race

Racial and cultural discrimination can have a negative impact on even the youngest children's wellbeing. Even very young children can be the victims of discrimination. For example, babies born of mixed ethnicity might not be fully accepted by either ethnic group and this can lead to poor attachments. Some cultural practices, such as dietary requirements, are not well understood by others, leaving children with limited choices of things to eat. This can mean that they miss out on having a balanced diet to support their growth and development.

Children who are in the minority within a childcare setting might feel self-conscious and unable to join in. If staff at the childcare setting do not consider the toys and resources they provide for children, children might not see any representation of themselves. This can affect their self-image and emotional wellbeing.

Look at the scenario below.

*Jessi is 4 years old. He attends a nursery every day. Jessi is interested in fire engines and fire fighters. The nursery wanted to support Jessi and has bought a book about fire fighters, a toy fire engine and firefighter figures. However, all the figures and pictures in the book have the same colour skin and this is different to Jessi's.*

If Jessi doesn't see a likeness of himself in the books and figures he might start to believe that he can never be a fire fighter. This might make him feel disappointed and could impact his self-esteem.

| How discrimination affects children |
| --- |
| • Children might become shy and withdrawn. |
| • Children might feel isolated from the people and the community where they live. |
| • Children might find it difficult to form relationships. |
| • Children could develop a lack of identity and confusion over who they are, affecting their self-esteem. |
| • Children could be less likely to want to join in with activities and mix with others. |

## Disability

Some discrimination is intentional, and some discrimination happens because people fail to consider what limitations some people have. An example of this might be where children, through disability, miss out on joining in. Providers of public spaces, such as play provision, need to consider how people with a disability can get around. It might be that the environment is not suitable for a child who uses a walking frame – for example, the doorways are too narrow or the tables are too high. This can mean

**BEST PRACTICE**

Nursery and pre-school workers can help to ensure that there is no discrimination in their setting by providing children with a variety of resources depicting diversity.

☐ Children who are discriminated against could become less likely to join in with activities and mix with others. How do you think that might affect their development?

that the child cannot join in properly with others. This could lead to the child feeling excluded and failing to make good progress in their development. In turn, this can affect the child's self-esteem. However, with reasonable adjustments there might a way of organising the environment to include everyone.

In early years settings, staff need to consider children with disabilities and how they can make sure that all children can access the full curriculum. Some settings are better at achieving this than others.

## Home situation

Everyone's home situation is different, and it is important that children see and hear positive representations of their home environments. Some children grow up in a home where they have two parents of the same gender. There might not be good representation of this – for example, story books and television programmes might not depict families with two parents of the same gender. This means these children do not have characters that they can relate to, which can make them feel excluded.

Some children grow up in low-income homes, meaning they might not have the same resources, toys or opportunities as others, which puts them at a disadvantage. **Discrimination can leave children open to being bullied, which can affect their confidence and wellbeing**.

### CHECK MY LEARNING

Explain what is meant by discrimination and how it affects children's emotional development. Suggest how early years settings can help to make sure that young children are included and learn about others.

### ACTIVITY

Write a plan to show how the nursery you are working at has resources in place to make sure no child is discriminated against. Make sure to consider:
- race
- disability
- home situation.

# Social factors that impact children's overall development: relationships with primary carers

It is important that children form close attachments to their main carers. This helps them to feel secure and loved.

There are ways that parents and carers can help their baby to develop close relationships with them and their main carers, such as:

- holding them soon after birth
- sharing feeding when possible
- holding and cuddling them
- talking to them
- meeting their need for food, warmth, affection and cleanliness quickly
- spending time with them.

Some things can deter the baby from forming close relationships, such as:

- having multiple carers
- not being held regularly
- being left to cry
- rough handling
- lack of eye contact and not being spoken to.

## Warmth and affection

Babies love and want to be cuddled. A Canadian study has shown that babies that are cuddled close to their mothers' bare skin after birth develop a more regular heartbeat and are better able to maintain a stable body temperature. This is especially important for premature babies who cannot easily regulate their own temperature.

Early years practitioners are aware of the need to cuddle babies and young children and show them affection. Young children are naturally trusting and will show affection to others. It is important that they get a positive and genuine response to their acts of affection in order for them to feel validated and secure. As children get older, practitioners teach them about boundaries and children become more sparing with their affection, saving it for those people closest to them.

**ACTIVITY**

Look at the daily routine below of an 18-month-old baby.

Write down some ways that the childminder can be affectionate and warm with the child to boost their sense of wellbeing at each time during the day.

| 7.30am | child arrives |
| 9am | child shares story with childminder |
| 9.30am | nappy change |
| 10am | childminder takes child to shops and park |
| 11.30am | child helps childminder to make lunch |
| 12pm | child eats lunch |
| 1pm | child gets ready for afternoon nap |
| 2.30pm | child wakes up and has nappy changed |
| 3pm | child plays with wooden bricks with childminder |
| 4pm | child gets ready to go home. |

# Giving children attention

Parents and carers need to be 'available' for children (see Figure 1.5). Parents and carers who spend their whole time looking at their mobile phones are unlikely to develop good relationships with their children (see Table 1.22). This is because eye contact and attention is important if children are going to thrive and develop strong attachments and good language and communication skills. Children who receive plenty of attention do not need to seek attention in negative ways, such as behaving badly. When adults take interest and play with children, these children make better progress in their learning and development. It also raises their self-esteem and confidence.

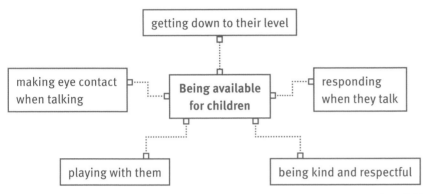

Figure 1.5: Ways that parents and carers can show children they are 'available'.

Table 1.22: The effects of relationships on children's growth and development

| Age | How relationships affect children's growth and development |
| --- | --- |
| 0–18 months | Children who have not had affection and attention might not develop bonds with their parent or primary carer. Poor attachments can affect children's ability to form relationships with other people. |
| 18 months–3 years | Children at this age might be starting to mix with other children. Children learn by copying others. Poor relationships might lead children to act aggressively, as they have not learned how to get along and play with others. This can mean they are not able to play and make friends. |
| 3–5 years | Children who have poor relationships might not be able to express themselves well. They might have emotional outbursts and demand attention. This can be difficult when children are in a group, such as a nursery, pre-school or school. It can affect their ability to learn and make friends. |

Children learn by copying others. How might an aggressive parent impact on a child's behaviour and development?

## CHECK MY LEARNING

Develop a guide for a new practitioner in a nursery.

Outline how important it is to show children care and affection.

You might want to produce a 'good practice guide' explaining the best ways to promote children's emotional, social, communication and language skills.

# Social factors that impact on children's overall development: siblings and extended family

A child's family circumstances will help to shape their early social experiences of forming relationships. Having a sibling can mean you have a friend to share in experiences and family activities. But not all brothers and sisters get along, and this can cause arguments.

## Only child

A child who does not have siblings does not have to compete for their parents' attention or share their toys and belongings. An only child might be accustomed to playing by themselves. Not having an annoying younger sibling borrowing all your things, or an older sibling bossing you around, might sound ideal. But only children can sometimes find it difficult when they start pre-school or nursery. This is because they might not be accustomed to being around other children and having to share.

Being an only child can feel like you are centre of the universe for children. So if a new brother or sister arrives, it can be extremely difficult for a young child to cope. Table 1.23 shows some of ways that a child might react to a new younger sibling.

## New baby

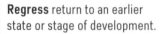 Table 1.23: How children might respond to a new baby

| Wanting to be babied | The child might **regress** in their behaviour. For example, they might start to wet themselves again. |
|---|---|
| Showing jealousy | The child might try to physically push the baby away or climb over the baby to get onto their parent's lap. |
| Temper tantrums | As children struggle to understand their strong emotions, they might have outbursts of uncontrollable behaviour, screaming and crying. |
| Being overprotective | It is not always negative. Children might take their role as a big brother or sister very seriously and be overprotective of their new sibling, wanting to look after them and care for them. |

## Large families

Being part of a large family means that there is always someone around to talk to, play with or argue with. Although parents will often find their children's squabbles and **rivalry** frustrating, children with siblings quickly learn how to negotiate and resolve conflict. This means that they develop a good set of social skills to help them when they start nursery or pre-school. Sometimes, children with siblings are more patient and able to share and take turns because they have experience of doing this with their siblings.

## Step-siblings

Due to marriage and relationship breakdowns and the forming of new relationships, children might find they need to accept a new step-sibling into their lives. This is a hugely complex situation. Getting used to a new step-parent and then step-sibling can leave children feeling pushed out. The step-siblings might be very different, having had a different parenting experience to the child's own. However, when children are young, they are generally accepting of a new playmate, especially if they are quite close in age. As step-siblings might not live with the family permanently, having a step-sibling that visits at weekends but goes home again can help children to adjust to the new situation.

## Relationships with extended family

During the COVID-19 pandemic in 2020 and 2021, many families faced long periods of being separated from their extended family and friends. This illustrated how important these relationships are to young children.

The wider relationships children share with trusted adults help them to begin to learn to separate from their parents and form loving relationships with other people who care about them. This is an important part of becoming sociable, independent individuals.

 **Extended family and friends play a big part in the lives of young children.**

Children learn about the different rules and expectations people have for them in different contexts. For example, they might learn that grandparents are more flexible with rules than their parents, or that aunties and uncles who do not yet have their own children have barely any rules. This helps children to learn about moderating their behaviour, developing negotiation skills and reasoning. In turn, this helps them to learn about feeling safe and confident.

Extended family very often step in to help families with childcare and during a crisis, which can provide essential support for children and their families' emotional and physical wellbeing.

### ACTIVITY

Complete the following table to consider the positives and disadvantages of each different type of family.

| Type of family | Positives | Disadvantages |
|---|---|---|
| Only child | | |
| Large family | | |
| Step-family | | |
| Extended family | | |

### CHECK MY LEARNING

Suggest two factors that might change a child's family structure and explain how this might make the child feel.

# Financial factors that impact on children's overall development: income

**GETTING STARTED**

How do you think the government tries to help families living in poverty?

Conduct some research to find out.

Living in poverty can lead to groups of people being isolated from others. Why do you think this is not a good thing for families with young children?

## Low income

You will have heard of the term 'poverty' but might not know what this means in detail. There are different types of poverty, and professionals use measures to identify those who are affected by poverty.

- Relative low income. This is where there is not enough income to afford an ordinary living pattern. Those in relative poverty cannot afford the activities that the average person enjoys.
- Absolute low income. This is when there is not enough income to afford the basics – food, clothing and shelter.

### Why do some families have a low income?

There are many reasons why some people find themselves without enough money to meet their personal needs, including:

- losing their job
- relationship breakdown
- borrowing more money than they can pay back
- death of a partner
- injury and inability to work
- mental health issues
- being a victim of crime
- disability or illness
- disasters, such as floods or fire.

Mental health problems are more common among people who have a low income. Why do you think this might be?

■ Research shows children who grow up in households where parents work are more likely to go on to further education and less likely to live in poverty when they grow up. Why do you think this is?

### Access to good early education experiences

One strategy that the government has used to help families to get into work is providing free early education for children. This means that all 3- and 4-year-olds and some 2-year-olds can go to nursery or pre-school for a set number of hours and their parents do not have to pay. This helps parents to be able to work. Good-quality childcare provides children with opportunities for learning that they might not have at home. This improves their chances of doing well in the future.

Although poverty has a negative impact on children, it is important to remember that many people go on to escape poverty and become very successful. Some families experience periods of poverty and go on to improve their situation.

### Support for families on low income

Despite the **welfare state** system, figures show that between 2020 and 2021, 3.9 million children in the United Kingdom were living in poverty (see Figure 1.6). The reasons why some people live in poverty are complicated, but it is a harsh reality that many families do not have enough money to feed their children. As a result, some have to rely on **food banks**.

**KEY TERMS**

**Welfare state** the system for protecting health and wellbeing in the United Kingdom. This includes financial and social support, for example through pensions and benefits.

**Food bank** a charity that provides food for free to people in need.

Children whose families are on a low income are sometimes eligible for free school meals.

Footballer Marcus Rashford started a campaign in 2020 to raise awareness of child poverty. The campaign highlighted that for some children, their free school meal is their only meal of the day. As a result, during school holidays many children go hungry.

■ Figure 1.6: In a typical classroom, 8 in every 30 children live in poverty.

Being hungry affects not only children's growth, as they do not get sufficient nutrients to grow, but also their mood, concentration and ability to sleep.

## Families on high income

It is generally accepted that children born to parents who have a high income have significant advantages in life right from birth. For example, they might have better healthcare, resources and toys.

Parents can afford suitable clothing and footwear and ensure that children have warmth, a good standard of housing and enough food to eat.

However, being able to afford such lifestyles often means that parents must work long hours. This means that they have less time to spend with their children. For children, this can mean that they spend long periods in childcare. Over time, they might have to adjust to different carers and different environments, which can be challenging for children. Parents might choose private education for their children, and this can sometimes mean that children spend a long time at school.

Having extra money after paying for essentials can mean that parents are able to give children added advantages, such as travelling abroad for holidays. This opens their minds to new experiences.

Parents on a high income might have stressful jobs. This means that although they might be free from financial stress, they find it difficult to have a good work–life balance, sometimes leading to a stressful environment for children.

It is important not to make assumptions about individuals based on the perception of their advantages and disadvantages. Despite differing circumstances, all families face similar concerns and worries and enjoy the pleasures and advantages of parenting.

**ACTIVITY**

Carry out some research about childcare in your local area.

Look for information on one type of childcare.

You might find information on your local authority website or nursery websites.

You could look for opening hours, the ages of children who can attend, how much it costs and what learning activities it offers.

Write a short review about the childcare you have found and explain how you think it might benefit children's physical, intellectual, social and emotional development as well as their communication and language.

**CHECK MY LEARNING**

State three disadvantages for children growing up in low-income families.

Assess why children who are born into high-income families might have more advantages.

# Financial factors that impact on children's overall development: access to services

Despite children growing up in different families and with different advantages and disadvantages, there are some services for families that are available for all such as the Family Information Service. Accessing these services has benefits for children's health and wellbeing, and for their overall development.

## Dentists

Many parents and carers do not realise that babies' teeth are starting to form in the gums before they appear in the mouth. Because of this, teeth can become damaged and decayed from a very young age. Tooth decay can be extremely painful for young children. It is the main cause of children being admitted to hospital for a **general anaesthetic** in the United Kingdom.

Parents do not need to pay for their child to visit the dentist and have treatment. Visiting a dentist from a young age can help to identify any dental problems early on. It also helps children to learn about caring for their teeth and can prevent them from suffering the pain associated with poor dental hygiene.

## Health visitors

Parents will often first meet their health visitor when the mother is pregnant or the baby is very young. Health visitors are midwives or nurses who specialise in public health. Their role is to work with families who have children under the age of 5. They can help families to prevent ill-health and offer advice and support (see Figure 1.7).

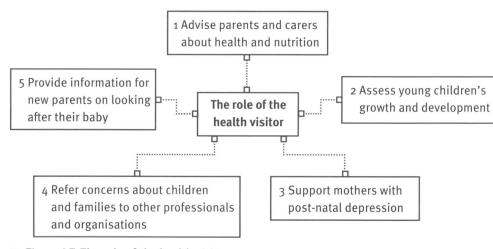

Figure 1.7: The role of the health visitor.

## Early years education

Most parents and carers choose some form of childcare for their children before they start school. For some parents and carers, this is because they need someone to care for their child while they work. Other parents send their children to childcare to help them to socialise and get ready for starting school. The main types of early education are pre-schools, nursery and childminders. Table 1.24 provides more information about early education.

◘ Table 1.24: Different types of early education

| Type of early education | Description | Advantages | Disadvantages |
|---|---|---|---|
| Pre-school | Usually for children aged 2–5 years.<br><br>It might operate from a community centre or purpose-built building.<br><br>Usually operates during school term time and school hours. | Helps children to socialise with others their own age.<br><br>Parents can usually choose what sessions their child attends. | Pre-schools are usually open for sessions, rather than full-time.<br><br>As pre-schools are open only in term time, parents might not have childcare in the holidays. Young babies cannot attend. |
| Nursery | Usually for children aged between 3 months and 5 years.<br><br>Generally operate from a building solely for the nursery.<br><br>Usually operate for the whole day and most of the year except public holidays. | Nurseries suit parents who need care while they work.<br><br>If a family has more than one young child, they can both attend. | Can be expensive if children do not receive free childcare.<br><br>Can be very popular, so spaces may be limited. |
| Childminder | This is an individual working from their home, possibly with an assistant.<br><br>They can provide care for babies from 6 weeks old up to 18 years old if needed.<br><br>Childminders will operate for varied hours. | Families can have all their children cared for in one place.<br><br>Childminders have smaller numbers of children, so children get more attention.<br><br>More homely environment. | As numbers are smaller, children do not get to socialise with as many children.<br><br>If the childminder is unwell the children will not be able to attend. |

**ACTIVITY**

Design a poster advertising a service for young families.

Your poster should include the following information:

Who can attend

A brief description of the service

What the benefit is of the service.

## Experiences outside the home

When parents and carers are at home with young children, they might take them to places to help them to socialise and learn. This has benefits not only for children but also for parents, who can meet up and develop friendships with other parents.

Singing groups are a great way for babies and young children to hear lots of different songs, rhymes and talking. Learning simple nursery rhymes and songs can help to promote children's early communication and language skills. Being within a group also helps children to be sociable and get used to being around others.

Parent-and-toddler groups often operate in local spaces, such as community centres. This helps parents to form relationships with people who might live nearby. This can be really positive for new parents' self-esteem and mental health and helps them to not feel **isolated**. Babies and toddlers can get used to mixing with other children with their parent's guidance and support. The toddler group might include singing or story-telling or a combination of both, called 'rhyme time' (often offered by local libraries), and some time for children to play together, do physical or craft activities, and have a drink and a snack. This helps them to prepare for moving on to pre-school or nursery.

Sports clubs can be particularly helpful for children who do not have an outside space or a garden at home and so miss out on playing outdoors in a safe environment. Being active from a young age can help young children to develop a positive attitude to exercising and being healthy. There will always be some form of rules to games, and this helps children to learn about playing with others and taking turns.

**KEY TERM**

**Isolated** being alone and away from others for too much of the time

**CHECK MY LEARNING**

Using your research about the Family Information Service, develop a table of or guide to services and their purpose.

# Learning outcome B: assessment practice

## How you will be assessed

When you have completed Learning outcome B you will be able to complete Task 2 and Task 3 of your set assignment. These tasks cover your learning across Learning outcomes A and B. You will be allowed 2.5 hours to complete each task. In each task you will demonstrate your knowledge and understanding of the principles of growth and development, and how factors impact on children's overall development.

Evidence includes:

- all expected milestones and all next immediate milestones
- a well-developed reasoning for the progression from one milestone to the next with fully accurate links
- four factors accurately selected from the case study
- a fully detailed account on how the factors could impact on development.

---

### TIPS

**Think about:**

- the progression from one milestone to the next
- how the factors could impact on a child's overall development
- how the different areas of development are linked.

---

### CHECKPOINT

**Strengthen**

- Identify one environmental, physical and social and financial factor that affects children's growth and development.
- Explain how each factor affects children's growth and development for children aged 0 to 18 months, 18 months to 3 years and 3 to 5 years. You could choose one specific age from each band.

**Challenge**

- Compare two physical factors that impact on a baby during pregnancy.
- Compare the impact of two factors from each physical, environmental and social and financial category and state how they impact on the growth and development of children aged 0 to 18 months, 18 months to 3 years and 3 to 5 years. You could choose one specific age from each age band.
- State which factor you believe has the biggest impact on children's learning. Explain your reasoning.

To complete this task you must work individually.

## Case study

Josie is 4 years old and has just started in pre-school.

Josie has previously spent most of her time with her grandmother, because both parents work full time. Josie enjoys telling and listening to stories with her grandmother. Josie and her family live in a small flat with access to a shared garden. They don't have much money and the family receive additional support for Josie to attend the pre-school.

At pre-school, Josie tends to stand and watch the other children and they tend to ignore her as they don't know how to include her.

Josie is a picky eater and doesn't like to eat fruit and vegetables. Her favourite food is a cheese sandwich.

Produce a written account on Josie's expected development. Your account must include:

- the expected milestones for her current stage of physical development
- the expected milestones for her current stage of communication development
- the next immediate milestones the pre-school will be focusing on to support her progression in physical and communication development
- the links between the current milestones and the future milestones of the two given areas with reasons for your choices.

For your second written account select four factors from the case study that will impact on Josie's overall development.

Your account must include:

- how these four factors can impact on Josie's overall development
- which of these factors may have the most influence on Josie's development and why
- which of these factors may have the least influence on Josie's development and why.

## TAKE IT FURTHER

Read the following case study.

Oliver was born at 28 weeks of pregnancy. He suffers from foetal alcohol syndrome. His mother and father are both alcoholics. Oliver went to live with his grandmother and then his uncle because his parents did not always ensure he had sufficient food. He was often left in a soiled nappy. Later he went to live with a foster family. His mother is currently not drinking alcohol so, at the age of 2, Oliver is now back living with her. He has just learned to say 'mama' and 'dada'. When his mother tries to cuddle him he often pulls away. He is smaller than other boys of his age and has just started to walk.

Write an account about how the different factors could impact on Oliver's overall development, making clear links between factors and the relevant areas of development.

# COMPONENT

# 02 Learning Through Play

## Introduction

Play is both fun and motivating for young children. It helps to promote areas of development and allows children to gain new skills. Can you remember what toys and games you played with when you were 3 years old? What about the activities that you joined in with when you were 5? Play can be different depending on the age of the child. You will learn the many different types of children's play that can be offered and how this play can help them develop, such as locomotive play and how this can improve gross motor skills. You will consider how you can support a child though play and how learning can happen during planned activities.

Singing nursery rhymes can help a child with their communication development; what other activities could help? Did you ever play with a doll or use puppets? Have you thought about how using them improved your emotional development? Using your knowledge and understanding from this component, you will be able to plan suitable activities that will promote learning across the five areas of development in young children.

### LEARNING OUTCOMES

In this component you will:

| A | understand how children play |
|---|---|
| B | understand how children's learning can be supported through play. |

# Stages of children's play: birth–2 years

Play is often seen simply as a fun activity for a child to keep them occupied. However, it is more than just fun; it is a vital tool that children use to gain a better understanding of the world around them. They are able to interact with others and learn mental, physical and **social skills** that are necessary in later life.

Children don't have to be taught how to play; they are born knowing how to do it. Play can be structured or unstructured, and at times children may need an adult to support them. As children grow up, they can use play as a way to express themselves and develop as an individual. Whatever form play takes, it is a very important part of growing up and learning.

How do you think play helped you to develop your social skills?

## Unoccupied play

**Unoccupied play** usually occurs between birth and 3 months old. It is one way that babies learn about their bodies and begin to understand how to control their movements. Have you ever watched a baby kicking their legs around and moving their arms? To us, it doesn't seem like play, but this is what is known as unoccupied play. Babies will make seemingly random movements with their bodies, kicking, stretching, grabbing and moving their faces. This is their attempt at learning about their environment and how their muscles move.

Movement of arms and legs helps to develop a baby's gross motor skills. Their muscles become stronger, which helps as they learn to hold their head up or begin to crawl. Without the development of gross motor skills, a child would find it difficult to perform basic everyday tasks such as walking or climbing. This could prevent them from being able to play with other children.

▢ The bright colours and moving objects of this mobile and mat are attractive for babies. There is plenty of room for this baby to move their arms and legs around.

# Solitary play

Playing alone is a natural step in the process of play. **Solitary play** occurs from birth to around 2 years of age. At this age, children are not curious about what others are doing and don't show an interest in playing with their peers. They will often sit and play with a toy and repeat actions, such as banging a spoon on a pan or moving parts on an activity cube. At times, older children may choose to play alone even when they have the skills to play with others.

A small child playing with a treasure basket, taking objects out and exploring them, will be improving their confidence and imagination.

## KEY TERM

**Solitary play** playing alone.

 Although there are other children in the room, this child is happy playing by themself. Why might they not be ready to play with others?

---

**ACTIVITY**

*Deborah is concerned about Harrison, who is 20 months old. She is worried that he is not joining in play with other children in the same way as his brother, who is 3 years and 6 months old.*

Make notes on what you could say to Deborah to reassure her that his stage of play is expected at this age.

---

**CHECK MY LEARNING**

1  Identify the age groups for unoccupied and solitary play. Give an example for each stage that identifies the characteristics of that play.

2  Describe how solitary play can give children the chance to:
   • use their imaginative skills
   • be able to explore.

# Stages of children's play: 2–3 years

After the age of 2, children are keen to explore their environment and try to understand what is going on around them. Play allows them to do this. They need to touch each toy or object to work out how it moves, how it makes noises or how to use it. Their imagination is used more and more when playing. As well as trying to understand their environment, they are also trying to understand other children.

How do you think 2–3-year-olds differ in play from younger children?

## Spectator/onlooker play

**Spectator/onlooker play** takes place at around 2 years of age. Watching other children is central to this stage of play. Children are beginning to explore the world around them but still lack the skills to join in with others. This stage is important as children learn through personal interaction with others and the objects in their environment. Children will often notice other children around them and may sit and watch them without talking to them. They are using this time to think about what others are doing and how they are doing it. A child may take part in social interaction, starting to speak to other children and ask questions such as 'What's that?' and 'Can I have it?' However, they do not take part in play.

During an arts and crafts activity in this stage of play, children will watch others play but not play with items, such as the paints or coloured markers, themselves. They may go over to the other children playing and ask questions about what they are doing with the paint or offer support by giving suggestions. They may ask the children what they are drawing or tell them what colour they should use.

◼ Limited social skills mean that a child could find it difficult to join in play with others.

## Parallel play

Around the age of 2–3 years, children have moved on from simply observing others to sitting near them and playing alongside them. This is referred to as **parallel play**. A child will play in close proximity to another child/children but will not join in play with them.

Playing alongside another child is one way of beginning to build trust around others and to help with social interaction. While playing alongside others, children are learning what their peers are doing and are starting the process of forming an understanding of others.

Parallel play can lead to new ways of playing and learning new skills. A child playing with blocks may watch another child stack them; this can lead to them mimicking that behaviour and learning the skills associated with construction play.

> **KEY TERM**
>
> **Parallel play** playing alongside others but not playing with them.

> **BEST PRACTICE**
>
> During parallel play, adults should watch over children as they have not yet developed their sharing skills and may take equipment from others.

▣ When taking part in creative activities such as playing with playdough, children will concentrate on their own model but will be able to see other children's creations, which will inspire them.

**ACTIVITY**

1 In small groups, create a role-play that shows spectator/onlooker play. You should think about the activity the children will take part in and what other children around them will do at the same time. Carefully plan the questions the children may ask each other. You should then present your role-play to the rest of the class.

2 In your groups, give an example of how a 2-year-old might play and the skills a child may develop from parallel play.

**CHECK MY LEARNING**

1 Identify some examples of parallel play and spectator play.

2 What social skills might a child use when in the parallel play stage?

3 Describe how parallel play can help a child to learn new skills.

# Stages of children's play: 3–5 years

By the time a child reaches 3 years old, they have developed a sense of what being social is. At this point in their lives they have started developing friendships and have a clear preference for who they want to play with. Children are now more co-operative; they are more able to wait for their turn and share resources and toys. As their communication is now more developed, others around them find it easier to understand them. Vocabulary has increased and children will try to find the words they need to have a conversation with others. They particularly like to ask questions. They are moving away from playing on their own and are now gaining an interest in playing with others. However, playing with other children does not happen straight away. Why do you think this is?

## Associative play

Between 3 and 4 years old, children start to interact with others, becoming more interested in other children than the toys that are around them. However, there is not a large amount of interaction. This is called **associative play**. This type of play is different from parallel play, as children are becoming more involved in what others are doing around them. Children may play the same game or even share toys, but they will be playing in their own way. Social skills are being developed when children start to take turns using resources/equipment and share their ideas and thoughts about what they are doing.

A group of children using the sand pit may look like they are enjoying play together; however, they are acting independently from one another and playing on their own. Children playing in the sand pit will share buckets, spades and other equipment and will talk to each other about what they are creating. But they will be playing on their own. Children are curious and at this age, as they play and watch others, they want to learn more. For example, watching others play with sand can lead children to ask questions such as 'Why is the sand soft?' and 'How do I make a sandcastle?'

This is an important time for children, as they are beginning to develop skills including:
- problem solving
- asking questions such as *How?*, *What?* and *Why?*
- socialisation
- communication.

◘ These children are sharing the blocks but each building something of their own. How can this activity develop skills such as problem solving or communication?

# Co-operative play

**KEY TERM**

**Co-operative play** when children are playing with each other.

**Co-operative play** occurs from 4 years onwards. By this time, children have acquired the necessary skills to be able to interact with each other for the purpose of play. They will have interest in both the activity and the other children involved. Children will begin to participate and work together towards a common goal.

Key features of co-operative play could include:

- sharing
- creating and following rules
- turn-taking
- negotiating.

At this age, the equipment or toys given to children will often require them to share and take turns, especially if the activity has limited resources. Children will begin to try to follow the rules of the game or activity and learn to understand that winning isn't the most important factor.

Table 2.1 summarises the different stages of play.

▪ **Table 2.1: A summary of the different stages of play**

| Stage | Description |
| --- | --- |
| Unoccupied | Physical movement of arms and legs by small babies. |
| Solitary | Children play alone. |
| Spectator | Children watch others play but may ask questions about what other children are doing. |
| Parallel | Children will play near others, often sitting next to them. |
| Associative | Children interact with others and share resources but will play on their own. |
| Co-operative | Children will interact with others and work towards a common goal. |

**ACTIVITY**

It is important for parents/carers to know the different stages of play their child will go through.

Design a leaflet for parents/carers that explains the different stages and gives examples of how children play at each stage.

Show your leaflet to the rest of the class. Have you missed anything?

**CHECK MY LEARNING**

1 Describe the difference between associative and co-operative play, giving an example of each.
2 Why are language skills important to support children in associative play?
3 Describe the social skills children need to take part in co-operative play.

# Types of play (1)

**GETTING STARTED**

Working in a small group, discuss the games/play activities you enjoyed playing as a child. Write down the names of the games/play activities that were similar to each other.

When children play, there are many activities they can take part in. These activities can be organised into different types of play (see Figure 2.1).

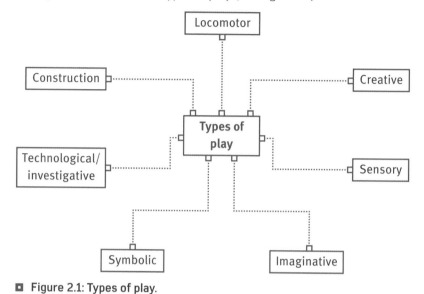

■ Figure 2.1: Types of play.

**KEY TERMS**

**Locomotor** relating to physical movement.

**Sensory** relating to one or more of the senses.

## Locomotor play

From birth, children are able to take part in locomotive play. This is because this type of play is based around the development of gross motor skills and physical activity. Any activity that uses gross motor skills or allows children to enjoy movement for movement's sake can be called **locomotor** play.

## Creative play

Learning about the world around them, children can take part in creative play. They are able to try to make something new, and they can do this in different ways. For example, a child may shake a tambourine, but they may also choose to hit it or bang it against another object to make a different sound. Creative play gives the child freedom to learn in their own way and to discover new things.

## Sensory play

Humans have five senses – touch, taste, smell, hearing and sight. Any activity that supports a child to use one or more of these senses is called **sensory** play. Sensory play helps children to discover the texture and function of things. For example, using scented slime or playdough is a good activity for small children, as it helps them to understand new smells whilst developing their fine motor skills when they touch, squish and squeeze it.

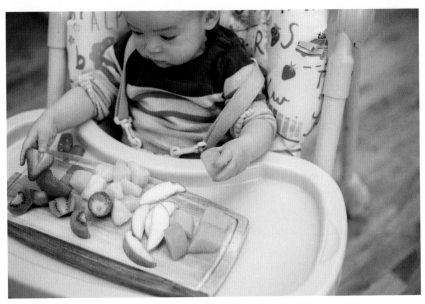

☐ This child is playing with a selection of fruit. What senses will the child use in this play? How does it help them learn and develop?

## Imaginative play

During this type of play, children are driven by their imagination; they will pretend in some way and act out what they have seen, heard or experienced in the real world. In role-play, children can dress up and use props to do this. Imagination can be sparked through small world play using miniature figures such as cars, people or animals. Children are able to practise their communication, emotional and social skills as they express themselves.

## Symbolic play

Children will often use objects to **symbolise** other items, such as a cardboard box becoming a space rocket or a block becoming a telephone. Symbolic play is a part of imaginative play that usually occurs from 18 months onwards, as children begin to understand that objects can represent other things.

**KEY TERM**

**Symbolise** (of an object) to represent something else.

**ACTIVITY**

1  Think of one play activity from your childhood. Write a paragraph to describe which type of play it was and give reasons.

2  There are five senses. Working with the person next to you, make an activity that could support one of them.

3  Create a list of three objects that a child may use in symbolic play. What could they symbolise?

**CHECK MY LEARNING**

You have learned about the different types of children's play. To check your learning of these, answer the following questions:

1  What is meant by locomotor play?

2  Why are children under the age of 18 months unable to play in a symbolic way?

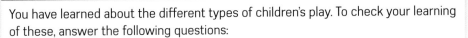

# Types of play (2)

## GETTING STARTED

Look back at your list of games that you enjoyed playing. Now sort them into different types of play. Can you think of a name for each of your types of play?

## BEST PRACTICE

The World Health Organization (WHO) suggests that children under the age of 2 years should have zero screen time whilst children aged 2–4 years should have 1 hour per day maximum.

## DID YOU KNOW?

According to Ofcom, around 1 in 5 children aged 3–4 years have their own tablet, with 50% of children going online for almost 8 hours per week.

## KEY TERMS

**Investigative** finding new information or facts.

**Construction** building or creating something new.

You have read that children can play using their senses, creativity, imagination and locomotive skills. Children also learn during other types of play. These types can help them to understand concepts such as balance, number, colour and basic science.

## Technological/investigative play

Many children now have access to technology such as tablets, laptops and mobile phones. Technological and **investigative** play allows children to access a large variety of activities and games that can support their development, including fine motor skills, hand–eye co-ordination, and recognition of number shape and colour. When children investigate the world around them and learn new concepts, information technology and equipment is a useful tool to help them. There are other ways that children can learn or investigate their world, such as through the use of science or maths equipment. Using counters, small children can begin to learn about number and colour. In water play, children can use objects that help them to understand the concepts of floating and sinking.

## Construction play

This type of play involves children building, stacking or joining things together to make something new. This helps them to make sense of the world, while developing fine motor skills, spatial awareness and problem-solving skills. Using blocks to make a tower or fitting a wooden train track together are examples of **construction** play.

▫ What fine motor skills can this child learn from building a block tower?

Table 2.2 gives some examples of activities for each type of play.

◻ **Table 2.2: Examples of activities for each type of play**

| Type of play | 0–18 months | 18 months–3 years | 3–5 years |
|---|---|---|---|
| Locomotor | Crawling to objects<br>Fetch – walking to collect different toys | Puddle jumping<br>Running | Hokey-cokey<br>Galloping like a horse |
| Creative | Mark making – using large crayons to make simple marks on paper | Finger painting | Musical instruments |
| Sensory | Sensory basket – contains different items such as ribbons, shells, wooden spoon, etc. | Musical shakers<br>Jelly play – objects are hidden in the jelly and children squish and squeeze the jelly to get to them | Blind box – contains different cooked and uncooked foods, which children feel and smell in order to describe them |
| Imaginative | Play telephone<br>Pull-along puppy | Playing families/mums/dads<br>Dressing up | Small world play – using action figures, dinosaurs, small cars, etc. |
| Symbolic | N/A | Using a cardboard box as a car or boat | Pretending to be a doctor and injecting a doll using a crayon |
| Technological/investigative | Drawing using electronic pen and tablet<br>Number match cards | Simple maths games apps using characters<br>Water play using measuring beakers | Apps that link sounds to letters<br>Using a magnifying glass to explore small animals outside |
| Construction | Large building blocks | Kinetic sand play<br>Sand or gravel digging pit with hidden objects | Putting a wooden railway together<br>Magnetic building activities |

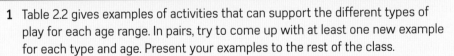

**ACTIVITY**

1 Table 2.2 gives examples of activities that can support the different types of play for each age range. In pairs, try to come up with at least one new example for each type and age. Present your examples to the rest of the class.

2 Using the table and your additional activities, create a leaflet for parents and carers that shows how they can support learning and development with different types of play.

**CHECK MY LEARNING**

You have learned about the different types of children's play. Check your learning of these:

1 List three activities used in technological/investigative play.

2 State the skills that are developed when taking part in construction play.

# Learning outcome A: assessment practice

## How you will be assessed

You will be assessed via a Pearson set assignment. This will be marked internally and moderated externally. Your assignment will be completed under formal supervision and carried out independently with no access to the internet.

When you have completed Component 2, your teacher will give you an assignment to complete. It will include three tasks. The first task relates to learning outcome A. For Task 1, you will demonstrate your knowledge and understanding of how a child of a given age plays. You will be allowed approximately 1 hour to complete the task. Evidence includes:

- a detailed and relevant account of stages of children's play
- a detailed and relevant account of selected play experiences
- well-developed reasons why selected play experiences are appropriate, with links to the given age and stage of development.

---

**CHECKPOINT**

### Strengthen

- State the six stages of children's play.
- State the age group linked to each of the stages of play.
- State the seven types of play.
- Describe examples of activities for each of the seven types of play.

### Challenges

- Explain the six stages of children's play.
- Explain how modelling clay can be used to support different types of children's play.

---

**PRACTICE ASSESSMENT ACTIVITY**

Task 1

To complete this task you must work individually.

Daisy is a 1-year-old child. Produce an article about how Daisy would be expected to play. In your article you must include:

- details of the stages of play that Daisy will be using
- details of one relevant play experience for each of the following types of play:
  - ☐ creative
  - ☐ sensory
  - ☐ construction.
- reasons why these play experiences are suitable for Daisy.

## TIPS

Remember that you should include examples to show your understanding of the different stages of play.

## TAKE IT FURTHER

*The manager of Happy Springs Nursery has asked that you write a guide for parents and carers that details how children play.*

Produce a booklet aimed at parents and carers that contains the following:
- Different stages of play between birth and 5 years old.
- Types of play, describing examples of each.

# Learning through play in different environments

**LINK IT UP**

To find out more about the EYFS framework, go to page 101.

When planning for play, adults need to consider the environment in which children will be playing. This is because the environment may not be suitable for specific activities or may not have the resources needed. How would play differ for children in a school compared with a nursery?

## Types of environment

### Home

A 'home' play environment could be the child's home or a childminder's house. If it is the child's home then it may also be used by siblings. If it is the home of a childminder then there may be several other children. Children feel comfortable in their surroundings, as they are used to the layout and it is not as big as a nursery or school. This means they are less likely to feel anxious or worried and are more likely to engage with adults or others.

Home environments can have limited resources and toys, as there is not always a lot of space for them to be stored.

### Nurseries

Nurseries are usually run as private businesses to make a profit, although some are part of primary schools. Children may attend on a full-time or part-time basis. The adults in the nursery follow the EYFS (Early Years Foundation Stage) framework to make sure that children meet their milestones and are developing properly. This means that adults will plan activities and select toys and games to make sure that the children are learning. Nurseries have qualified staff who are trained to work with children and promote development. There are lots of toys and activities available to all children.

### Pre-school

A pre-school provides care for children of 3–5 years and helps them to learn the skills needed for starting school, such as reading and writing. Some pre-schools are part of nurseries and some are part of primary schools. Children usually attend part time; this can include a morning or afternoon session each day. Activities will include drawing and practising pencil grip, as this will help children when they are learning to write. These skills are included in the EYFS *Development Matters* guidelines.

### Reception

A reception class is usually the first class that children go into when they start school at around 4 or 5 years of age (unless the school offers a nursery), and they attend for the full school day. Play and learning in a reception class still follows the EYFS framework supported by the guidelines. Games and activities are planned to promote learning and development. In reception, teachers will build on the skills children have already learned. This might include listening and speaking activities, which build on communication skills.

## Community-based groups

Community-based groups for play are usually for children under the age of 5. They will often have different groups based on the age of the child – for example, baby group, toddler group, or parent and tots group. This is a good way for parents or carers to play with their children and also to meet up with others. New parents who are unsure about supporting children as they learn through play can get advice and talk to others about their experiences. Community-based groups often use volunteers. They often take place in churches, community halls or libraries. Typically, children will attend on a part-time basis, often two or three sessions each week. As these groups are run locally they may have less money than a school or nursery. This means that resources and toys can be limited. The activities may be less structured than in a nursery or reception class. Usually, children have a choice of toys to play with and can freely move between toys.

## Learning through play at different ages

All children learn through play. The type of play and learning develops as they get older.

### 0–18 months

Children are more reliant on adults in this age range. Games and activities will use bright colours and noises to attract the child's attention, such as singing nursery rhymes or using a walker. Activities are used to encourage small children to explore and learn how things work and the noises they make.

### 18 months–3 years

Children now have a better understanding of their environment. They are interested in everything around them and have some skills in movement, such as jumping and climbing. Younger children in this range still rely on adults and may have tantrums if they do not get what they want. Play activities help children to learn some of the social skills they will need when they are older, such as sharing and taking turns. Activities that use shared resources, such as painting or using playdough, are one way of teaching children to share with others.

### 3–5 years

Within this age range, children have already developed some of the key skills for communication and are mastering the use of their fine motor skills. The focus of play moves to letters, numbers and rhyming activities such as singalongs. Activities, such as Post Office role-play, help children to develop their imaginative skills, and playing outdoors on climbing equipment and using tricycles and bikes improves their physical skills, such as co-ordination and balance.

**ACTIVITY**

1 Create a mind map that shows the different learning environments and a summary of how they differ.

2 Working together in groups of three, make a list of all the nurseries, pre-schools, reception classes and community-based groups in your area. Add these to your mind map.

3 Share your list with the rest of the class. Are there any similarities?

4 Make a poster to advertise the different play opportunities at one of the learning environments. You should include the name of the learning environment and how children are able to learn through play there.

**CHECK MY LEARNING**

1 If a child is nervous about leaving their parents, in which environment do you think they will prefer to learn? Why?

2 In what way are community groups beneficial for new parents?

3 How is play in a reception class different to play in a community-based setting?

# Children's learning supported through physical play: 0–18 months

Physical play for small children supports the development of their fine and gross motor skills. To help with fine motor control, children are given opportunities to interact with objects and manipulate them with their fingers. Gross motor skills are developed when children use their larger muscles to help them walk and balance. Do you think an activity that promotes gross motor skills would be the same for a 3-month-old baby as it is for an 18-month-old child?

## Physical play

### Spatial awareness

Babies have very little eye co-ordination, foot and leg co-ordination or **hand–eye co-ordination**. This is because their muscles have not developed fully enough. By the time they reach 18 months, they show more control over their body and are generally able to walk. There are several ways to encourage **spatial awareness**:

- Simple ball games such as *rolling a ball* to a non-mobile baby will encourage them to touch and push the ball. As they try to reach it, they are learning a basic understanding of distance. When they get older and are mobile, children may attempt to kick the ball or even catch it.
- Obstacle courses are a good way of improving spatial awareness. As babies begin to crawl, objects can be placed on the floor so they start to learn to co-ordinate their bodies. Older children will be able to negotiate an *obstacle course* as they learn how to get over and under objects.

### Hand–eye co-ordination

Adults can provide children aged 3–12 months with toys with sound, such as *rattles*, to help to promote hand–eye co-ordination. Children will look towards the sound and be encouraged to reach out and grab the toy. *Baby gyms* feature bright, dangling toys to inspire babies to reach up and touch them. Older children, 12–18 months, can hold and manipulate objects, so they will enjoy *scribbling on large sheets of paper* and *building with blocks*.

### Activities to stay healthy

Staying healthy is important regardless of age. Babies are encouraged to understand their environment through movement such as crawling and walking. Being physically active is important for growth and development. Babies can be given *walkers* to encourage them to grasp, pull and push. At around 12 months of age, children are more active and should be encouraged to take part in activities that allow them to use all their muscles, such as using *ride-on toys* or taking part in outdoor play. Giving children space to play and run can get them moving and help to keep them healthy.

### How to take care of yourself and self-care

A baby cannot take care of their own body. They rely on adults to change their nappies as well as feed and clean them. As they grow older, the basics of hygiene should be taught. Up to 18 months of age, babies will place many objects into their mouths as they do not understand what 'clean' means. The lack of understanding can lead to accidents or illness. Children can start learning to take care of themselves by taking part in the following activities:

**GETTING STARTED**

Close your eyes! Now try to grab your pen from the desk. What about walking over to the opposite desk and grabbing the pen on that desk? It's difficult when you have limited spatial awareness. What do you think that means?

**LINK IT UP**

For a reminder on the difference between fine and gross motor skills, go to learning outcome A of Component 1.

**KEY TERMS**

**Hand–eye co-ordination** co-ordinated control of eye movements with hand movements.

**Spatial awareness** understanding where you are in relation to the objects in your environment.

**DID YOU KNOW?**

According to the NHS, to be healthy, toddlers who are able to walk should be physically active for at least 3 hours a day.

▪ This child is learning to brush their teeth. How could it be made a fun activity?

- Routines such as hand washing after a nappy change and before eating can be taught through demonstration but also through song and dance. Singing 'Wash, wash, wash your hands' to the tune of 'Row, row, row your boat' will help children to remember what they are doing.
- Practising brushing teeth helps to develop the use of children's fine motor skills as they manipulate the toothbrush in their hands.

## Gross motor skills

The movement of larger muscles and **body management** begin when a baby is born. **Bodily co-ordination** comes from a child kicking their legs and moving their arms around in an attempt to understand their body and the world around them when they are non-mobile. As they become more mobile (by around 9 months), children begin to sit unsupported. Giving toys that encourage children to sit up and to attempt to crawl will develop their gross motor skills (see Table 2.3).

◻ **Table 2.3: Activities to help develop gross motor skills at different ages**

| Age range | Activity |
|---|---|
| 3–6 months | *Prop pillows* will encourage children to sit up. A baby can be placed on their stomach, resting on the prop pillow. They are soft and colourful and will often make noises. This encourages the baby to try to touch and move and become more inquisitive. This helps them to explore the world around them and sparks their imagination. |
| 6–12 months | Children have developed their balance enough to be able to sit without falling. A *ride-on toy* is a great way of improving balance and co-ordination. The muscles in the child's legs become stronger as they move and distribute their weight evenly. It can also promote the use of other areas of the body such as hands, feet and arms. In this age range, a child's hand–eye co-ordination and foot–eye co-ordination is not yet fully developed, so they will struggle with balance and co-ordination of their body. |
| 12–18 months | Going to a *local park* is an activity that would be suitable for older children in this age range. Children can run around and attempt to pull themselves up onto some of the equipment. The different floor surfaces, such as grass to sand, will make the children think about how their *walking* or *running* has to change so they can move around. It will also spark their imagination. |

## Fine motor control

Children will master the control of their limbs before they develop control over their fingers and toes. At around 6 months old, a child can hold an object; at 9 months they will use their finger and thumb to pick it up. The further the development of a child's fine motor control, the more **accurate** they are at **manipulating** objects. At around 15 months, children will attempt *mark making* and will hold a *crayon* with their hand wrapped around it. Other activities to improve fine motor control could include the following:

- Using *playdough* strengthens fingers, hands and wrists as children squish, poke and squeeze it. This develops their smaller muscles so they are able to work on the manipulative skills that will be needed for writing and using technology when they are older.
- Creative activities such as mark making allow children to practise their grasp and to understand how to make marks on paper.
- To further improve grasping skills, different-sized *crayons* or *paintbrushes* can be used.
- *Finger painting* is another way in which children can develop fine motor skills, while being creative.

**KEY TERMS**

**Body management** skills used to control the body.

**Bodily co-ordination** movement of different areas of the body.

**Accurate** free from mistakes.

**Manipulating** handling or control over objects.

**ACTIVITY**

1 Create a table for non-mobile and mobile babies. In it, describe toys/activities that the children can use/play with to support their fine and gross motor skills.

2 Write down how an adult could make brushing teeth a fun activity for an 18-month-old. Share your ideas with the rest of the class.

3 Make a colourful and bold poster that shows a play activity for a 12-month-old that can promote spatial awareness and staying healthy.

**CHECK MY LEARNING**

1 A 10-month-old baby is crawling; its parents want to encourage walking. What physical activities would you suggest to help the parents?

2 How can promoting fine and gross motor skills to a child under 18 months help them to take care of themselves?

3 Which fine and gross motor skills are used when taking part in play activities that promote staying healthy? Why would these be important for a child's cognitive development?

# Children's learning supported through physical play: 18 months–3 years

At 18 months most children will be able to walk without any help. Their gross motor skills are developing, and over the course of the next 18 months they will be able to run, climb, throw a ball and pedal a tricycle. As well as promoting physical skills, these activities will promote other areas of development such as cognitive skills and social skills. What type of gross motor skills do you think are needed to use a tricycle?

## Physical play

### Spatial awareness

A child's sense of spatial awareness becomes more developed from 18 months. Children now have a better idea of where objects are in relation to them. This makes *kicking a ball* easier, as foot and leg co-ordination are now improved. Being able to see the ball and know where to kick shows that hand–eye co-ordination has also improved. Children will still miss the catch, or stumble when trying to kick, but these skills will further develop with practice, and the following activities could help:

- *Bat and ball games* will further improve spatial awareness and allow children to practise their hand–eye co-ordination and balance. A 'T ball' game set uses oversized bats and balls and allows children to practise hitting the ball off a T.
- Foot and leg co-ordination can be improved with '*walk the line*' activities. An adult can draw a line outside in chalk and children have to stand on it and walk.

### Activities to stay healthy

Between 18 months and 3 years, children can be picky eaters and will sometimes not eat if they feel uncomfortable about what is put in front of them. It is important that children see mealtimes as a relaxed event and not a time when they are forced to eat foods they don't like. If mealtimes become stressful, children will not want to eat. The following activities can help promote healthy lifestyles:

- *Role-play* can allow children to understand more about living a healthy lifestyle. Taking part in a mealtime role-play can open discussions about different foods, such as vegetables and fruit. These help children to feel comfortable around new foods.
- Making a '*food cupboard*' with children can get them thinking about healthy food options. It can be placed in a real cupboard or drawn on a wall with a piece of paper to act as the door.

### How to take care of yourself and self-care

At this stage children may be beginning to go to the toilet independently and will be learning about washing their hands and being hygienic. They may not yet understand the reason why they need to wash their hands. However, they will be becoming familiar with the routine. Adults can make it clear when children need to wash their hands and model how to do it properly.

■ Helping with food preparation can encourage children to want to eat healthier foods.

Children can help with food preparation, enabling adults to discuss with them which foods are healthy and which are not. Children can be introduced to a range of fruits and vegetables, which they can peel and cut.

Resting is important. Sometimes children are so involved in play and what is going on around them that they don't realise they are tired. Children can move to a quiet area of the room and rest their eyes and listen to a story. The story can be read by an adult, or it could be an audiobook. Being in a calm environment and concentrating on the sound of the story will encourage some children to fall asleep.

## Gross motor skills

Physical play gives children a chance to become more co-ordinated in their movements as they develop their gross motor skills even further. It also gives children the opportunity to play with others and develop their social skills, which builds self-esteem.

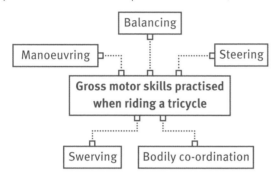

◘ Figure 2.2: Gross motor skills practised when riding a tricycle.

Figure 2.2 shows the gross motor skills children develop from using a tricycle. Other activities to improve gross motor skills could include the following:
- To strengthen arms and core muscles in the body, children can *crawl* around.
- Squatting and bending improve strength and balance. Playing hide and seek with toys encourages children to search for them and squat to pick them up. This activity can also promote cognitive development, as it encourages children to be curious.
- *Climbing frames* encourage children to co-ordinate their body while they hold onto bars and climb. When other children are using the climbing frame at the same time, children can practise their skills of manoeuvring as they move around each other, as well as improving their social skills.

## Fine motor control

Accuracy and manipulation of objects improves as children get older. At 18 months they should be confident in using a palmar grasp to *build a tower of bricks* and are likely to enjoy *scribbling* with crayons. By the time they are 2 years and 6 months old, children often show a hand preference and start to use a simple tripod grasp to hold a crayon.

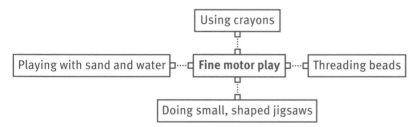

◘ Figure 2.3: Fine motor skills practised during play.

Activities to improve fine motor skills, as shown in Figure 2.3, could include the following:
- A *sand table* or *sand pit* allows children to use different tools to manipulate the sand. Scooping and raking will strengthen the small muscles in the hand and wrist.
- *Wax crayon etching* is a colourful way to develop fine motor skills.

**ACTIVITY**

1 Which gross motor skills are promoted when a child rides a tricycle?

2 Create a mind map to show how riding a tricycle can promote each of the other areas of development (social, emotional and cognitive).

**CHECK MY LEARNING**

1 Jacob refuses to eat any vegetables. What play activity and resources could be used by the adults at his nursery to encourage him to try them?

2 Bella damaged her hand several months ago. She is not as developed as others in her fine motor skills. What activities could Bella try to promote her learning and development of fine motor skills?

# Children's learning supported through physical play: 3–5 years

Between 3 and 5 years of age, children's fine and gross motor skills advance rapidly. Children improve in their balance and co-ordination and have a good sense of their surroundings when playing. Being physically fit and healthy is important, as it promotes all other areas of development.

By taking part in a physical activity with others, children are able to build on relationships and friendships, which can promote communication and language skills. Can you think of other areas of development that physical play can help to develop?

## Physical play

### Spatial awareness

Spatial awareness has developed quickly. Children can sense where an object is in relation to them. Their foot and leg co-ordination has improved significantly and they can now kick a ball with some force, hop on one foot and walk along a line. They are able to catch and throw a large ball, showing that their hand–eye co-ordination has also improved.

### Hand–eye co-ordination

Fine motor play activities can help children to co-ordinate their eye movements with their hand movements. Children will need to have well developed hand–eye co-ordination to be able to draw and write; the following activities can help to develop this:
- Using a *plastic needle* (these are blunt and cannot hurt the child) to *thread beads* onto string can help to improve a child's hand–eye co-ordination.
- *Creative activities* such as making cards using paints, crayons and scissors, also require hand–eye co-ordination.
- To further improve co-ordination and control, children can be introduced to tricycles, balance bikes and *bicycles*. By around 4 years, children are usually confident with riding a tricycle or a balance bike. At around 5 years, children can be introduced to bicycles although this will vary from child to child. Stabilisers or balance bikes will help with their balance, co-ordination and control.

◻ Using crayons encourages children to work carefully to avoid colouring over the lines of a picture.

### Activities to stay healthy

As children are more active in this age range, they are using all parts of their bodies and keeping fit. Besides teaching about physical fitness through play activities indoors and outdoors, it is important to consider other aspects of staying healthy. Children need time to rest, to eat healthy foods and to be able to take care of their bodies through *washing and brushing their teeth*.

In a nursery, pre-school or school, adults can ask children to choose the fruits and vegetables they would like for snack time. They could pick them from their garden area if they have one. Children can help to *wash and cut the fruit and vegetables* while having discussions with the adults.

### How to take care of yourself and self-care

Most children have a good sense of how to take care of themselves, as they are likely to be self-feeding, but they should be reminded about hygiene. At this age, a lot of activities will take place outdoors to improve gross motor skills. This means that children can often play in the mud or pick things up that could have germs and bacteria on them. Good hygiene, such as *washing hands* after playing outdoors and after using the toilet, should be taught to the children.

Knowing which foods are high in sugar can also be useful for children, as well as an awareness that too much sugar can be bad for their teeth.

Adults can help children learn about healthy and unhealthy food in group activities. In groups, children can place two hoops overlapping each other on a table. There can be a selection of food (real or plastic) on the table too. Children can discuss in their groups where to place the food: healthy in one hoop and unhealthy in the other. Anything they are unsure about can go in the middle. Adults can then open up discussions about eating healthily.

## Gross motor skills

When a child is between 3 and 4 years old they can jump from a low step, run, kick a large ball and stand on one leg for a moment. By 4–5 years, most children can *run, avoid obstacles* and *swerve* around things and *skip*. They are significantly stronger and have better control over their bodies. They are confident in running, *hopping* and skipping and they have refined their balance, so they can stand on one foot for longer than ten seconds without falling.

Through physical activity, children develop the gross motor skills that will help them develop in other areas. Being able to run and play outside can promote emotional development, as children will feel good about themselves. Taking part in physical games together, such as the following, can promote cognitive skills such as problem solving:

- Using a *climbing frame, swings* and *slides* allows children to have control over all of their body. They will stretch, reach, swing and pull themselves up.
- *Bat and ball games* encourage the movement of swinging, balance and bodily co-ordination.

## Fine motor control

At 3–4 years, children are usually able to button and unbutton, can generally use scissors and thread beads and use a knife and fork well. At 4–5 years, children will be able to form letters, write their name and colour pictures in more accurately, plus colour within some lines. Further development of fine motor control can be learned through activities.

- *Construction toys* using different materials that allow children to push, pull and twist can encourage the use of fingers and also promote imagination.
- Further activities that are useful for strengthening the hand muscles include creative play with *crayons*, pens, paintbrushes and *scissors. Junk modelling* encourages children to feel textures and different materials and then to manipulate them to create something. This also promotes cognitive development as it sparks their imagination.

◘ **Playground climbing equipment will improve children's balance and co-ordination.**

### CHECK MY LEARNING

1 Discuss how role-play can promote a child's learning across all areas of development.

2 Describe the motor skills used when a child is colouring or painting.

# Children's learning supported through cognitive and intellectual play: 0–18 months

To small children, everything around them is interesting. Hearing new sounds, seeing bright colours and understanding how things work and fit together: their brains are trying to make connections with every new piece of information. What do you think when you hear a siren in the street? How do you know what it is?

Planning play activities allows a child to make connections with each new piece of information.

## Cognitive/intellectual play

### Problem-solving skills

By 4 months old, babies are using all their senses to find out about themselves and the world around them. They have developed enough muscle control to be able to move objects towards their mouth. This is the first step towards problem solving. At around 8 months old, babies begin to see a cause-and-effect relationship when playing with toys. Banging and shaking can cause movement and noise. As they get older, around 12 months old, they become more interested in solving problems. The activities below require children to be active while promoting fine and gross motor skills.

- Children are naturally inquisitive. *Shape sorters* and simple *jigsaws* are a good way to support problem-solving skills. Children will begin to learn about shape and size and understand the link between the spaces available and the pieces to put in them.
- When a child has set their mind on wanting a particular toy then nothing will stand in their way. *Placing colourful toys under a box* that has holes in and then leaving *obstacles* around the room encourages children to work out how to get to the toys.

### Imagination and creativity

By around 8 months old, children will begin to use their **imagination** when playing with toys and games. Providing activities that stimulate their imagination opens them up to new ideas and possibilities.

- A simple *digging activity* can encourage the imagination of a child aged 15–18 months. *Coins or small toys* hidden in sand or mud can allow a child to create a story. Adults can ask questions as children are digging to ensure that their imagination is being sparked.
- *Playdough* helps to unlock imagination and creativity. If children are also given other objects, such as *blocks and sticks*, they can use them all together.

◻ This child is having fun in the mud. How could this help to promote their imagination?

### Listening and attention skills

Younger children in this age range do not have the focus to pay attention for long periods. Early signs of listening and **attention skills** are seen when babies move their head to follow familiar sounds or when they move their arms and legs when they hear someone they know. Eventually they will become quieter when someone is talking or singing to them. Listening and attention skills can be developed through play and songs.

- Playing 'peek-a-boo' is one way of developing listening and attention skills for small babies. Children usually become quieter as they are waiting for the face to reappear from behind the hands.

- As small babies are interested in everything, their attention can move from one thing to the next quite quickly, so their focus can be held by *singing songs* accompanied by a rattle.
- Singing *rhymes with actions* that adults can demonstrate to children can help with focus – for example, 'Three little pigs' or 'Round and round the garden'. Children will want to copy the movement while they listen to the song and are more likely to pay attention and focus on the song.

## Numeracy skills

Early on, children will begin to understand the basics of quantities, knowing if they want more or less of something. However, they will not understand quantity in terms of the number of objects. In this age range, children will imitate others when attempting to count. Activities that could help to develop numeracy skills include the following:

- Using large *colourful counters* or blocks can encourage numeracy development. When playing with them, adults can talk/sing the number of counters. Children will begin to mimic this, which will lead to them developing their understanding.
- *Dressing and feeding* a child can become a numeracy learning activity. Counting 'one arm in, two arms in' when putting on a coat or 'one spoonful, two spoonful' when feeding will encourage children to think about numbers.
- In this age range, children are also able to complete pre-numeracy activities such as comparing sizes. For example, they could be given a selection of sea shells to sort into size order.
- Matching *picture cards* can also be used.

## Exploration of environments inside and outside

When trying to make sense of their environment, children will pay close attention to every sound, smell, touch or experience. Often they will 'explore' indoors as they navigate around their own home or nursery. However, allowing a child to be outside can help promote cognitive development, as they learn to understand how the outside environment is different. Activities to explore indoor and outdoor environments could include the following:

- Non-mobile babies can be moved around so they are able to experience a different view of the room or outside environment. This will stimulate their interest.
- Taking a small child to the *park* will allow them to experience new things such as trees and ducks on the pond.
- *Hide-the-toy* is a great activity for indoor exploration. Children's toys are hidden and they have to find their favourite toy by searching through areas in the room.

## Confidence using technology

Small children are beginning to recognise technology around them. From around 9 months they are using toys that have simple buttons, flaps or knobs that make sounds or have actions. These can prepare children for using technology.

## Understanding of others' experiences

From birth to 18 months, a child does not understand differences in culture. It is important that adults encourage learning in this area so that all children are able to empathise with others' experiences. This can be done by saying nursery rhymes from other cultures and using words from different languages. Adults can also:

- celebrate festivals from different cultures with the children
- show photographs of people and places from around the world to celebrate and acknowledge diversity

**ACTIVITY**

*To improve the numeracy skills of children in the local community centre, you have been asked by the manager to plan two play opportunities for them. They want them in a poster format so they can display these around the community centre for all volunteers to see. This means that if staff need ideas, they can use yours.*

Each play opportunity must be on a separate sheet of A4 paper.

**CHECK MY LEARNING**

1 Explain how the 'This little piggy went to market' rhyme can improve a child's listening and attention skills.

2 How can a story such as 'Goldilocks and the three bears' promote numeracy skills for an 18-month-old?

# Children's learning supported through cognitive and intellectual play: 18 months–3 years

You have learned that younger children are very interested in everything around them but lack attention and listening skills. This changes between 18 months and 3 years.

## Cognitive/intellectual play

### Problem-solving activities

Children in this age range are likely to have a tantrum or show their frustration if the activity they are working on doesn't go to plan. They are not as resilient as older children and will often give up on an activity if they find it too challenging. Problem-solving activities could include the following:

- *Counters and weights* can introduce a child to problem solving in maths and science. A child could hold a weight while an adult encourages them to find objects in the nursery that are lighter or heavier.
- Puzzles such as *magnetic puzzle boards* can encourage children to be creative as well as practising their problem solving. Magnetic puzzle boards contain different colourful shapes and characters. They need to be able to understand how the shapes fit together and how to create an image that fits the space given. In what way could these types of activity promote fine motor skills too?

☐ Adults can support role-play by joining in to help act the story out. But they must let the child stay in charge.

### Imagination and creativity

Between 18 months and 2 years, many children will use their imagination and act out *pretend scenarios*. Usually, these are based on home-life situations: answering the 'phone', going to work, doing laundry and looking after a 'baby'. Children might create a 'play' but it will usually be based on what they have witnessed at home. Adults can help with this by providing a role-play area with costumes. Pretend play can help children to build friendships as they play alongside and with other children, sharing and communicating with them.

From 2 years of age upwards, children will use their imagination to pretend items are different objects.

- Using the environment inside or outside can spark imagination in children. An empty cardboard box could be a rocket ship! An outdoor hose could be a snake!
- Using *natural resources* found outside is one way of encouraging imagination. Children may see a twig or branch as part of a tree, but when they have collected enough of them, they could begin to build a small den. Adults can suggest ways in which they could use them safely while encouraging children to come up with their own ideas, which will boost their self-esteem.

### Listening and attention activities

Children in this age range can often seem to ignore adults. This is a busy time for children, as their brains are in overdrive as they develop. To be able to listen effectively, children need a quiet area free from distractions. The following activities can help develop listening and attention skills:

- Play a pattern or shape activity with **wipe boards**. Show the pattern or shape to the children and encourage them to copy it on their wipe board. They then answer questions about what they have heard and understood.
- There are some apps that can promote listening and improve attention in children, such as *phonics apps*. Phonics apps aim to help children with their language development.

The apps keep children's attention by using fun characters, songs and rhymes. Children need to listen carefully to be able to learn new vocabulary and how to say it.

## Numeracy activities

By 2 years old, most children will know what 'one' and 'two' mean and they will be able to show how old they are using their fingers. When playing with water, they are able to show which container has more water in it. 'Numeracy' isn't just numbers: it also involves shape and number patterns. Other activities can help to develop numeracy skills:

- *Puzzles* can develop numeracy skills as children are looking at shapes and moving them to fit.
- *Counters* can be used to support learning of numbers and colours. Adults could ask younger children to sort the counters by colour. Children around 2–3 years old could be asked to count them.

## Exploration of environments inside and outside

A child's environment, whether it is inside or outside, is a useful tool for learning new things. There are a range of objects and new experiences that can promote learning between 18 months and 3 years.

- Using outdoor materials can allow children to explore size and weight. Adults can ask children to collect *stones and pebbles*. They can then play a comparison game where children are asked which is the biggest, the longest or the heaviest.
- Children like to feel and smell and try to work out what objects do. Making a *den* or placing a tent outside (or even inside) and setting up camping equipment is one way of encouraging children to learn about new things and allowing them to explore.

## Confidence using technology

Children may not be confident at using technology at this age but they will have been introduced to it. Technology can be used in learning activities to support other areas of development.

- A *drawing program* on a tablet can promote confidence with using technology while allowing children to practise their fine motor skills. Children can draw shapes and create pictures by using either their finger or the electronic stylus/pen.
- Using a *tablet* can also allow children to access colours that they might not be able to mix using paint.

## Understanding of others' experiences

Some children may have limited knowledge or experience of the cultures of others at this age. Adults can support learning by celebrating different cultures' religious festivals throughout the year, acknowledging and celebrating the cultural heritage of the children and talking about the meaning of the festivals.

Children are now asking more questions about who they are and how other children and families might be different to them. They are at an age where they are able to understand basic concepts, so it is important to teach them about different cultural and religious experiences in a positive way.

- Cooking activities can help children recognise that food differs across cultures. Circle time is a good opportunity to talk to children about different cultures in a relaxed atmosphere. Read books that show diversity.
- Show video clips of dances from different cultures. Encourage children to copy the moves.

◘ Children can use their imagination to play games inside a tent or den.

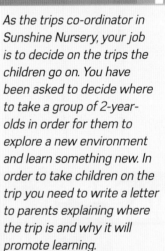

**ACTIVITY**

*As the trips co-ordinator in Sunshine Nursery, your job is to decide on the trips the children go on. You have been asked to decide where to take a group of 2-year-olds in order for them to explore a new environment and learn something new. In order to take children on the trip you need to write a letter to parents explaining where the trip is and why it will promote learning.*

Your letter should include:

1 where you plan on taking the children

2 why the trip would be beneficial for the children

3 how it can promote learning.

**CHECK MY LEARNING** ■ ■

1 How can cognitive/intellectual activities help to promote emotional development?

2 In what way can technology be used to teach children about colours?

# Children's learning supported through cognitive and intellectual play: 3–5 years

Between 3 and 5 years, children become more sophisticated in the way they think. They can usually count, have better problem-solving skills and are able to use their imagination in new ways. Children's cognitive and intellectual learning depends on the adults around them. New topics or learning opportunities need to be pointed out to children, as they may not realise they have an opportunity to learn. If you were outside and saw a slug, would you see the learning opportunity? Can you think of ways this can promote each area of development?

## Cognitive/intellectual play

### Problem-solving skills

At this age, problem-solving skills are becoming well developed. Children are usually more confident and are less likely to have anxiety over new situations. They are more likely to be tackling things head on and trying to solve problems rather than giving up. It is still important for adults to continue with the development of this skill.

Simple maths problems such as *counting play money* in shop role-play are one way to develop problem-solving skills further. They will also help with the understanding of numbers and number patterns, which will be needed for school.

### Creativity and imagination

Creativity and imagination are more than just fun for children: they are a way of expressing emotions and building friendships. As time goes on, children become more creative and experiment with games, toys and other resources. They will begin to make up their own games with their own rules and become interested in sharing the world of their imagination with others.

- At 3–4 years, children enjoy building with large *cardboard boxes* and imagining they are castles or boats.
- Children around 4–5 years will be developing their skills ready for school. One way to support this, and also benefit their creativity, is for them to use *wipe boards*. Children can *practise writing skills* on the boards and remove mistakes easily. They can draw characters and *tell a story* to adults.

### Listening and attention skills

At approximately 3 years, children show an interest in *listening to stories* and talking about what is happening in the pictures. Their attention can be held for longer. When there is a story that they love, they are happy to hear it repeated many times. Around 4 years of age, children are able to use their listening skills to follow three-step directions.

■ Taking children out to farms or zoos can spark their interest and encourage them to listen and ask questions. It is also important that they learn to listen to instructions you give them in order to keep them safe.

As children now have better listening and attention skills it makes it easier to go on trips and visits. This could include the following:

- Visiting a farm or a zoo, where children can listen to animal sounds, discuss the animals and learn about the animals from the farmers, animal carers or zoo keepers.
- Visiting a *museum* where they can also practise listening to an adult or museum curator talking about a display.

## Numeracy skills

At 3 years old, a child can tell if an object is heavy or light, is able to arrange objects into categories and can understand the term 'more than'. By the time they reach 5 years, children can usually count accurately up to ten, are able to add two sets of objects together and can understand matching of equal objects. Activities that can help practise numeracy skills include the following:

- Using *play money* in role-play situations can improve numeracy skills. *Playing 'shop' or 'post office'* allows children to use simple sums for the 'money'.
- Using wipe boards as part of a quick *basic numeracy activity* like adding and subtracting. Adults can ask numeracy questions and children can guess the answer and write it on the board.

## Exploration of environments inside and outside

The exploration of inside and outside environments continues in this age range. As children are more confident in their body management, can communicate effectively and are able to express themselves, activities that support exploration should be more challenging. Challenging activities will allow children to think carefully about what they are doing, which will help them to learn.

- In *'loose parts play'* children are encouraged to explore their environment to find and play with different objects. A pipe could be turned into a pirate's spyglass, or an old cable reel could be a bird's nest on a boat.
- A *woodland walk* can allow children to explore the natural environment. Children can feel different textures of leaves, twigs and the bark of trees. This promotes questioning and sparks the imagination as well as promoting the development of fine motor skills.

## Confidence using technology

Different technologies can be used to help children to understand their world. Children should be encouraged to use a range of different technologies so they are more familiar with them. As well as electronic items like *digital cameras*, *tablets*, *PCs*, computer games and apps, more traditional items, such as mechanical toys/pulleys and construction kits, can also be used.

## Understanding of others' experiences

By the time children are 3–5 years old, their attention span has increased and they are able to sit for longer. To support learning about other cultures and religious festivals, guest speakers can visit to talk to the children or children can be encouraged to share and talk about their culture and experiences. The children can be shown where different countries are on a world map and the different cultures that are celebrated around the world.

Children are now more inquisitive. If something is not the 'norm' for a child they will want to learn more about it and will ask questions. It is important to celebrate the diversity of our culture, and this can be done in many ways. One way is acknowledging and celebrating different festivals, such as Chinese New Year, Diwali and Eid-al-Fitr. Encouraging children to share stories or speak in their first language (mother/father tongue) will also be beneficial for all children as a way of celebrating different cultures.

**ACTIVITY**

1 Using sheets of paper, create a set of memory cards that will help a child develop their problem-solving abilities. They should not contain too many words and should look simple and colourful.

Don't forget that you should have six matching pairs (12 cards).

2 Once you have made your cards, swap with someone else in the room and try theirs.

**CHECK MY LEARNING**

*Caleb is 4 years old and finds it difficult to concentrate and listen during story time.*

1 How can taking Caleb to the local zoo help to develop his attention and listening skills?

2 Explain why the development of listening skills is important for cognitive and social development.

# Children's learning supported through communication and language play: 0–18 months

In the first year of their life, children are busy trying to focus on the sounds they hear. They have the difficult task of trying to work out which sounds are from humans and which are not. They also need to understand what words mean. Early on, babies make lots of sounds; these are mainly babbling noises, as they are unable to form words. By the time a child is 12 months old, they are able to say a few words, such as 'mama'. Do you know what your first word was?

## Communication and language play

### Listening skills

Listening is an important step on the way to developing good communication and language skills. By listening, children are able to pick up on new words and their meanings, and to begin to understand how to pronounce them and how to place them in a sentence.

At 1 month old, most babies will turn their head when they hear a familiar voice, showing that they are listening. However, as they are learning so much about the world around them, their attention is limited. This can mean that it is difficult for a child of 0–18 months to listen well and refine their speech like an older child.

- It is important that adults role model **interaction** skills such as making eye contact when they are talking and allowing for pausing. This is a foundation in later communication development.
- The repetition of *nursery rhymes* such as 'Twinkle, twinkle little star' encourages children to listen for patterns and sequences, which can help with refining their speech later.
- Listening to a song or rhyme that has a steady beat can allow children to develop their language and help them to talk. To support this, *listening/action games* can be played, such as 'If you're happy and you know it', where children need to listen to know when to clap their hands.

### The process of following instructions

By 9 months, a child will understand what 'no' means but will not always obey it. In this age range, a child is learning new words and trying to understand them. As vocabulary increases, the child will start to follow simple instructions such as 'wave goodbye'.

### Vocabulary and literacy skills

Vocabulary is limited early on in this age range. By the age of 6 months, most children will understand the word 'no' and will babble. Within a short time (around 15–18 months) children will have learned approximately 15 words, although some may know more.

Early literacy skills are learned through listening to an adult reading a book. This interaction also allows children to **refine** their speech sounds as they attempt to mimic the words they are hearing. Questioning skills are important when exploring new words and literacy skills. Children who ask questions are practising their language and using their question to clarify what has been said. Different types of books can improve literacy and vocabulary skills, for example:

◻ How could this lift-the-flap book improve questioning?

- **Lift-the-flap books** allow children to develop their literacy and vocabulary skills. This might be by matching the written word to an object that is revealed.
- **Textured stories** are another way in which small children can engage with literacy. In a book about animals, for example, children might feel the 'fur' of a bear, which could prompt questions about where it lives and what it eats.

## How to express and discuss feelings appropriately

Small children will find it difficult to express their feelings appropriately, as they have not yet developed communication techniques. Babies cry and scream when they want attention or they feel pain; older children will have tantrums. Table 2.4 shows some of the differences in how children express emotion before and after 12 months of age.

◨ Table 2.4: Differences between children when expressing emotions

| Under 12 months | 12–18 months |
| --- | --- |
| Cry | Tantrum |
| Scream | Laugh |
| Gurgle noises | Cry |
| Social smile (smiles at anyone) | Co-operative when happy |
| Frown | Unco-operative when unhappy |
| Laugh | Clingy when anxious |
| | Wanting attention when jealous of others |

There are a number of activities that can help children to learn to express emotion.
- *Books with finger puppets* are a good way of allowing small children to understand emotions and begin expressing them.
- *Simple songs* such as 'If you're happy and you know it' can be sung to children or older children in this age group can join in.

## Having conversations with other children/adults

By 12 months children will start to use language in a way that is more recognisable, although only a few close carers may actually understand what is being said. Singing nursery rhymes that have actions such as 'Incy Wincy Spider' will help to connect the words to the actions. It is also a good way for children to remember words.

**ACTIVITY**

Lift-the-flap books are a fun way of introducing information to young children and keeping them engaged. The book follows a story and on each page there is a flap with something underneath.

1 In pairs, design a short lift-the-flap book for an 18-month-old child (2–3 pages). Carefully consider the topic you want to write about. The book should be colourful and the font easy to read, and it should be at the right level for the age group. You should have a flap on every page with new information or an image under it.

2 When you have completed your book, find another pair and read your stories to each other.

**CHECK MY LEARNING**

1 Why are listening skills so important in the communication process?

2 How can improving the listening skills of young children help them improve their speech?

3 List the differences in how children of 6 months and 18 months might express emotions.

# Children's learning supported through communication and language play: 18 months–3 years

### LINK IT UP

For more detail on how children's communication and language develop, look back at learning outcome A in Component 1.

### KEY TERM

**Listening walk** being silent whilst walking in order to hear what is going on around you.

◼ Having a strong vocabulary allows children to feel confident when they are asking questions and promotes cognitive development.

Language and communication skills have improved significantly by the time a child reaches 18 months old. It is important that adults plan activities that make the most of children's language abilities in order for them to improve and develop new skills in all five areas of their development. Did you ever struggle to say a particular word? How do you think adults can help children who have speech difficulties? How important is language for building friendships?

At 18 months, the majority of children are already saying a few short words and can understand simple requests such as 'get your book'. By the time they reach the age of 2, most children will have developed approximately 50 words and will be learning several new words per week. Sentences at this point are simple and will usually consist of two words placed together, such as 'drink gone'. By 2 years and 6 months, the average child will have developed approximately 200 words and be able to ask simple questions, such as 'What's that?'

## Communication and language play

### Listening skills

Between 18 months and 3 years, children are learning lots of vocabulary, so listening is important. Good listening skills will enable children to master new words and have confidence in what they say. Interaction with others is an essential part of the communication process, as children will refine their speech as they listen to, and later understand, new words. Listening to each other can promote social development by helping children to build friendships. Other activities to develop listening skills could include the following:

● Reading storybooks with children allows them to use their imagination. It also allows them to use the vocabulary that they have learned as they talk about the book.
● Books that are not familiar to children will encourage them to learn new words. As children begin to learn new words, adults can help to refine speech by pronouncing words in the correct way. This supports children as they master the word.
● To encourage listening skills, adults can take children on **listening walks**. On a listening walk a child visits a wooded area and they are asked to be silent and listen to what is going on around them. By not talking, children can hear the wind in the trees, birds and other woodland noises. This will encourage discussions about what they hear.
● Simple action games such as the 'Five little ducks' allow children to practise the rhyming of words and improve their listening skills as they focus on the instruction of the song.

### The process of following instructions

From 2 years, vocabulary has increased significantly and children are able to put two words together. This is also true for following instructions. Adults can ask children to do something in two parts, such as 'put the toy in box'. Children need time to process what is being asked of them, and instructions will need to be repeated as they may lose focus.

## Vocabulary and literacy skills

Typically children will match the sounds of an object that they are playing with, such as 'moo' when playing with a toy cow. They are very good at copying the sounds from adults but need specific help when trying to pronounce words.

By 3 years old, children may ask a lot of questions. These questions are a way of finding out about the world from a person that they trust.

Children can now form sentences that can be fully understood and should be encouraged to use their vocabulary and build on it with new words. Singing nursery rhymes and songs will allow children to practise the words they know and learn new ones.

Mixing with children of different ages can improve vocabulary. Adults can mix age groups for a role-play activity. Younger children can learn from older children and pick up new words. Older children may find it difficult to understand some younger children who may not have developed their vocabulary as much. Because of this, the older children will have to think of new ways of expressing themselves in order for the younger children to understand them.

## Expressing and discussing feelings appropriately

At around 18 months, children will seek out immediate attention. As they can't always get what they want or have trouble in expressing themselves, they can have tantrums and become argumentative. By 2–3 years, children can become jealous of their peers or siblings, especially when they are getting adult attention. This can stop children developing friendships and relationships as well as learning. By 3 years, children are becoming more rational and will begin to appreciate the needs of others; the following activities could help them develop their skills in this area:

- Role-play activities such as 'dress up' can allow children to express themselves safely without fear. Encouraging children to act out their feelings towards others in a safe environment can lead to them overcoming any frustrations they have.
- Using books, children can develop their knowledge of emotions. Stories such as *The Angry Ladybird* or *The Happy Bear* allow them to explore feelings.

## Having conversations with other children/adults

Adults should regularly have conversations with children to promote communication and language development. This can be done by asking questions about their favourite things or what they have done in the day. Adults can also read the child's favourite book and encourage the child to join in. Children rarely have conversations with other children and still lack the social skills to make friends. During play, they may ask another child a question but interaction is limited.

### CHECK MY LEARNING

1 How can sharing stories with each other promote communication and intellectual development?
2 If you were a nursery nurse, how would you get a 2-year-old to calm down and try to express their feelings in an appropriate way?

### BEST PRACTICE

Modelling behaviour when discussing feelings shows children how to act appropriately.

### ACTIVITY

*Quinn and Harvey are 3 years old and are twins. They were born prematurely and this affected their learning abilities. They are struggling with their communication and language and find it difficult to say words or understand what the words mean. One of their favourite songs is 'Old MacDonald'. They don't know all the words to the song but they love to make the animal noises. Gemma is the nursery nurse in charge and she has decided that it is important for all children to learn to associate the noise of an object with the sound it makes. She tells you that this basic association can lead to new vocabulary and improved speaking skills. Gemma has asked you to create a poster to help children like Quinn and Harvey.*

1 Create an A3 'word-sound' poster. Pick one of the following themes:
   - animals
   - transport.

You should draw pictures of the theme you have chosen and include a word that best describes the sound it makes.

2 How will the poster help to develop Quinn and Harvey's communication skills?

3 How would the poster help to promote Quinn and Harvey's social and emotional development?

# Children's learning supported through communication and language play: 3–5 years

Children's language has now become more fluent; this is important for them, as communication and language is one of the main ways that children will learn. As they develop emotionally and socially, communication becomes a key part in the development of friendships and relationships. Children need to be able to communicate so they can express themselves without feeling frustrated. Sentence structure will start to become more complex as they get ready to start school. Imagine that you had tape over your mouth; how could you tell someone you were upset or hungry if you couldn't speak?

## Communication and language play

### Listening skills

Children between 3 and 5 years often have difficulty when pronouncing words – for example, 'spaghetti' is often pronounced as 'pasgetti' and animal as 'aminal'. This should not be a concern to adults unless it continues after the age of 5. Play in this age range should be aimed at refining speech sounds through interaction with others. Playing with other children and talking to adults allows children to practise their communication skills but also allows them to refine how they say words.

Many children at this age will already know nursery rhymes and songs. The rhythm encourages children to refine their speech to help them to pronounce the words correctly. Having a singing session while acting out the rhyme will allow children to have fun while learning how to say the words correctly.

Older children can be recorded while singing. When it is played back to them they will be able to hear themselves, which they will often find quite funny. It is a useful way to pick up on any mispronounced words.

As children are more active and are able to pay attention for longer periods, action games such as 'Simon says' can develop listening skills. As the adult gives commands such as 'touch your toes' or 'spin around', the children have to use their listening skills to work out if the adult has said 'Simon says' at the beginning of the sentence. If they do not listen properly and make a move when the adult has not said 'Simon says', they are disqualified from the game.

◻ This adult is using a large book to read to the children. Why do you think it is important to let children see the pages of the book?

### The process of following instructions

At around 3 years old, children are more confident following instructions, as their vocabulary and listening skills have improved. They have moved on from two-step instructions and can follow three- or four-step instructions. At this stage of development, they may also ask questions to help them understand or clarify what has been said.

### Vocabulary and literacy skills

By the age of 3, most children have a good understanding of words such as 'on', 'under' and 'in' and are able to use pronouns such as 'I', 'we' or 'you', and some plurals. Most sentences are easily understandable and children now use questions to gain further knowledge and to expand their vocabulary.

By the age of 5, children can usually use complex sentences with words such as 'because' and 'can' and talk about what has happened in the past and what might happen in the future. They are more articulate and are also able to argue with others and to answer back. Literacy skills have developed and most enjoy listening to and talking about storybooks and will make an attempt to read and write. By the time a child is 5 years old they begin to match words to what is being said and can usually recognise letters and their sounds.

**Story sacks** are a great way to get children to develop their literacy skills and vocabulary. A story sack will have a theme based around a book (for example, a train driver). It will also contain supporting material based on that theme, such as train-themed snap cards, pictures that could be coloured in or a simple comprehension task based on the book. Children can choose their story sack.

## How to express and discuss feelings appropriately

Children will now know some basic feelings and are likely to apologise if they have done something wrong. They are beginning to use more complex words to describe their feelings, like 'embarrassed'. Children are usually better at managing their emotions and tend not to have tantrums as much, but they still need help. The following activities could be useful:

- Puppets are a good way for a child to address any emotional issues they may be having. For example, some children may feel anxiety when away from parents or parents may be going through a difficult time (for example, a divorce). Hiding behind a screen can help children to feel more comfortable talking about their feelings.
- Picture books that depict emotions can also help children identify which emotions they are feeling if they are unable to say them. These books show pictures of children with different facial expressions. Usually under each facial expression it will give the emotion that the child has. It may also have a story to describe the feeling.

## Having conversations with other children/adults

Children can now form full sentences and have conversations with both adults and other children. They have mastered the social skills to make friends, so they will talk more with others. To continue support, adults should plan activities that are group-based, such as treasure hunts, as this allows children to work together and discuss what they are doing.

**KEY TERM**

**Story sack** a sack or box that contains a storybook and resources that are linked to the story.

---

**ACTIVITY**

Work in small groups to write a list of words that children may struggle to say.

1 Using your word list, describe how adults can help to promote communication and language through play, in order to help children to say the words correctly.

2 How can supporting speech help to promote a child's intellectual, social and emotional development?

---

**CHECK MY LEARNING**

1 Why is it important to listen carefully when playing a game like 'Simon says'?

2 How can puppets help a child who may find it difficult to control emotions?

# Children's learning supported through social and emotional play: 0–18 months

## GETTING STARTED

Can you remember how you felt when you first started school? Discuss your feelings with the person sat next to you. Why do you think you had those feelings?

## LINK IT UP

For a better understanding of social and emotional development, look back at learning outcome A of Component 1.

## KEY TERMS

**Social bonds** attachment to other people.

**Emotional bonds** having a connection with a person.

Children form attachments to those around them. When they are babies this is with their parents or carers. When they get older they also form attachments with other children and people who are important to them. In this age range, social and emotional play involves planning activities that allow children to begin to understand how to interact with others, and the rules of sharing and turn-taking that will help them form relationships in the future. How would you feel if someone took a pen from you as you were writing with it? Would you want to be friends with them?

## Social play

### Developing relationships

Relationships are limited in this age range, as children are usually not confident with strangers. Babies will develop strong **social** and **emotional bonds** to their primary caregivers and this will be shown when separation anxiety emerges. As a child becomes mobile and is more active in play, anger and frustration can occur when they can't get what they want. Having a reliable, familiar person to carry out play activities with can help to calm them and help them to feel at ease. Play activities, such as the suggestions below, can help to build stronger bonds and trust between adults and children.

- Although friendships do not emerge in this age range, it is important that adults allow children to watch during activities with others. This will then form the basis of them understanding how to interact in the future and form relationships.
- *Singing in groups* such songs as 'Five little monkeys' teaches children about having fun with others.
- A calming play activity for babies can be based around *massage*. Adults can sing or talk to the baby as they massage legs and arms. This helps to build trust and strengthen emotional bonds.

### Sharing, turn-taking and compromise

Children 0–18 months old find it difficult to share with others and to understand the concept of taking turns. They want everything their own way and struggle to understand social skills such as compromise. Activities to build sharing and turn-taking could include the following:

- From around 6 months a child will actively hold a toy; simple sharing can be encouraged by *passing the toy back and forth* between the child and adult.
- Getting children to make prints of their hands and feet for a *group collage* on the nursery wall is one way to encourage social skills. Children may have to wait their turn to share the resources.

## Emotional play

### Expression of feelings

Sometimes it can be difficult for younger children to express themselves, as they do not fully understand their own emotions. Practising recognising their own facial expressions can help them identify how they feel.

- Younger babies can have a place to be calm where they can have special toys and *comfort blankets*.

- *Messy play* using mud, sand, water and paints can help children learn the foundations of emotions control – slapping the water in an angry way, then stopping to slosh water happily, for example.
- By 18 months, children have more understanding. *Finger puppets or dolls* can be used to show expressions of feelings.

## Promoting independence

Children under 18 months tend to be very attached to their main caregiver, and rely on them for everything; because of this they are not very independent. Having independence is an essential life skill that is needed for confidence. It is important that young children are given activities that promote independence so that, in the future, they are less reliant on adults (see Figure 2.4).

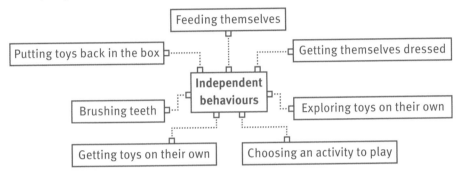

◘ Figure 2.4: It is important that young children are given activities that promote independence.

Puppets can help to promote independent behaviours. Finger puppets or dolls can be used to show children how to feed themselves and what not to do when eating dinner. Children around 18 months will try to mimic this behaviour.

## Improving self-confidence, self-esteem and self-awareness

At the age of approximately 15 months, children will begin to develop a sense of who they are; they will also begin to develop self-confidence and self-esteem. There are several ways adults can help with this.

- Playing with children 0–18 months old and paying full attention to them, using *safe play mirrors* and talking about them can encourage self-confidence.
- Self-esteem can be encouraged by making a child feel *involved in decision making*. When choosing an activity to play, giving a choice to the child and allowing them to 'choose' will make them feel important (even if the decision is actually the adult's).

## Building on relationships

- Young babies are attached to their caregiver and will often show distress when they leave. Adults can use *carpet time* to show photos of and talk about people who are special to them. Adults can also have one-to-one time with children to create stronger bonds.

◘ Children do not begin to develop self-awareness until around 15 months old. What could this girl be thinking? How could an adult help her understand?

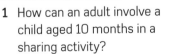

CHECK MY LEARNING

1 How can an adult involve a child aged 10 months in a sharing activity?

2 How can taking part in sharing activities help to promote the social development of children aged 18 months?

ACTIVITY

1 Write a script for a puppet show that you will perform to the rest of the class. It should be based on an independent behaviour you want to promote in a child. You will need to design your puppets from paper and make them large and colourful.

2 Evaluate how well you performed your puppet show. What can children learn from it?

# Children's learning supported through social and emotional play: 18 months–3 years

## GETTING STARTED

Have you ever heard of the 'terrible twos'? Write down a brief explanation of what you think it means. Share this with the rest of the class.

## LINK IT UP

You have previously learned about the stages of play a child goes through. If you need help to remember, head back to the 'Stages of children's play' sections on pages 62–67.

◘ This child is trying to comfort their friend who is upset. How can comforting one another build on relationships?

## BEST PRACTICE

Caregivers should allow children to make their own choices when interacting with others – for example, deciding if they want to kiss/hug someone rather than being told they have to.

At this age, children are well on their way to developing a sense of themselves and understanding who they are. As they learn, they can often get frustrated and jealous of others, which can lead to tantrums. Around the age of 2 years and 6 months, children begin to react well to praise and positive attention when it is given by adults and will try to do their best to get it. Have you ever been shopping and seen a small child screaming at their parents? Why do you think some children do this?

Towards the age of 3, children are not as easily frustrated if they do not get immediate gratification, as they now find it easier to wait. They find it easier to share and take turns and usually show concern for others when they are upset.

## Social play

### Development of friendships and relationships

Through parallel and associative play, children have had some interaction with their peers. At 3 years, children lack some social skills but are beginning to develop friendships with others. They are likely to have a sense of trust with a familiar adult. As children are more comfortable around others they will ask questions; this can be seen during associative play. Adults should start introducing activities that encourage children to work together.

Many nurseries have their own *mud kitchen* for play or garden area for planting. *Gardening* is a beneficial activity for the future development of friendships between children. They are becoming aware of each other and the activity can lead to questions. This can promote cognitive development, as asking questions can develop problem-solving skills and imagination.

### Sharing, turn-taking and compromise

Children in this age range crave immediate gratification and this can mean limited sharing and compromise with peers. To support the development of social skills, adults can plan activities that encourage sharing and compromise with others.

By the end of this age range, most children will have learned to share and enjoy playing with others. Adults can plan activities to build on these skills. This encourages children to think about their feelings and the feelings of others.

- At around the age of 2 years and 6 months, children can kick a ball. Children could take turns *rolling or kicking the ball* to other children or an adult.
- Using '*sharing bins*' in role-play can help children to understand sharing. The bin contains different props and all children are told that anything in the bin can be used by anyone in the nursery. When one child takes a prop, other children will learn that they can no longer use it and learn to compromise by using something else instead.

## Emotional play

### Expression of feelings

Children can have some issues with controlling their behaviour and feelings in this age range. That is because they are not fully aware of how they feel or the appropriate way to deal with it. Activities to encourage expression of feelings could include the following:

- **Emotion face** activities can begin the process of children linking a facial expression to a feeling. At this stage of development, children will find this difficult, so it is important that adults take the lead and prompt questions.
- During *circle time* children can be given a teddy to pass around. The children can talk about '*how teddy feels today*'. This can encourage children to express their own feelings.
- *Emotion check-in*, where older children in this range are able to choose a face that matches how they feel. An adult can then talk about what they can do to improve that emotion. This helps children to understand how to control emotions.

## Promoting independence

At 18 months, children are still heavily reliant on their caregivers. As children want to be independent, frustration can arise. Children at this age should be guided into becoming independent and given activities that can promote it without overwhelming them. Having a sense of independence can lead children to develop a sense of self and begin to be more aware of themselves. It can also help children to build friendships with others. Activities that can help to promote independence include the following:

- *Role-play* or pretend play is a useful activity to show children different ways of becoming independent. Pretending to have a family meal will encourage setting the table, serving food and self-feeding.
- Role-play that uses *dressing up* encourages the child to undo their zip or buttons and work out how to take clothes off and put them back on.

## Improving self-confidence, self-esteem and self-awareness

Children often appear to be full of self-confidence; however, a lot of the time they are struggling to understand their own emotions. To try to encourage children to tackle their shyness and worry, they need to know what those feelings look like and what can be done to help cope with them.

*Finger puppets* can be used to show children how a child might act if they were upset in a specific situation. 'Look, Alice is feeling sad today because she misses her mummy.' Adults can use characters to show children what can be done in that situation. This will teach them how to improve their own confidence but also how to be self-aware and aware of others.

## Building on relationships

Although children can have tantrums and be argumentative, they are learning that it is more important to get along with others, as there will be a reward. This reward can be spending time with someone they like or taking part in a fun activity. Children begin to develop empathy and will help others if they see them in distress. They are also more likely to stop a tantrum if they know it upsets someone else.

Children will start having a preference as to who they want to play with. Activities should encourage group work using role-play in order for children to build on the relationships they already have.

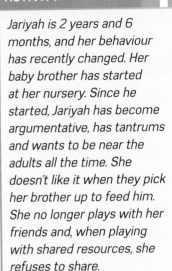

### ACTIVITY

*Jariyah is 2 years and 6 months, and her behaviour has recently changed. Her baby brother has started at her nursery. Since he started, Jariyah has become argumentative, has tantrums and wants to be near the adults all the time. She doesn't like it when they pick her brother up to feed him. She no longer plays with her friends and, when playing with shared resources, she refuses to share.*

1 Why might Jariyah's behaviour have changed?

2 Describe how emotion faces could help.

3 How can using emotion faces promote Jariyah's emotional, communication and language development?

### KEY TERM

**Emotion face** showing different emotions on your face. This can be done by a child or adult, or shown through images or video.

### CHECK MY LEARNING

1 Describe how group activities can promote compromise.

2 How can activities that promote compromise also promote social development?

3 Olivia is 2 years and 6 months, is very shy and barely talks to the other children or staff. What activities do you suggest the nursery could provide so that she can gain some confidence?

### LINK IT UP

For a range of activities and resources related to social and emotional play, see pages 94–99.

# Children's learning supported through social and emotional play: 3–5 years

Children are now becoming more independent. If they are with someone they know, being away from their primary care giver is much easier. Children are less likely to have tantrums and will usually deal with situations in a more co-operative way. Emotions have become more complex, with some children showing embarrassment and excitement.

Around 3–4 years, children will show a preference for a friend, but they will only develop close friendships around the age of 5. Sharing with others has become much easier and children can usually understand the rules of games, although they will often fail to follow them. What games did you play with other children when you were younger? Did you ever try to change the rules?

## Social play

### Developing friendships and relationships

Children have moved away from simply observing others as they play and towards forming relationships. Bonds with other children are built on trust and sharing and develop into friendships. While children will play with others of either sex in this age range, typically same-sex friendships occur around 5 years. As children are more emotionally developed, they understand when a friend is upset, shy or needs help. Activities to develop friendships and relationships could include the following:

- Setting up *team games* and activities that allow children to work together and co-operate will develop trust between them and deepen their friendships. For example, children can pass a balloon to each other using their knees to hold it. This will also help to develop balance and co-ordination.
- A *treasure/scavenger hunt* can build bonds as children work together to find the hidden objects.
- *Doctor, dentist or vet role-play* will require children to co-operate and talk to each other. It will also promote speaking and listening skills.

### Sharing, turn-taking and compromise

In this age range, sharing and turn-taking has become easier for children. They are less likely to have a tantrum and cause an argument when they do not want to share, as they have more of an understanding of others' feelings. However, there can be times when some children choose not to share or take turns. At this point, adults should act as a role model or suggest a solution.

- *Board games* such as 'snakes and ladders' are particularly good for developing turn-taking skills. As each child's turn is short, the game keeps their interest.
- Have you ever played 'keep it up' with a balloon? This group activity can encourage sharing, as there is only one balloon with a group of children. Children stand in a circle and the balloon is thrown into the air. Only one child at a time can hit it to keep it up. Some children may reach out to hit the balloon but realise that another child is doing the same thing. They will learn to compromise and let the other child hit the balloon, in the hope that they can hit it the next time.
- A joint project of a *collage* based on the current season can also help children with sharing resources and compromising.

◻ These two children are sharing the blocks. If one child wanted to use all the blue blocks, what do you think would happen? How do you think an adult could help in that situation?

## Emotional play

### Expressing feelings

By the time a child reaches the age of 5 they are more aware of how to self-manage their feelings. They are less likely to argue back and have tantrums, as they have learned to express themselves. It is important that adults continue to promote the expression of feelings so that children can express themselves in a positive way rather than a negative way.

- Some *dolls* have been specifically made to help children express their emotions. The dolls show an emotion on their face. If a child is sad, they may want to play with the sad doll. This will help adults identify that the child is upset, but it also helps the child as they try to understand their own feelings.
- A *'how I feel today' mirror* can encourage children to look at their own faces and say how they feel. The mirror needs to be large enough so children can see all of their face. On the mirror it says 'how I feel today'. The words encourage children to think about how they feel while looking at their facial expression in the mirror. Adults can support them with new vocabulary that expresses their feelings, such as 'frustration' or 'anger', while they form links between new emotions and their facial expressions.

### Promoting independence and building relationships

Creating an *'I can do' play* for children to take part in encourages them to think about what they are good at. They get to dress up, sing or dance and show others what they can do well. This promotes their independence and the sharing of their feelings with others, which in turn can help them create relationships and friendships.

### Improving self-confidence, self-esteem and self-awareness

Being self-aware requires children to think about their feelings and how they think others see them. Having strong self-awareness allows a child to gain confidence and self-esteem, as they are able to recognise their strengths and weaknesses, understand their own behaviour and identify what they need to do to complete a task.

At *circle time*, children can be asked to stand and talk about what they did during the day. Adults can ask each child to nominate one other child for doing something good. As each child takes a turn, they praise someone else. This activity makes children feel good about themselves and increases their self-esteem as they praise other children, but it also increases the self-esteem of the children who have been praised.

**ACTIVITY**

*The local pre-school is keen to make sure that every child has a friend and doesn't feel left out. They want to make sure that, as the children turn 5 and are getting ready for school life, they have the skills to make friends so they don't find it difficult when they start school.*

*The manager has asked you to create a leaflet that includes several activities that staff can plan for children in order to improve their friendship skills.*

Your leaflet should include:

1 different activities

2 any resources needed

3 an explanation as to why building friendships is important for all areas of development.

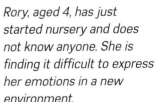

**CHECK MY LEARNING**

Rory, aged 4, has just started nursery and does not know anyone. She is finding it difficult to express her emotions in a new environment.

1 Explain how circle time could help Rory with her emotions.

2 What could adults do for Rory to promote friendships through play?

# Activities and resources to promote more than one area of development

Many activities promote a number of different areas of development at the same time. Here are a few examples. Can you think of others?

| Type of play and learning | Age range 0–18 months | 18 months–3 years | 3–5 years |
|---|---|---|---|
| **Physical development** | • Using a rattle that is colourful and noisy is one way for babies to improve their grasp. It will also encourage their cognitive and intellectual development as they begin to develop their listening and attention skills.<br>• An obstacle course for babies can help them improve spatial awareness and promote their gross motor skills as they crawl around objects in front of them. It also encourages them to problem solve as they work out how to get around an object.<br>• A baby gym allows a child to develop their gross motor skills through kicking and grabbing. They are able to increase their muscle strength and co-ordination and problem solve as they work out how to reach objects. | • Playing outdoors on a tricycle can develop balance, bodily co-ordination and steering skills. It also encourages children to socialise and builds confidence and self-esteem.<br>• Push-along toys encourage young children to push up from the floor and get into a standing position. Holding a push-along toy will give support as the child is learning to walk. Walking can increase confidence too, as the child is proud to learn a new skill. | • Using a plastic needle, children can thread beads onto string. This will help to improve their hand–eye co-ordination. The activity will allow children to share the beads with each other and to problem solve if they find it difficult to thread the bead. Children may also discuss with others what they are making or the colours they are choosing.<br>• As children use climbing frames they increase their balancing skills and upper body strength when they hold on to bars. Playing on play equipment can be a social activity too. |
| **Cognitive and intellectual development** | • A digging activity, searching for coins or hidden toys, can allow children to use their imagination to create a story. Communication and language are also promoted as children talk about what they have found.<br>• Taking small babies and children on trips and visits can help them learn about the world around them and also begin to understand social differences. | • Magnetic puzzle boards can encourage children to be creative as well as practising their problem-solving skills. Manipulating the magnetic pieces is one way of improving dexterity and promoting fine motor skills.<br>• Using small weights can help children learn about 'light' and 'heavy'. This helps with intellectual development and language.<br>• Small world toys such as farmyard animals can help children to learn about the colours of animals and where they live. Fine motor skills are also developed with small world toys. | • Children can practise their writing skills and improve pencil grasp and dexterity whilst writing on a wipe board. As mistakes can easily be removed, it will help improve a child's confidence and self-esteem.<br>• Computer games, apps and tablets with educational games suitable for this age range can help with word, colour and shape recognition. They also help to develop language.<br>• Children use their imagination to make up stories with small world toys such as dinosaurs. These toys also help to develop fine motor skills. |

| Type of play and learning | Age range 0–18 months | 18 months–3 years | 3–5 years |
|---|---|---|---|
| Communication and language | • Lift-the-flap books can allow children to develop their literacy and vocabulary skills as they are introduced to sentence structure. As a child helps to turn the pages, this activity can also help to develop their fine motor skills. | • Action songs such as 'Five little ducks' allow children to practise rhyming and improve their listening skills, as they need to focus on the instructions. It is also one way of enabling children to work together in a group. This means that children are able to begin to build friendships with others as they sing. | • Children's literacy and vocabulary can be improved when using story sacks. As a story sack can also contain puzzles and comprehension tasks, children can also develop their problem-solving skills and social skills as they work with others when completing the puzzles. |
| Social | • Making prints of hands and feet for a group collage on the nursery wall will promote sharing and turn-taking but also allow children to use their gross motor skills. | • Group gardening activities, such as planting vegetables, allow children to develop friendships as they tend the soils and plant seeds and bulbs. It is also a great way for children to use their cognitive skills, such as problem solving, when placing seeds. The activity can also lead children to ask questions about the vegetables they are planting. | • Team games, such as children passing a balloon using only their knees, will allow children to work together and co-operate. It also helps to develop a child's balance and co-ordination.<br>• Board games can be used at this age, as older children start to learn about rules. Board games help to improve social skills but also fine motor skills. |
| Emotional | • Using finger puppets or dolls to show expression of feeling can also allow a child to use their fine motor skills and their communication skills as they attempt to say how they feel. | • Emotion face activities can allow a child to link facial expressions to emotions. As adults will help with this activity, it can lead to children talking about emotions and also answering questions. This activity can take place during circle time with other children, allowing everyone to share in the time they talk and begin to develop friendships. | • Allowing children to have 'share time' where they can share what they like about their favourite game allows them to improve their self-awareness. They can also develop friendships as they find other children with similar interests, while improving their communication skills as they talk in a group setting. |

# How play can be organised to promote learning: adult-led play

Because it is fun, play is a useful way of helping children to learn and develop new skills. To make sure that children are learning appropriately, adults can organise play. There are three types of play structure that promote learning. Can you think back to when you played games? Was there any structure to them?

## Adult-led play

This type of play requires an adult to plan, organise and lead children in an activity. The adult tells the child what to do and how to play. As the activities are focused, children often don't see them as play. **Adult-led** activities are planned with an awareness of the child in a particular setting. They build on what the child already knows and can do and what they are interested in. The adult should carefully plan the activity based on the particular needs of the child and the milestones that they need to meet. The activity will follow a sequence of steps or tasks that children need to complete.

Did you ever sing 'The wheels on the bus'? This song needs an adult to lead. Other examples of adult-led play can include:

- cutting fruit for a fruit salad
- a writing activity to develop pencil grip
- making cards
- cutting shapes
- bat and ball games.

## Potential benefits

### High-risk activities

Some activities would be high risk for children if they were to carry them out on their own, as they could be putting themselves or others in danger. This is especially true if they are using high-risk equipment such as scissors, knives or cookers. Having an adult plan and lead the activity means that children can take part without the risk of hurting themselves. They learn specific skills and how to use the resources and equipment safely.

Taking children on a trip to the local park can also be high risk, especially if children need to cross roads. Having an adult lead this activity means that they can help children to cross safely, and to climb down from equipment safely once they are at the park.

An adult is needed when children cook to make sure that they know how to use equipment safely.

Adults can give children the confidence and skills to use play equipment safely.

### New vocabulary

Communication is important, and adult-led play can support language development in children. When taking part in role-play, children take on new characters, and adults can prompt them to express their feelings and thoughts about a particular topic. This will help children to increase their vocabulary.

Discussions with older children can lead them to share their ideas, likes and dislikes. For example, having a discussion about food can encourage children to describe their favourite foods or their most hated foods. They can learn new vocabulary such as 'tasty', 'scrummy', 'slimy' or 'salty'.

## Potential disadvantages

### Learning is limited by the adult's choice of activity

As the adult chooses the activity or task for children, there will be a focus on a particular kind of learning. Although this may be good in terms of meeting particular milestones or targets, it means that children's overall learning is limited to that learning outcome.

When a child becomes distracted, adults are likely to bring the focus back to the task. This means that children do not have the opportunity to explore new concepts or skills.

### Learning is limited by the time given to the activity

Learning can also be limited if an adult has planned for an activity to take a specific length of time. This can mean they stick to their plan and do not allow children the time to develop their own thoughts and ideas about a topic.

### Limited repetition

**Repetition** allows children to practise the skills they have learned. It can increase confidence and **enhance** learning of new skills. However, if adults have a set duration in mind, this can also mean that children do not have enough time to repeat the actions/skills they have learned. Without repetition and practice, children will struggle to master skills.

For example, learning to write requires children to hold a pencil in a tripod grasp; this can take time to learn. Without repetition, a child may struggle to hold the pencil in the right way, as they have not been able to practise, which can affect how they learn to write.

**KEY TERMS**

**Repetition** doing something more than once.

**Enhance** increase or improve something.

---

**ACTIVITY**

*At ABC Nursery, Mark is planning activities for a group of 3-year-olds. He has decided to get the children to create a 'shape' display. All the children will cut out different shapes and paint them, then stick them to the wall. When they have completed this activity, Mark will talk about the activity and ask questions.*

1 Describe the benefits of Mark leading this activity.

2 In pairs, discuss, and then write down, the potential disadvantages of Mark leading this activity.

---

**CHECK MY LEARNING**

1 What is 'adult-led play'?

2 Describe two potential benefits and two potential disadvantages of adult-led play.

# How play can be organised to promote learning: adult-initiated play

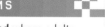

**GETTING STARTED**

What types of resources could be provided that would encourage mark making?

Do you think children would play with them in the way you wanted? Explain your answer.

It is not always necessary for an adult to lead an activity. Adults may want children to learn at their own pace with the security of having resources/equipment chosen for them. Why do you think adults might want children to learn at their own pace?

## Adult-initiated play

In this style of play, an adult sets up a play scenario for children but does not lead it. The childcare worker or parent/carer will leave tasks and resources out for children but will allow them to complete the activities in their own way and in their own time.

Providing resources encourages children to play with them in a certain way, leading them to develop new skills. For example, play money could be placed on a table with empty dishes. This would encourage children to sort the money. Smaller children could be given buckets and spades in the sand pit. Other examples of **adult-initiated** play can include:

- potato printing (leaving potatoes and paint out on tables)
- small world play (farmyard, city block, etc.)
- beads and string.

**KEY TERMS**

**Adult-initiated** where adults provide resources for an activity but let children play with them in a way they choose.

**Independent learning skills** being able to think, problem solve and act without an adult helping.

### Potential benefits

#### Children will play in new ways

Adult-initiated play allows children to explore the resources they have been given, which helps them to learn new skills and concepts. This is because children can choose their own resources and play in their own way. By doing this, they are more likely to become engaged and concentrate on the activity.

In the arts and crafts corner, a nursery worker could leave out different-sized brushes, sponges, cut potatoes and apples, and a selection of coloured paints. Children will begin to explore the objects. They could stamp apples and potatoes onto paper, squeeze paint from the sponges and mix up paint colours.

#### Promotes independent learning skills

When an early years setting uses adult-initiated play, it encourages children to develop **independent learning skills**. Adults should step back and allow the children to discover things for themselves. Children are able to learn new skills and concepts independently through problem solving and using resources/equipment in new ways.

◘ Leaving a child with a jigsaw they have never seen before will encourage them to problem solve on their own.

## Potential disadvantages

### Children may not learn the expected skill or concept

Adult-initiated play relies on children understanding the activity that the resources have been laid out for. Unfortunately, children may not always understand what the aim of the activity is and may not play in the way that is expected. This will mean that they do not learn the skills or concepts that adults expect them to learn. For example:

- a child may not use the bucket and spade in the sand but use their hands
- children may choose to use only one colour when painting and not learn how to mix a range of colours.

**ACTIVITY**

*Taryn is 3 and has just started nursery. Taryn's mother is unsure how adults at the nursery will provide adult-initiated play and how it will benefit Taryn.*

Create a leaflet for Taryn's mum and other parents that:

1 describes adult-initiated play

2 has a range of play activity examples

3 describes the benefits of these activities.

**CHECK MY LEARNING**

1 In what ways can adult-initiated play encourage new skills/concepts?

2 Explain the potential disadvantages of adult-initiated play.

3 Describe the difference between adult-led and adult-initiated play.

# How play can be organised to promote learning: child-initiated play

 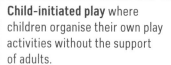
Play should not always be about what adults want a child to do or learn. To make sure play stays fun for children, they should have their own time for discovery so they can play and learn how they want to. When a teacher gives you an activity to do, are you always happy to do it? Could you learn in a better way if you thought of your own activity?

## Child-initiated play

**Child-initiated play** is sometimes called 'free play'. Adults provide a safe environment for the child to explore and try out their own ideas. Children are free to choose their own activity. They are in control of how they play, how long they play for and who to play with.

This type of play is usually more creative and imaginative, as children are deciding what they would like to do rather than following instructions.

Adults are able to join in with the children but they must follow the instructions of the child.

**KEY TERM**

**Child-initiated play** where children organise their own play activities without the support of adults.

### Potential benefits

#### Developing social skills

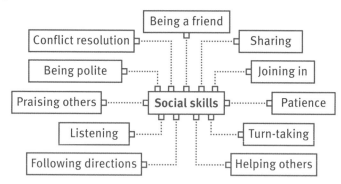

Figure 2.5: Social skills that children may develop from child-initiated play.

Child-initiated play provides an opportunity for the development of social skills (see Figure 2.5). As children have chosen the game or activity, they are more likely to play for longer and want to interact with others. As children use the resources and activities around them and begin to interact with others, they are improving social skills such as turn-taking and sharing.

At times, during this type of play, children will make up games with their own rules. Children may not always agree, but this is no bad thing, as it encourages negotiation skills and helps children to find ways to work things out themselves.

**BEST PRACTICE**

It is important to consider a child's preference when setting up child-initiated play. This will increase the likelihood of children joining in and not being left out.

#### Developing ideas freely

When children choose an activity or game, they often do not see it as a learning experience and are more likely to spend time on it and focus. Children often see the environment differently and will play with activities/games in their own way. Child-initiated play allows a child to develop their own ideas more freely.

**LINK IT UP**

In learning outcome A of Component 1 (see Table 1.5, page 11) you learned about fine and gross motor skills. Look back to refresh your memory.

## Potential disadvantages

### Children focus on one area of learning or development

During child-initiated play, children may have a strong preference for a particular activity. This can lead to children excluding other play opportunities in favour of their preference. By choosing the same play activity over and over again, children are limiting the skills they are learning and so could be limiting their development.

For example, a child that chooses to stack blocks each time may improve fine motor skills and could learn to sort by colour, but they are not developing gross motor skills or skills in expressing themselves.

🔲 Children may move quickly between resources without fully exploring them.

### Children may ignore others

Play is an opportunity to learn, develop and interact with others. However, child-initiated play can lead some children to isolate themselves. Children who prefer to be alone or those who are focused on a particular form of play may not socialise with others. This can lead to a lack of development in social skills.

### Learning may be limited

- Children may not learn new concepts or vocabulary, as there is often limited contact with adults.
- Without adults encouraging and supporting play, children may find it difficult to expand their knowledge.
- Children with learning difficulties may also find it challenging to participate in some of the activities and could miss out on opportunities to learn/develop new skills because they do not receive sufficient adult support.

**ACTIVITY**

Draw a table on A4 paper with three columns and three rows. List the three learning styles and outline advantages and disadvantages of each.

| Learning style | Advantages | Disadvantages |
| --- | --- | --- |
| Adult-led play | | |
| Adult-initiated play | | |
| Child-initiated play | | |

**CHECK MY LEARNING** 🔲🔲

1 Define the term 'child-initiated play'.

2 Why might some children not achieve learning goals through child-initiated play?

3 How can this type of play develop social skills?

# The role of adults in promoting learning through play: a variety of activities

**GETTING STARTED**

Make a list of five activities that children from 0–5 years old can do. Consider which ones can be played outside, inside, in a group or alone. Which of your activities can help promote a child's senses?

It is important to allow children to have access to a variety of play activities. Do you think that playing outside alone is better than inside in a group? How could children take part in group sensory activities?

## Organising activities

Play needs to be planned carefully in order to offer a variety of exciting and challenging opportunities to children. In a school or nursery, adults can organise activities and games to promote learning and allow children to develop and meet their milestones. When planning, adults need to consider the types of activity, the location and whether the activity will be for a group of children or just one child.

**DID YOU KNOW?**

Good-quality play should include a range of indoor and outdoor play opportunities. This will enable children to access different resources as well as promoting different areas of development.

Some activities can be organised either indoors or outdoors. Sand play is an example of this; a sand tray can be used indoors and a sand pit can be used outdoors.

It is the role of the adult to provide children with resources that are suitable for their age and stage of development. Adults may set out activities and lead play (adult-led play), direct children towards activities and resources and engage them in play (adult-initiated play), or set out accessible resources and supervise while children choose and experience different types of play independently (child-initiated play).

### Indoor activities

**KEY TERM**

**Circle time** a time when children sit together with an adult to take part in an activity or a discussion.

Indoor play can include:

- messy areas
- book sharing
- small world play
- domestic corners for role play.

Indoor play is organised by adults, for example creative/messy areas, quiet areas for **circle time** and sharing books, construction or small world play, and domestic play corners.

### Outdoor activities

Children should be given extended periods of time outdoors. Activities should allow children to make noise and move freely. As outdoor areas are usually larger, children will be able to access activities/toys they may not be able to use indoors.

Adults should create different areas for the children to play outdoors. They should plan activities suitable for the stage of development and help children to participate in all activities, as well as supervising the use of equipment and resources.

Outdoor play should include woodland and digging areas that allow children to explore and the opportunity to talk about the natural environment. Equipment such as climbing frames and trikes can be used to promote physical development, while areas to make dens can be provided to spark a child's imagination. Outside activities should also be provided for babies and small children, such as giving them a soft area to play in.

☐ This child is enjoying playing with cooked green pasta. How is this supporting them to learn through their senses?

### Individual activities

Activities may be organised for individual children or a group of children. Individual activities can be targeted towards the development stage of a child, their interests and their individual needs.

Between birth and 18 months old, individual activities are planned for children who are still in the unoccupied or solitary play stages. They are planned to promote development, for example rolling a ball back and forth or using a treasure basket. From around 2 years of age, individual activities can be organised based around a child's particular interest, such as construction or water play.

Activities should be carefully planned for children with a developmental delay, as their individual needs have to be considered. Adults should provide an individual activity that may focus on a specific area of development for that child. For example, a child that has a speech delay may take part in reading or singing a nursery rhyme with an adult. This will allow them to practise and improve their speech and communication skills.

Benefits of individual play could include:

- time to think
- a chance to be creative
- a chance for children to explore on their own
- few distractions
- a chance to use imaginative skills.

## Group activities

Group activities allow children from 3 years to socialise with others and develop their social skills as well as learning to co-operate and understand rules. Group activities can also include playing games such as 'If you're happy and you know it' or playing simple board games. They allow children to have fun together and begin to understand how games work and why they have rules. Examples of group activities could include:

- making classroom displays
- group construction play
- a tallest tower challenge.

## Sensory activities

From the moment a child is born they are constantly exploring the world through their senses. They do this by touching, tasting, seeing, smelling, hearing and moving. Babies will often place things in their mouths, small children make funny noises, and older children want to touch things.

It is important that adults plan for sensory play so that children are able to learn about texture, taste and smell.

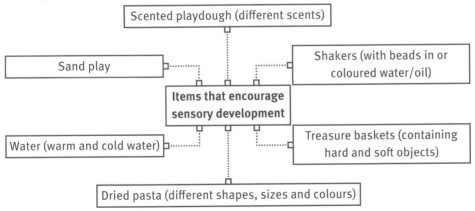

**Figure 2.6: Items that encourage sensory development.**

The role of the adult is to provide suitable sensory materials/resources for the children to use (see Figure 2.6). The materials should encourage children to use a number of senses such as smell, touch and sound. During sensory activities, adults should help children to explore the resources and ask questions.

## LINK IT UP

In learning outcome A of Component 1 (see page 14) you learned about physical development and the senses. Sensory play encourages children to use those senses. Take a look back to remind yourself of the senses.

## ACTIVITY

Tinkerbelle's Nursery is opening soon and they are planning their outdoor space. They have asked for your guidance.

1 Write a report detailing:

   a what adults should consider when setting up an outdoor area

   b why outdoor play is important for children's learning.

2 Create a poster for the nursery that shows activities for one day for children aged 18 months–3 years. Against each activity, outline the role of the adult.

## CHECK MY LEARNING

1 Why is it important that adults plan some activities to take place outdoors?

2 What is sensory play?

3 Describe the role of the adult in adult-initiated sensory play.

# The role of adults in promoting learning through play: supporting children

A key part of an adult's role in play is to make sure that learning is taking place. Helping children to understand what they need to do during an activity helps them to learn effectively. It is also important for adults to consider the personal interests of children. A child that has no interest in an activity may find it difficult to learn. Why do you think a child may not learn if they are not interested in the activity?

## Explaining and demonstrating how equipment and resources work

How does a child know to spin a hula hoop around their waist? It isn't obvious. Is that the only way to play with it? When children are given an activity, they often don't know what to do. Adults need to explain what the equipment is called and what children should do as well as demonstrate how to use it safely.

■ A 2-year-old is unlikely to have the language to understand an explanation of how to stack blocks, but if they are shown how to, they will usually pick it up very quickly.

There are several reasons why it is important for adults to explain equipment and resources to children:

- safety
- so children know how to use the equipment
- so children know the rules of the activity
- to help children to develop confidence.

Sometimes, simply explaining what a piece of equipment is and how it should be used is not enough for children to fully understand. This is especially true for very young children or children who have special educational needs. An activity should always be demonstrated.

## Adapting activities to suit personal interests

Adults need to be able to meet the **personal interests** of children in their care. Planned activities should consider what children like to do or what they are interested in at that particular time.

If their interests are considered, children are more likely to feel valued, as adults are thinking about their likes and dislikes. It also means that children will be more motivated to take part and enjoy the activities. This will promote learning, as children are more active when engaged in an activity that they enjoy.

**KEY TERM**

**Personal interests** topics that children are interested in or things they like to do.

**BEST PRACTICE**

Asking a child to help demonstrate a piece of equipment allows the other children to fully understand, and boosts self-esteem.

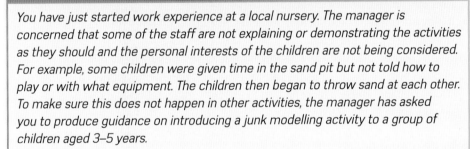

**ACTIVITY**

*You have just started work experience at a local nursery. The manager is concerned that some of the staff are not explaining or demonstrating the activities as they should and the personal interests of the children are not being considered. For example, some children were given time in the sand pit but not told how to play or with what equipment. The children then began to throw sand at each other. To make sure this does not happen in other activities, the manager has asked you to produce guidance on introducing a junk modelling activity to a group of children aged 3–5 years.*

In pairs:

1  a  Identify the resources and equipment needed.
   b  Detail how the adult should explain and demonstrate how to use the resources and equipment.
   c  Explain how to adapt the activity for a child who has delayed fine motor skills.

2  Present your work to the rest of the class, demonstrating your explanations. Did the class understand your explanations? Could you improve them?

**CHECK MY LEARNING**

1  Why do adults need to explain activities to children?

2  How can demonstrating an activity help a child to understand what they should do?

3  If an adult takes a child's personal interests into account and plans an activity, how can this affect a child's learning?

# The role of adults in promoting learning through play: equipment and resources

**GETTING STARTED**

In groups, think about activities that you took part in when you were younger. Did you always enjoy them or learn from them? If not, why do you think that is?

**KEY TERM**

**Motivate** to give someone a reason to do something.

◘ Why do you think these children are fully engaged in the activity?

When planning play activities for children, it is important that adults select the right equipment and resources to promote learning. Resources should be suitable for the age group and the interests of the children. For example, giving 5-year-olds large building blocks for a fine motor activity would not be suitable. At their age they would need something more challenging, such as different-sized and -shaped blocks.

## Choosing equipment and resources

When considering a learning activity for a child, adults should focus on equipment and resources that will promote learning. It is important that the activity allows children to want to learn and face some challenges. There are many things that adults need to consider when choosing equipment and resources.

### Motivating children to engage

If you thought an activity was boring, would you want to do it? What about if the equipment or resources looked difficult to use? When creating an activity for children, adults need to **motivate** children to want to do it. They can do this in a number of ways.

- Adults could provide young children around 10–12 months with balls with bells or toys with wheels to encourage them to move around and explore their environment.
- If they are offered colourful and attractive resources, children are more likely to want to take part and learn.
- When children are practising handwriting, it can be helpful to try different approaches, for example using paintbrushes and paints on windows or using chalks outside. These allow children to use their imagination and can help to engage them in the activity.

### Promote exploring

Children learn through first-hand experience; this can be on their own or with others. Resources should allow children to use their imagination so they are able to explore their environment and ideas freely. Children should be given a range of resources to play with so that they can choose how they want to explore.

Children like to play with water because they like how it feels. If they are given a range of different resources to use in the water, children can learn in their own way. Resources can include marbles, ping-pong balls and recycled containers. Using these, children can learn about sinking and floating.

### Encourage questioning

When children ask questions they are trying to understand their world. Children will learn more from an activity if they feel they are free to ask questions about what they are doing. Asking questions is one way of improving communication and language development and encourages reasoning. There are lots of ways to use resources to enable children to ask questions.

- Selecting stories suitable for the age group that will capture children's imagination and encourage questions about what is happening or how the characters are feeling.

■ New environments can promote exploring. Taking children to a petting zoo allows them to touch the animals and interact with them.

- Using resources that allow children to use their senses can also lead to questions. They may ask why, what and how questions. For example, an animal listening game, where children have to guess what the noise is, can lead children to ask why a goat sounds similar to a sheep or learn the difference between a goose and a duck.

## Set challenges

Equipment and resources should be chosen carefully so that they challenge children but do not make the activity unachievable. For example, giving a posting box with shapes for a child who has not yet developed hand–eye co-ordination will result in them becoming bored and disengaged. If the equipment or resource is too difficult then children often feel upset that they can't do it. A gentle challenge can encourage them to think about something in a different way and to develop and practise their problem-solving skills. For example:

- When threading beads on string, children can be given a range of different-sized beads or thicknesses of string.
- Playing dominoes can start with matching pictures. Then, to make it more challenging, children could move on to dominoes with dots on them. This will allow them to practise their counting. Finally, the dominoes could have numbers on them and children would need to try to remember what the number represents.

## Sufficient time

Allowing children enough time to complete an activity gives them an opportunity to learn. If a nursery doesn't have enough resources and children must share, it can mean that not all children have enough time to play with the equipment. This can lead to some children missing out on learning opportunities. Always consider time when planning an activity.

- When planning outdoor time and using the climbing equipment, it is important to consider the weather, as this could also limit the amount of time for the activity.
- Reading takes a long time for children to master. When planning reading sessions, adults should choose an appropriate book for the age of the child. Children aged 18 months–3 years are only able to concentrate for a few minutes, so books for this age range should be short.

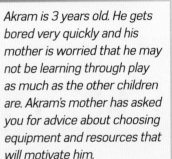

**ACTIVITY**

*Akram is 3 years old. He gets bored very quickly and his mother is worried that he may not be learning through play as much as the other children are. Akram's mother has asked you for advice about choosing equipment and resources that will motivate him.*

1 Give three reasons why Akram may not engage with the equipment and resources he is given.

2 Why is it important to choose resources and equipment that challenge Akram?

3 Give examples of equipment and resources that could encourage Akram to ask questions.

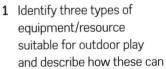

**CHECK MY LEARNING**

1 Identify three types of equipment/resource suitable for outdoor play and describe how these can motivate children to explore.

2 What are the disadvantages of giving children resources that they do not have time to use or explore fully?

# The role of adults in promoting learning through play: social skills and health awareness

Children often try to mimic the actions of adults. This can be useful for adults, as it is a good way to show children how to behave. Adults can also model specific behaviours or skills that they would like children to mimic, such as communication techniques or how to share and take turns. Why is it important that adults are careful how they behave in front of young children?

## Modelling communication

Communication and language are important for a child's development and are essential for building relationships with others and making sense of the environment.

There is a difference between communication and language.

- Communication is the way messages are passed between people.
- Language is the structure for words, such as sentences and the order in which words are used.

Communication and language can be difficult for children to grasp and they will often make mistakes such as pronouncing words incorrectly, not listening and making up words.

For example, small children often have difficulty pronouncing the letter Y. They often say 'lellow' instead of 'yellow'. Parents and childcare professionals can support them with this by encouraging the correct pronunciation early on and modelling the correct way to say Y words.

Language structure can often be a problem for children starting to form longer sentences. They are still trying to understand the rules of language and can get confused easily.

By taking time to talk to children, asking questions and listening, adults are modelling the communication behaviours they want children to mimic.

☐ When trying to say, 'I went to the pet shop and saw a mouse', children may say, 'I gone to the pet shop and saw mouses'.

## Joining in with play activities

When adults join in with play, children can understand what they need to do during the activity. It gives parents and childcare workers an opportunity to demonstrate how to play. It also gives children confidence in what they can do, as they tend to feel more secure with an adult near them. Playing with children allows an opportunity for questions to be asked, which can encourage communication and further learning.

- A child under 18 months won't automatically know what to do with an activity cube and is likely to need an adult to show them. On their own, a baby is unlikely to realise that the shapes should be placed into the cube in a certain way.
- Games such as 'follow my leader' wouldn't work without a parent or childcare professional to lead the activity and start the game.

☐ During small world play with farm toys, adults could encourage a child to talk about what the animals are doing and what they think a farmer does.

### Sharing

Sharing is a social skill and needs to be learned. Children often need help to enable them to share properly. Arguments between children can occur if there is not enough equipment for each child or if all of the children want to play with the same thing.

Sharing is an important part of building relationships and attachments. Modelling sharing practices will demonstrate to children how they should act.

## Turn-taking

Turn-taking encourages sharing and is important for communication. Children who struggle with the concept of turn-taking may find it difficult in the future to have a conversation without interrupting.

Baking cakes is a useful activity to encourage turn-taking. A parent or childcare professional ensures safety and can pass the bowl around to each child so they get a turn at mixing the cake batter. They could also monitor children for negative behaviours such as snatching or arguments. Questions can be asked about the cakes and children can be encouraged to take turns to talk.

Examples of turn-taking can include:
- 0–18 months: peek-a-boo, rolling a ball back and forth
- 18 months–3 years: hand printing, sharing ride-on toys
- 3–5 years: simple dice games, playing on a slide.

## Awareness of health and safety

If parents or childcare professionals lack an awareness of health and safety, children may hurt themselves or others. There are two factors that adults need to consider: is the toy or activity suitable for the age of the child and is it used appropriately?

Adults can check how suitable a toy or activity is based on the age of the child who will be playing with it. For example:
- children under the age of 18 months place objects in their mouths
- for these children bigger blocks are safer, as they cannot choke on them
- the blocks need to be wiped clean so no bacteria can get into a child's mouth
- smaller blocks can be given to older children, as they are less likely to put them in their mouth.

It can be a health and safety risk if children do not use toys properly or do not listen to instructions from an adult about an activity. For example, children taking part in role-play may want to use a belt as a dog lead. Although this is creative and they are using their imagination, it could be very dangerous, as a child could choke with a belt around their neck.

Adults should also make sure that when they give equipment to children they have the right skills to be able to use it properly. Risky items such as scissors should not be given to children who do not know how to use them in the correct way.

### LINK IT UP

Safety is discussed in more detail in learning outcome B of Component 3.

### CHECK MY LEARNING

1 Why should adults join in with play with young children?

2 Give some examples of how an adult could join in with play.

3 What is the adult's role in promoting turn-taking, and what activities could they choose for children at 0–18 months, 18 months–3 years and 3–5 years?

### ACTIVITY

*It is UK Health and Safety week. Your voluntary placement at the nursery is coming to an end. Your team leader is keen to promote health and safety in the nursery and has asked you and other volunteers to produce an A3 poster before you leave.*

The poster should focus on how the staff at the nursery should consider health and safety when planning activities. When complete, present it to the class and discuss what you included on the poster and why.

# Planning play opportunities for children: considerations

The content that you have covered in this Component will help you to think about how children learn and develop and how to plan for activities to support them. When planning activities, there are a number of factors that you need to think about (see Figure 2.7).

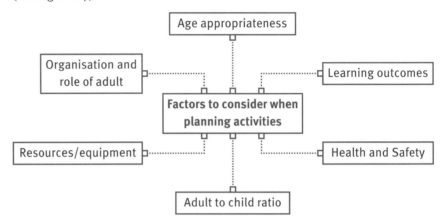

Figure 2.7: Factors to consider when planning activities.

## Age appropriateness

When you buy a toy for a child it will be labelled with an age range. This is to show what age that toy is appropriate for. It is important to think carefully about the ages of children taking part in a play activity. Some children may not be able to take part or access the resources because it may be too dangerous for them. For example, using a climbing frame would not be appropriate for a 6-month-old baby, as they haven't developed their gross motor skills enough. However, children's individual level of ability should also be considered, as each child develops at a different rate and may need more or less support to access play opportunities than other children their age.

## Learning outcomes

All play activities should have a learning outcome. This is what you want the child to achieve and learn by the end of it. For example, a child who may need more practice holding a pencil correctly could do drawing or painting activities so that they can practise their grip. Having a learning outcome helps the adult to focus the play activity so it can support the child's development.

## Resources/equipment required

An activity such as painting requires many resources, including paints, water, a selection of brushes, aprons, paper and mixing trays. When planning play activities, adults need to think carefully about all the resources and equipment that is needed. If they do not have enough, it could mean that a child misses out on learning and developing a new skill. For example, when practising writing skills with older children, if there are not enough pencils and they have to take turns, it may mean that some children miss out on dedicated time to practise.

## Adult-to-child ratio and health and safety

There is a legal requirement in the UK to maintain a specific adult-to-child ratio in childcare settings. This means there have to be the right number of adults to supervise children in order to keep them safe. Keeping children safe is a priority when planning play activities. It is also important to consider whether any of the resources you are planning to use could be dangerous, depending on the age and stage of the children. For example, giving a 5-year-old scissors so they can cut out shapes is usually appropriate, as most 5-year-olds understand how to use them responsibly and can use them in the correct way. Giving scissors to a 2-year-old is not safe. They are unaware of the dangers and may hurt themselves or others. It is also important to think about how the children will be supervised.

◪ Why would only one adult be needed to supervise two children? Do you think the age of the child would make a difference?

## Organisation and role of adult

Once the adult has thought of an activity and the resources that could be needed, they will also need to think about how they organise it. This means they need to decide what their role will be while the children take part. The activity can be adult-led, adult-initiated or child-initiated.

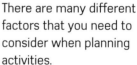

### ACTIVITY

*You have been hired by a local nursery to create information resources for new staff.*

1 Create a guidance booklet for new staff that describes what a member of staff needs to consider in order to plan play activities.

2 Swap your booklet with a friend and review their booklet. Give them feedback on what they did well and how they can improve their booklet.

3 Share your experience with the class.

### LINK IT UP

You will learn more about health and safety in Component 3. This will include risks/hazards and how to prevent them, and adult-to-child ratios.

### LINK IT UP

Remember that organising activities has been covered previously and can be found on pages 102–107.

### CHECK MY LEARNING

There are many different factors that you need to consider when planning activities.

1 Why is it important to consider whether the activity is age appropriate?

2 How might a lack of resources in a painting activity affect learning and development?

# Learning outcome B: assessment practice

## How you will be assessed

You will be assessed via a Pearson set assignment. This will be marked internally and moderated externally. Your assignment will be completed under formal supervision and carried out independently with no access to the internet.

When you have completed learning outcome B you will be able to complete Task 2 and Task 3 of your set assignment. These tasks cover your learning across learning outcomes A and B. You will be allowed approximately 2.5 hours to complete each task. In each task you will demonstrate your knowledge and understanding of a suitable play experience/activity based on a case study.

Evidence includes:

- detailed and relevant learning outcomes for the play experience/activity
- a detailed and relevant account of the resources needed to support the activity
- a detailed description of the activity with details of preparation, health and safety, implementation and tidying away
- a detailed account of how the activity will support a child's/children's overall development in the specified area
- details of what the adult will do and how these actions will support the child's/children's development
- justification for the choice of activity
- benefits and disadvantages of how the play is organised.

---

### CHECKPOINT

**Strengthen**

- Describe how play can promote physical development across the three age groups:
  - ☐ 0–18 months
  - ☐ 18 months–3 years
  - ☐ 3–5 years.
- State two activities and the resources required to promote gross motor skills.
- Describe how play can promote communication and language across the three age groups.
- Outline two activities and the resources required to promote learning for emotional development.
- Outline the three ways play can be organised by adults.
- Describe examples of activities for each of the three styles.

**Challenges**

- Explain the role of an adult in promoting play and give examples to show your understanding.
- Discuss how explaining and demonstrating an activity can affect a child's learning.
- Discuss how considering health and safety in play can benefit children.
- Assess how different styles of play could benefit or disadvantage a child's learning.

## PRACTICE ASSESSMENT ACTIVITY

Task 2

**Play activity A**

Plan a suitable play experience/activity for a child aged 12–18 months in a home environment. The activity must be child initiated and encourage communication and language play. Use the plan below as a template for your own activity plan.

Task 3

**Play activity B**

Plan a suitable play experience/activity for a small group of children 2–3 years old in a pre-school setting. The activity must be adult-led and encourage social play. Use the plan below as a template for your own activity plan.

| Area of play | Age of child/ren |
| --- | --- |
| How play is organised | Type of setting |
| Adult-led/Adult-initiated/Child-initiated | |
| **1** Activity title | |
| **2** Proposed learning outcomes: What do you want the children to learn? | |
| **3** Number of children and adults | **4** Resources/equipment required |
| **5** Health and safety | |
| **6** Description of the activity | |
| **7** How will this activity support the child/ren's development? | |
| **8** Role of the adult – what will the adult do? | |
| **9** Evaluation – justify your choice of activity | |
| **10** Benefits and disadvantages | |

## TIPS

When writing about the activities you should also think about how they benefit the child.
- Problem-solving activities such as computer games can promote listening and questioning skills because they spark children's imagination.
- Developing socially when taking part in team games or board games with others is beneficial, as it means children can form friendships and relationships. It also benefits them because they can talk to other children, which will improve their communication and language.

## TAKE IT FURTHER

- Explain how the use of construction blocks can develop fine motor skills and a child's imagination.
- Discuss how beneficial role-play is at supporting communication and cognitive development.
  - Example: Role-play is very beneficial to a child when they are learning new vocabulary as it can allow them to practise new words and sentence structures.
- Assess the extent to which board games can support the development of friendships.

# 03 Supporting Children to Play, Learn and Develop

## Introduction

Did you know that every child is different, and all have different needs?

Thinking about your own childhood, can you remember a time when you needed more support?

Can you think of all the professionals who give support to children, helping them to develop?

Even those children who seem to have a really positive start in life may develop additional needs due to different circumstances and situations, which happen either to them or their families. These circumstances can be related to any of the following factors: physical, cognitive/intellectual, communication and language, or social and emotional, all of which can affect a child's learning and development.

Would you like to feel confident in supporting children who have additional needs, to play, learn and develop in a safe environment?

Would you like to move onto a Level 2 or 3 course as a step to a career in Early Years Education?

This component will give you the knowledge and skills to begin your journey as an Early Years Educator. You will learn how adults can support children of all ages to achieve their full potential. This can be in keeping children safe and adapting activities so that children can have fun as they learn and develop, whatever their needs are.

## LEARNING OUTCOMES

In this component you will:

| A | investigate individual needs that may impact on play, learning and development |
|---|---|
| B | create safe environments to support play, learning and development in children aged 0–5 years |
| C | adapt play to promote inclusive learning and development. |

# Physical needs that may impact on play, learning and development

## KEY TERMS

**Delayed gross motor skills** the large movements of a child's body are not progressing as quickly as other children of the same age.

**Delayed fine motor skills** the small movements of a child's hands and fingers are not progressing as quickly as other children of the same age.

There are a range of physical needs that children may face that could have an impact on their play, learning and development. Some children experience delayed gross motor skills, which could create additional challenges in many areas of learning and development. Children's physical development can be restricted, which means they are unable to move in the same way as other children.

In Component 1, you learned that children acquire skills at varying rates in different areas of development and that not all children develop at the same rate physically. Some children's gross and fine motor skills may be delayed, which means these skills are not reaching the expected milestones for a child's age and stage of development.

Can you think of any reasons why children's physical development may be delayed?

## Sensory impairment

If a child has a sensory impairment this means that they have difficulty in seeing (visual impairment) or hearing (hearing impairment). This may impact on different areas of a child's development and learning.

■ **Table 3.1: The possible impacts of sensory impairments**

| Area of development | Possible impact of visual impairment | Possible impact of hearing impairment |
|---|---|---|
| Physical development | Motor skills can be affected as a child may be reluctant to move because they are unsure what is around them. They may not move towards things because they cannot see them. A child aged 0–18 months who can see well may be stimulated by a brightly coloured ball and reach out to try to grab it. A child with a visual impairment may not be able to see the ball clearly, or at all, so will not reach out. | Some conditions that cause hearing impairment may cause discharge from a child's ears. Some children may need to tilt their heads or lean forward in order to hear properly, which can affect their posture. |
| Cognitive and intellectual development | If a child is not moving around much, they will not fully explore the environment, which is important for the brain to develop. This may mean that they do not develop concepts such as shape or space. | A child may have difficulty with reading and mathematical concepts. |
| Communication and language development | A child may have difficulty learning to talk because they cannot read lips and notice the way adults' mouths are moving. | A child may have difficulty learning to talk because they cannot hear the sounds required in order to speak. |
| Social development | If a child is unable to make eye contact this will affect their ability to engage in social situations. Social interaction includes non-verbal language such as body language and facial expressions. Children who cannot see will not pick up on these, which will make it difficult for them to read social situations. | Restricted language can affect communication with others, which can prevent a child from interacting socially. |
| Emotional development | A child may be less independent because they rely on adults to complete tasks for them. This can affect their self-esteem and make them feel they cannot do things. | The effects on the other areas of development can cause a child to have low self-esteem and feel left out because they cannot communicate effectively. |

■ Which areas of a child's learning and development could visual and hearing impairments affect?

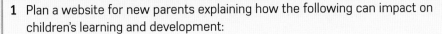

LINK IT UP

To remind yourself that children acquire skills at varying rates in different areas of development, go to learning outcome A of Component 1.

To remind yourself of the growth and development across the ages of birth to 5 years, go to learning outcome A of Component 1.

To remind yourself of the different physical factors that affect growth and development, go to learning outcome B of Component 1.

## ACTIVITY

1 Plan a website for new parents explaining how the following can impact on children's learning and development:

   **a** sensory impairment

   **b** long-term health or physical condition which restricts physical activity or movement

2 Produce a fact sheet for professionals working with children aged 3–5 that includes information on the impact of the following on children's learning and development:

   **a** delayed gross motor skills     **b** delayed fine motor skills.

## Delayed gross motor skills

If a child has **delayed gross motor skills** the large movements made by their bodies are not progressing to expected milestones of their age and stage of development.

Most play incorporates physical movement. A child with delayed gross motor skills may find it hard to explore the environment, which can affect other areas of development.

- Communication and language development: a child who finds it hard to explore the environment will not have opportunities to talk about what they are experiencing.
- Social development: a child may have limited opportunities to join in with other children's play, which means they may not make friends easily.
- Emotional development: a child's self-esteem may be affected as well as the way they see themselves; they will be aware that they cannot do things that other children the same age can do and this may make them feel inadequate.

## Delayed fine motor skills

If a child has **delayed fine motor skills** the movements of their hands and fingers are not progressing to expected milestones of their age and stage of development. A child with delayed fine motor skills may find it hard to explore new materials using their hands.

Children can usually hold a crayon and draw simple shapes by the age of 3. A child who has delayed fine motor skills may not be able to do this at 3, which can make them feel frustrated and delay them starting to form letters and write.

## Other physical needs

Children may need to use a wheelchair or walking frame to move around which could mean access to a playground or outdoor space, or to some inside spaces and activities, is restricted. Other children may have a long-term physical or health condition that affects their ability to join in with some activities, especially if they involve physical exercise and their gross motor skills are restricted.

How might a child's physical needs be impeded by being in a wheelchair?

BEST PRACTICE

Remember each child is an individual; what works for one child with a specific physical need may not always work for another.

CHECK MY LEARNING

1 State the different physical needs that can affect a child's play, learning and development.

2 Explain what is meant by 'sensory impairment'.

3 Explain the difference between delayed gross motor skills and delayed fine motor skills.

# Cognitive and intellectual needs that may impact on play, learning and development

There are several cognitive and intellectual needs that may impact on children's learning and development.

## Learning disabilities

Children may have learning disabilities in one area, for example, cognitive or communication and language skills. Some children may have general learning disabilities and this is known as global developmental delay.

## Poor concentration levels

Some children have a short attention span and find it hard to focus on what they are doing. This can lead to disruptive behaviour, which will be looked at later in 'circumstances that may impact on learning and development'.
- Children who find it hard to concentrate may talk a lot and interrupt people. This can affect their communication and language development and also their social development, as they find it difficult to take turns in a conversation.
- Children with **poor concentration levels** can be restless or fidgety. They may not persevere with learning a new physical skill like riding a tricycle because they lose interest quickly. This can affect their physical development.
- Poor concentration levels may have a significant impact on cognitive development as children find it hard to pay attention, follow instructions and complete activities. This can affect children aged 3–5 years significantly as this is the period within which they start full-time school.

Remember children's levels across the age ranges will be very different and you should consider their ages and stages of development before coming to the conclusion that they have poor concentration levels.

 **Table 3.2: Concentration levels across the different age ranges**

| 0–18 months | Children have a very short concentration span and become distracted easily because everything is very new to them. |
|---|---|
| 18 months–3 years | Children are still learning about the world and exploring. Their levels of concentration will still be developing but they are usually able to concentrate for a few minutes. |
| 3–5 years | Children can usually sit still for longer periods and concentrate for long enough to complete a task or activity. |

## Memory issues

Some children may have difficulty remembering instructions. This could be due to one or more of the following reasons:
- Developmental disabilities such as Attentional Deficit Hyperactivity Disorder (ADHD), autism, or **Down's syndrome**.
- The result of concussion or traumatic brain injury.

- Medical conditions such as epilepsy.
- Because of other, unknown/unspecified reasons.

Children who have memory issues may need additional support from specialist professionals including child psychologists and therapists. These professionals will work alongside the setting staff to support the child during the day. They may also contribute to a child's Education Health and Care Plan (EHC), which could affect the way you work with the child in the setting.

## Difficulties in problem solving

Some children may find problem-solving difficult. This could be because they have not reached the expected milestones for cognitive/intellectual development. There could also be other reasons, for example, if children are born with a developmental condition such as Down's syndrome, which can mean that children have problem-solving difficulties due to their level of cognitive development.

Other reasons could be: following trauma, accidents that have injured the brain, or the excess use of alcohol or illegal substances by a person during pregnancy.

## Delayed literacy skills

If a child has **delayed literacy skills**, this means their reading and writing skills are not progressing through expected milestones for the child's age and stage of development.

A child who is left-handed may have delayed writing skills as they struggle to find a comfortable grip when holding a pencil and their grip can be awkward when they are starting to make marks and write. This may mean it takes them a little longer than other children to form letters.

A child with delayed literacy skills may develop learning difficulties or behavioural problems. This is why it is important to support children whose literacy skills are not meeting the expected milestones.

It is important to understand the development of children's literacy skills across the different age ranges in order to provide the child with the correct support.

 Table 3.3: Literacy skills across the different age ranges

| 0–18 months | Children are developing their hand–eye co-ordination skills ready for writing by picking up objects and using toys such as shape sorters. They may begin to make marks with brushes and chunky crayons. Children this age will enjoy looking at simple books and will learn which way up books are held and which way the pages are turned. |
|---|---|
| 18 months–3 years | Children will be starting to show a preference for a particular hand for writing. They will use a palmar grasp to hold crayons and pencils, which means they grip with the palm of their hand. Children this age are learning that print has meaning, for example, that the sign outside the supermarket actually says its name. |
| 3–5 years | Children grip crayons and pencils using a tripod grip, which means three fingers are used. They make shapes and start to form letters and write their own name. They can usually read their own name too and recognise other familiar words such as names of family members and names of their favourite snacks or television programmes. |

### CHECK MY LEARNING

1  Explain the term: 'poor concentration levels'.

2  Which areas of a child's development can be affected by poor concentration levels?

3  State the meaning of 'global developmental delay'.

4  Discuss what could cause a child to have memory issues.

### DID YOU KNOW?

There are lots of resources available to support children who are left-handed such as easy grip crayons, pens, pencils, scissors and rulers.

 How could being left-handed delay a child's writing skills?

### KEY TERM

**Delayed literacy skills** when a child's reading and writing skills are not progressing to expected milestones of their age and stage of development.

### LINK IT UP

To remind yourself of cognitive and intellectual development across the ages of birth to 5 years, including the development of attention span, go to learning outcome A of Component 1.

To learn about social and emotional circumstances that may impact on a child's development and learning, including disruptive behaviour, go to 'Disruptive behaviour' in this component.

To remind yourself of planning play opportunities for children, including vocabulary and literacy skills, go to learning outcome B of Component 2.

# Communication and language needs that may impact on play, learning and development

One important need that may impact on a child's play, learning and development is if they are learning **English as an additional language**.

Many children learn English alongside a different language because their parents do not speak English or their parents can speak more than one language.

Some children attend childcare settings where the staff and children may not speak the language the child uses at home. This could create some challenges for the child and can lead to a delay in language development because the child is processing more than one language. However, it is important to remember that being able to speak more than one language can have a positive impact on a child's play, learning and development. How many different languages can you speak? Can you think of the benefits of being able to speak more than one language?

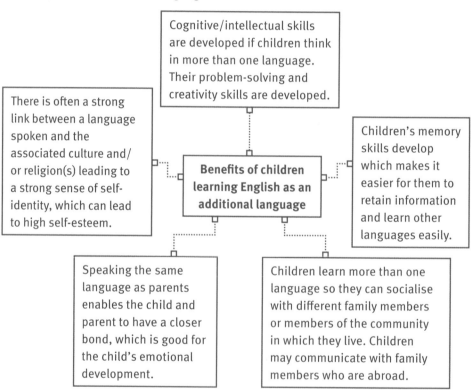

■ Figure 3.1: The benefits of children learning English as an additional language are varied.

As well as the positive impact that learning English as an additional language can have on a child, there can also be a negative impact.

A child who enters a setting where all the other children speak a different language may:

- be frightened – they will not understand why others cannot understand them and why they cannot understand others
- feel different to other children and that can have a negative effect on their self-esteem
- take a long time to settle in because they will need to tune in to the language around them and make sense of it – this means they may find it difficult to leave their parents when starting a new care or educational provider.

A child may lose the ability to speak their 'home' language because they are exposed to English more than the language spoken at home. However, this can depend on their age and the amount of time they have spent away from their parents.

A child learning English as an additional language may have gaps in their English vocabulary (the words that they know in English). Sometimes a child who is learning English as an additional language may develop a speech delay. This can happen when different languages are spoken to them by the same person. Speech may become delayed because it will take more time to process the different words and phrases than if only hearing one language.

## A child who is learning more than one language

As society becomes more multicultural, many children entering childcare and education are learning a second language. Some children hear and learn more than one language from birth if parents are fluent in other languages and use them with their children. Some children learn their second language (often English) when they start nursery or school. It is important for childcare teams to respect the child's first language and support them as they develop a second.

Growing up with two languages is beneficial to children. It helps them to celebrate their culture and customs and to relate to their wider family and community. Experts have found that speaking and thinking in two languages supports children's cognitive and intellectual development. Talking to children, reading to them and showing them pictures, will help children to learn their second language in a positive way.

## A child who has language or communication delay

All children develop at different rates. Some are early talkers, and some start later. As a guide, most children have about 50 words by the time they are 2. By 2 years and 6 months old, they may have started to use two-word phrases. At age 3, children can have about 200 words or more. A child may have a speech delay if, at 3 years old they:
- are hard to understand
- don't ask for things by name
- learn words but do not remember them
- know fewer words than you might expect.

There are several possible causes for language delay. Some are medical, including problems with the mouth, or the result of trauma, which could be accidental or non-accidental. Delayed language could also be caused by a lack of stimulation. If children do not hear language, they will find it hard to learn. Children should be spoken to, sung to and read to, from birth. As a childcare worker, it is part of your duty of care to ensure that all children you work with have opportunities to interact and learn language throughout the day.

■ Why might a child be distressed when they cannot understand the language around them?

**LINK IT UP**

To remind yourself of children's communication and language development across the ages of birth to 5 years, go to learning outcome A of Component 1.

**DID YOU KNOW?**

Many settings employ adults who can speak different languages so they can communicate with children who are learning English as an additional language to support their play, learning and development.

**CHECK MY LEARNING**

Explain how the amount of time a child spends hearing different languages can determine what becomes their preferred language.

**ACTIVITY**

You have been asked to appear on a television documentary called *The Impact of Learning English as an Additional Language.*

Prepare some notes for your television appearance.

You should include:
- the positive impact of learning English as an additional language on children's play, learning and development
- the negative impact of learning English as an additional language on children's play, learning and development.

Practise reading out what you will say with a partner.

# Social and emotional needs that may impact on play, learning and development

Adults are a very important influence on children's social and emotional development. Children learn by observing adults and will copy them. This means it is important that adults are **positive role models** and always demonstrate best practice.

Part of being a good role model is interacting positively with children and giving them the attention they need. It is also important that adults are good role models in developing children's understanding of **social norms and values**. Adults should provide play opportunities to enable them to be happy and to develop in all areas.

The amount of time children spend playing has changed over time. Think about your memories of playing as a child. What about children today? Are their opportunities for play the same as yours? What has changed?

## Limited interaction with adults

Children begin to interact with adults as soon as they are born. They enjoy spending time with adults and soon learn how to respond positively to play experiences and develop skills such as taking turns. Playing with adults helps to create a **bond**.

◘ Table 3.4: Adult interactions with children differ across the age ranges

| | |
|---|---|
| 0–18 months | Children will prompt adults to play with them, for example, by putting up their hands to show that they want to be picked up. |
| 18 months–3 years | Children often follow familiar adults around and may tug on their clothing or call their name in order to get their attention. They will start to transfer the skills they have learned from playing with adults into play with other children. |
| 3–5 years | Children will sometimes ask adults to play with them. Children this age need support to play fairly and follow the rules. |

It is very important that adults give children the attention they need, or there could be a significant impact on children's learning and development. **Limited interaction with adults** could mean that children:

- have a lack of interest in things
- do not learn how to join in and play with other children
- behave unacceptably in order to gain the adult's attention
- do not develop their language skills (because they are not being spoken to by adults).

◘ How does interaction with adults support children's learning and development?

## Poor awareness of social norms and values

The expression 'social norms and values' refers to the attitudes and behaviours that are expected in society. For example, in society it is expected that we will queue at the counter in a shop rather than push in, or not interrupt when people are talking.

Some children have a poor awareness of social norms and values, which means they may display inappropriate and unwanted behaviour in social situations and public places. This can make it difficult for children to concentrate and to make friends. They may become withdrawn and not join in with others because they feel different and have low self-esteem.

## Difficulty forming bonds with adults

By the time children have reached 18 months they have usually formed bonds with familiar adults; however, some children can have difficulty with this due to individual circumstances.

◘ **Table 3.5: Some children have difficulties forming bonds with adults**

| Premature birth | Children born prematurely may need care away from home, for example, they may spend their first days in an incubator at the hospital, which may prevent them from building an attachment to their parents. |
|---|---|
| Postnatal depression | This can affect the mother's ability to cuddle, show affection and interact with her baby, which can prevent her building an attachment with the child. |
| Child's health | If a child spends time away from home, for example in hospital, they may not spend as much time with their parents as other children. |
| Parents' health | If a parent/parents are ill, they may not spend a lot of time with their child and play with them, which could mean relationships are not developed. |
| Abuse | Some children are abused by their parents. This can mean they do not build positive relationships with them. |

If a child has difficulty forming bonds with adults, this will have an impact on their play, learning and development.

## Limited experience of play

Play is important for children's health, wellbeing and development. However, some children may have limited experience of play. This could be for a number of reasons, such as: overcrowding in the childcare setting or home, lack of outdoor space, or not having the opportunity to mix with other children.

It is the role of the adult to provide play opportunities that support all areas of learning and development and to play with children, being a positive role model.

If a child has not been given enough opportunities to play this can have an impact on their learning and development. Without play children will:
- not be given opportunities to find out what they like and are interested in
- find it difficult to control their emotions
- be unable to make friends and learn to get along with others
- not learn how to use resources and equipment
- not progress in all areas of development
- find it difficult to adapt to different situations.

Children are happy when they are engaged in play; therefore, limited experience of play can lead to anxiety and depression.

### LINK IT UP

To remind yourself of social development and emotional development of children across the ages of birth to 5 years old, go to learning outcome A of Component 1.

To remind yourself of the different factors that affect growth and development, including socio-economic factors such as poor relationships with significant adults, go to learning outcome B of Component 1.

To remind yourself of the role of the adult in promoting learning through play, go to learning outcome B of Component 2.

### BEST PRACTICE

Be a role model for social norms and values by showing respect, listening carefully and taking turns in conversations.

### CHECK MY LEARNING

1  State what is meant by social norms and values.

2  Explain the reasons why some children have difficulties forming strong bonds with adults.

3  Explain the impact of limited play opportunities on children's learning and development.

### ACTIVITY

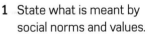

Willow is 3 years old and is new to the pre-school. She lives in a small flat with her parents and three siblings and does not have many opportunities for outdoor play. When you take Willow outside at the pre-school for the first time, she does not try out any of the large play equipment and becomes stressed when one of your colleagues tries to encourage her to join the queue for the slide.

State three ways Willow's learning and development might benefit from using large play equipment outside.

# Social and emotional needs that may impact on play, learning and development: friendships

**GETTING STARTED**

Think about reasons why children may find it difficult to form friendships. Make a list and compare this with a partner's list.

**KEY TERM**

**Friendships** relationships between friends.

**BEST PRACTICE**

Encourage children to work in pairs to support friendship building.

**Friendships** are important to children as they grow and develop. Friendships enable children to have positive interaction with other children and show children they are accepted, giving them confidence. Friendships form easily if children have well-developed social skills and the confidence to interact with others. However, some children have difficulty forming friendships with other children and, because children learn a lot by playing with others, this can affect their learning and development.

Think about your own friendships and why these are important to you. At what age did you first develop friendships? How did friendships support your learning and development growing up?

## Difficulty forming friendships with other children

Children's expected social development is shown in Table 3.6. But some children do not find it easy to make friendships. This can be for a number of reasons.

- A child may not have the skills required to form friendships, for example, delayed social skills, making it difficult for them to share and take turns.
- A child may not have formed strong bonds with adults, which makes it easier to make relationships with others and form friendships because they have learned to trust and to understand the needs and feelings of others.
- A child may have delayed language skills or may be learning English as an additional language, which means they may find it difficult to communicate with other children.
- Some children's personalities mean they like to take the lead, do things their own way or win at games. They may not be tolerant of others and may respond inappropriately when there is a disagreement. This can put other children off from wanting to play with them.

◻  **Table 3.6: Expected social development across the age ranges**

| | |
|---|---|
| 0–18 months | Children will look at other children, get excited when they see them and begin to play alongside them. |
| 18 months–3 years | Children usually start to form friendships at the end of this period. |
| 3–5 years | By this time children have usually developed one or two close friendships and may have a best friend. |

You can support children's social development in different ways, for example:

- design home and pretend activities so that children have different roles that need co-operation, such as shops, hairdressers, vets
- include opportunities for simple conversations in play.

Remember to find out about customs and festivals so that these can be celebrated as part of a day's activities, to make sure all children feel included. Encourage friendships that are forming by including activities where children play in pairs.

◻ How can you tell that these two children have developed a friendship?

## ACTIVITY

*Ruby is 4 and likes to tell the other children what to do when they are playing. She often gives each child a role that they must take, for example, baby, mum or dog. Sometimes Ruby pushes the other children to make them do what she wants them to do. Today, she began to scream and cry loudly when another child said they wanted to play somewhere else. She hit the other child and threw some toys and equipment around. She then became unhappy and sat in the corner.*

Write down your answers to the following questions.

1 Why might other children not want to play with Ruby?

2 How might Ruby's behaviour affect her ability to make friendships?

3 If Ruby doesn't make friendships, how might this have an impact on her development?

## LINK IT UP

To remind yourself of social and emotional development of children across the ages of birth to 5 years old, go to learning outcome A of Component 1.

To remind yourself of planning social play and learning opportunities for children, including development of friendships, go to learning outcome B of Component 2.

## CHECK MY LEARNING

1 Explain why forming friendships is important to children's learning and development.

2 State two reasons why children may find it difficult to form friendships.

# Social and emotional needs that may impact on play, learning and development: disruptive behaviour

## GETTING STARTED

What do you think causes disruptive behaviour? Discuss this in a group and make a list.

## KEY TERM

**Disruptive behaviour** unwanted behaviour that disturbs and interrupts activities.

## BEST PRACTICE

Use a calm tone when managing disruptive behaviour and positive, non-aggressive body language, e.g., not crossing your arms.

You have just learned about friendships and how some children can have difficulty forming these. One of the reasons children may find it difficult to form friendships with other children is that they display **disruptive behaviour**. This is attention-seeking behaviour that disturbs and interrupts activities. If a child displays disruptive behaviour this will affect not only their learning and development but will have an impact on the children around them too. Imagine someone in your class is behaving disruptively. How do you think this would affect you?

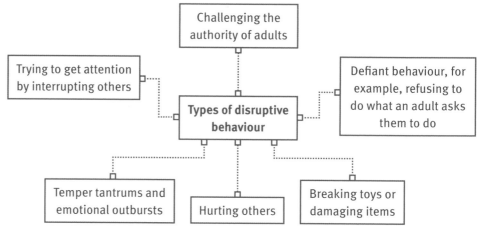

Figure 3.2: Disruptive behaviour disturbs and interrupts activities.

It is important to remember when recognising disruptive behaviour that expectations for behaviour change across the age ranges, as shown in Table 3.7.

Table 3.7: Expectations for behaviour across the age ranges

| 0–18 months | Children do not understand the needs of others and do not understand that toys may belong to others. |
| --- | --- |
| 18 months–3 years | Children are easily frustrated and may have tantrums. They do not like attention being given to other children. |
| 3–5 years | Children can follow simple rules and play more co-operatively with others. By 5 children usually understand the difference between right and wrong. |

A child may display disruptive behaviour for a number of reasons. For example, they may have difficulty forming friendships because of delayed language, sensory impairment or poor concentration levels.

At what age do children usually have temper tantrums?

If a child is displaying disruptive behaviour this can mean they may not make friendships with other children. A child may continue their behaviour because they feel they have 'nothing to lose'.

A child with disruptive behaviour may find it difficult to concentrate. This will have an impact on their cognitive/intellectual development and eventually on their academic performance.

◼ How is the girl in this photo being disruptive?

**LINK IT UP**

To remind yourself of the stages of play, go to learning outcome A of Component 2.

# Social and emotional needs that may impact on play, learning and development: transitions

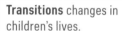
## KEY TERMS

**Transitions** changes in children's lives.

**Care or educational providers** settings that provide formal care or education for children. For example, a school.

**Sibling** a brother or sister.

**Significant family member** a close family member, such as a parent, sibling or grandparent.

**Family structure** the way in which a family is organised.

◼ How might starting school be an exciting time for children?

A **transition** is a change in a child's life. There are several different transitions that a child may experience between 0 and 5 years.

A transition often brings a new environment or a new relationship to a child, which can have different effects on different children. During a transition, a child may experience a range of feelings that could impact on their learning and development. Even though a child may feel excited they can still feel stressed, anxious and nervous.

Children like things in their lives to stay the same (be consistent) as this helps them feel safe and secure; therefore, changes can be unsettling. Often, transitions mean that a child will be separated from their parent/s. The effects of this can depend on the child's age and stage of development.

Can you remember the first time you were separated from your parents/carers? How old were you? How did you feel?

## Starting care or attending an educational provider

Almost all children will experience this transition.

◼ Table 3.8: Starting day care across the age ranges

| 0–18 months and 18 months–3 years | Children may attend a day care setting because their parents work. |
|---|---|
| 3–5 years | Children in this age group will be starting school. |

Starting with a new **care or educational provider** can be exciting for a child but can also be a stressful time. They will be nervous and will not know anyone or where anything is. They may suffer from separation anxiety, which is a form of distress caused when children are separated from their parents/carers.

Reactions of children to this transition depend on their age and stage of development. For example, children aged 0–18 months may cry and become clingy, whereas older children may ask lots of questions, such as people's names and where things are, for example, the toilets or their favourite types of toys.

## Moving between care/educational providers

Sometimes children move between care or educational providers. For example, they leave the childminding setting because they have reached school age.

This can be a distressing time because the child will have formed bonds with their previous carers. These bonds will be broken, and they will need to form relationships with new people and make new friends. This may cause them to feel unsafe and insecure. The routine at the new setting could be different to the previous one, which can be confusing for children and make them feel unsettled.

## Birth of a new sibling

A new baby in the family is a huge adjustment for a child. They may feel that the new baby is going to take their place. Many children experience feelings of jealousy towards a new **sibling**, and they may start to behave like a baby to get the adult's attention, for example, cry and have tantrums or wet themselves even though they are toilet trained. This is called regression. A child may behave aggressively and may try to hurt the baby by hitting them or taking toys from them.

## Change in family structure

The way in which a family is organised (the **family structure**) can change through birth, divorce, separation or death. This means that there can be new additions to families. For example, children can find themselves with a new step-parent or step-sibling. As with the birth of a new sibling, a child may experience feelings of jealousy or resentment towards the new additions to the family.

The family may need to move house or the child may be spending time at two different homes, which can be confusing and make them feel unsettled. This can also disrupt their sleep patterns; therefore, they may find it difficult to concentrate, which can have an impact on their cognitive/intellectual development.

Change in family structure can also mean that children are cared for by the local authority. These children are called 'looked after children' and they may move into a home with a foster family because their own family is unable to care for them.

Children may find it difficult to adjust to the new family. They may not understand why they have had to leave their parents and will need caregivers to be understanding and patient as they adjust to their new circumstances. It is important not to treat 'looked after children' differently. They may have additional needs, but they will still have all of the same needs of a child of their age and ability.

## Moving house

Moving house can be an exciting time for a child but can also be distressing, particularly if the new house is a long way from their old home and they have to move to a new care or educational provider and get used to new adults and children.

There can be an impact on the child's emotional development, as they may feel sad because there is a sense of loss. Their routine is likely to be disrupted during the move, which will make them feel anxious. They may become clingy to significant family members and regress in their development. They may even feel angry about the move.

---

**ACTIVITY**

*You are completing your work experience in a pre-school where many of the children are experiencing different transitions. You have been asked to create a section of a staff training guide to explain to staff the effect of transitions on children's learning and development.*

The training guide must cover the following:
- starting care/educational providers
- moving between care/educational providers
- birth of a new sibling
- moving house
- change in family structure.

---

**DID YOU KNOW?**

Some children who are looked after and 'in care' (for example, living with a foster family rather than with their birth parents) are likely to experience multiple transitions in their lives.

**BEST PRACTICE**

If you know a child is experiencing a transition give them time to settle and get used to the new situation.

**LINK IT UP**

To remind yourself of the social and emotional development of children across the ages of birth to 5 years, go to learning outcome A of Component 1.

**CHECK MY LEARNING**

1 State three types of transitions that a child may experience.

2 Explain the effects of starting with new care or educational providers on children of different ages.

3 Explain how the impact of the birth of a new sibling can impact family structure.

# How not meeting milestones may impact an individual's play, learning and development

## GETTING STARTED

Working in pairs, make a list of milestones expected in the following age groups:
- 0–18 months
- 18 months–3 years
- 3–5 years.

How do you think children's learning and development can be affected if they are not meeting expected milestones?

Write down your ideas.

## KEY TERMS

**Expected milestones** development that is expected at a particular age.

**All areas of development** physical, cognitive/intellectual, communication and language, social and emotional.

**Initiate play** to start play.

## DID YOU KNOW?

Observations of children are carried out in settings to check children's development against milestones.

It is important to remember that milestones are approximate and that no two children the same age, even identical twins, will develop at the same rate.

Children may have specific additional needs in one area that may impact on their play, learning and development in all areas of development – physical, cognitive/intellectual, communication and language, social and emotional.

Milestones are aspects of children's development that are expected at particular ages. Milestones have been decided by professionals who have studied large groups of children and reached a conclusion about the normal pattern of development for different ages. Think about the following milestones. At what age is the development expected?
- Starting to walk
- Starting to talk
- Riding a tricycle.

Milestones are used to measure children's development to see if they are developing at the expected rate. In Component 1, you learned about the growth and development of children across the ages of birth to 5 years old and what is expected at different ages.

## Not meeting expected milestones

A child may not be meeting **expected milestones** because they have additional needs known as 'developmental disorders', which prevent them from developing at the expected rate in one or more areas of development.

If a child's rate of progress across **all areas of development** is a lot slower than what is considered 'typical' for their age, this is called 'global development delay'.

Some children have a delay in one aspect of one of the areas of development.

Where children are not meeting the milestones in one area of development, this can impact on other areas of learning and development, as shown in Table 3.9.

 Table 3.9: The impact of not meeting milestones

| | |
|---|---|
| Impact of not meeting physical development milestones | • May be unable to access learning activities set up at different levels in the room<br>• May be unable to grasp small objects or manipulate materials in a constructive way, for example, playdough<br>• May tire easily and not be able to stay involved in activities<br>• May be unable to move around the play areas to access different activities |
| Impact of not meeting cognitive/intellectual development milestones | • May be unable to understand rules in play or sustain attention in activities<br>• May have difficulty with problem solving and mathematics<br>• May become overwhelmed by choice |
| Impact of not meeting communication and language development milestones | • May have difficulties communicating preferences and choices<br>• Play with others may be limited<br>• May lack confidence<br>• May not be able to build friendships or share |
| Impact of not meeting social and emotional development milestones | • May find co-operative play difficult<br>• May have poor emotional resilience<br>• May isolate themselves or be isolated by others<br>• May find it difficult to join in group activities<br>• May have limited expression of thoughts and feelings<br>• May find it difficult to join in group activities<br>• May find it difficult building positive relationships with adults<br>• May find it difficult to cope with change/routines/new situations<br>• May have low self-esteem |

# The effects on play of not meeting expected milestones

Not meeting developmental milestones can affect a child's approach to play. They may not be able to invite other children to join in because they are likely to be less confident and independent. This could be for a number of reasons, for example: low self-esteem, delayed social or language development. It is important not to assume developmental delay, it could just be that children have little experience of play due to family circumstances, illness or trauma.

Their learning and development can be affected in several ways, as shown in Figure 3.3.

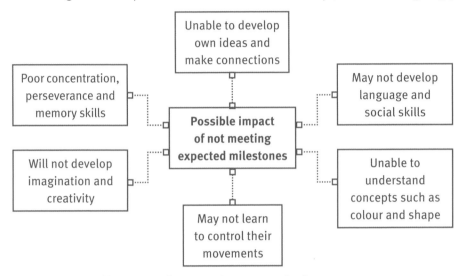

■ Figure 3.3: Possible impact of not meeting expected milestones.

## LINK IT UP

To remind yourself of growth and development of children across the ages of birth to 5 years, go to learning outcome A of Component 1.

To remind yourself of the factors that affect growth and development, go to learning outcome B of Component 1.

To remind yourself of child-initiated play, go to Component 2, 'How play can be organised to promote learning, child-intiated play'.

## BEST PRACTICE

Provide opportunities to practise skills and praise achievements to support confidence and self-esteem.

## ACTIVITY

*You are working in a large day nursery. Some of the children appear to not be meeting expected milestones.*

Produce a booklet to explain to the staff the impact of not meeting expected milestones in children's physical development.

Your booklet should focus on the impact on other areas of development.

## CHECK MY LEARNING

1 Describe what is meant by 'expected milestones'.

2 State one reason why a child may not be meeting expected milestones.

3 State two reasons why being unable to initiate play may impact on a child's ability to socialise.

■ Why might some children find it difficult to initiate play?

# How individual needs may impact on physical learning and development

There are several individual needs that may impact on children's physical learning and development. Some children have difficulty with their gross motor skills, which means they are unable to access learning activities at **varying levels** or **navigate** their way around play areas and activities. Some children's fine motor skills development means they are unable to pick up and grasp small objects or manipulate materials to use them correctly. What impact do you think this can have on their physical development?

## Unable to access learning activities at varying levels

In both indoor and outdoor environments, activities and resources may be situated at varying levels. The pictures below show some examples of varying levels.

■ How many different 'levels' can you see in these pictures?

A child who has a sensory impairment or delayed gross motor skills may be unable to access learning activities at varying levels because their physical skills of co-ordination and balance are not as good as other children. This can have an impact on their learning and development, for example on their:

- physical development – they may not develop stamina
- social development – they may not develop friendships.

## Unable to grasp small objects or manipulate materials in a constructive way

Some children have delayed fine motor skills. This means they may be unable to grasp small objects such as buttons or beads because the movements of their hands and fingers are not as well-developed as other children. They may find it hard to manipulate materials such as clay, playdough, paint, building bricks or jigsaw pieces to make something **constructive**. This can have an impact on children's learning and development, for example, on their:

- cognitive development – they may find it hard to think and make choices
- emotional development – they may find it hard to express their emotions and may lack a sense of achievement.

Some children may find it difficult to manipulate equipment and resources too, so they will find it hard to handle these skilfully enough to use them in the way they are intended to be used. Examples that they may struggle with include fastening buttons and cutting with scissors.

## May tire easily and not be able to sustain involvement in activities

It is not uncommon for children to feel tired occasionally. However, some children tire easily, and this can affect their ability to **sustain involvement** in activities, which means they are not involved in activities for long before needing a rest.

There are several reasons why children may tire easily. They may be going through a transition or not getting enough sleep. In 'How resources can be organised and the use of specific areas' and 'Health and safety considerations for outside environments' you will learn that, when looking at health and safety considerations for inside environments, the indoor and outdoor environments should provide quiet, comfortable spaces for children, so that they can rest when they are tired.

◘ Table 3.10: How children's learning and development can be affected if they tire easily

| Physical development | May lack the energy to take part in physical activities |
|---|---|
| Cognitive/intellectual development | May struggle to learn and remember things |
| Social and emotional development | May display disruptive behaviour, which can affect relationships |

## May be unable to navigate the play areas and activities

Some children may find it difficult to navigate round the setting. Children with restricted or delayed gross motor skills or a physical disability may find it difficult to control their movements to gain access to the play areas and activities. Those with a sensory impairment may be unable to see clearly, making it hard for them to explore the environment. Children's learning and development can be impacted if they are unable to navigate play areas and activities.

- Physical development – children may move less because they find it difficult to control their movements.
- Cognitive/intellectual development – children's learning could be affected if they cannot access activities and resources.
- Social and emotional development – children may not play with other children because they cannot move in the same way as them. This could affect their self-esteem.

Adults should ensure that furniture and equipment is positioned to allow all children to navigate to play areas and activities.

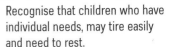

### BEST PRACTICE

Recognise that children who have individual needs, may tire easily and need to rest.

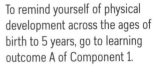

### LINK IT UP

To remind yourself of physical development across the ages of birth to 5 years, go to learning outcome A of Component 1.

To remind yourself of sensory impairment, restricted and delayed fine and gross motor skills, go to 'Physical needs that may impact on play, learning and development' in this component.

### DID YOU KNOW?

Most children aged 18 months–3 years still need an afternoon nap. This usually stops when they reach 3–5 years.

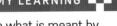

### CHECK MY LEARNING

1 Explain what is meant by varying levels.

2 State three examples of materials that children who struggle with their fine motor skills may find difficult to manipulate.

3 State one reason why children may tire easily.

### ACTIVITY

Write a report about how individual needs may impact on physical learning and development. Your report should include information about children who:
- are unable to access learning activities at varying levels
- are unable to grasp small objects or manipulate materials in a constructive way
- may tire easily and not be able to sustain involvement in activities
- may be unable to navigate the play areas and activities.

You will need to include headings in your report to check you have covered everything.

# How individual needs may impact on cognitive and intellectual, and communication and language, learning and development

**GETTING STARTED**

Some children may find it difficult to understand non-verbal as well as verbal communication.

Working with a partner, make a list of all the different ways in which we communicate besides speaking.

Imagine your friend 'gives up' speaking to you because they think you are not listening? How would this make you feel?

**KEY TERMS**

**Preferences** things that children prefer to do.

**Perceived** interpreting something in a particular way.

**Lack of responsiveness** not responding to people.

**BEST PRACTICE**

Treat children with respect and show you value them. Always show patience, so children have a positive role model.

You have already learned about children's cognitive/intellectual and communication and language development across the age ranges of birth to 5 in Component 1, but did you know that they are closely linked together?

Language allows us to process our thoughts. If children struggle with language this means their thinking skills will be affected, which can have an impact on their ability to communicate and socialise with others.

Language is the way in which we communicate our **preferences** and choices, for example, how we are feeling or what we want. Some children have difficulties with this, which can lead to them feeling frustrated. Language difficulties can also prevent children from building friendships. For these children play with others may be limited, as they may be **perceived** as not wanting to play due to **lack of responsiveness**. Other children may think a child is ignoring them when really they do not understand what has been said. This could be because they have English as an additional language, or communication needs, or that the stage of development they are at means that they do not understand some words yet or the rules of language.

## Cognitive and intellectual learning and development

### Difficulty understanding the rules in play

Some children have difficulty understanding the rules in play because they have not learned these. This could be because they have poor awareness of social norms and values or a limited experience of play. They may not be able to sustain attention long enough to understand the activity or may find the choice too much to cope with and become distressed.

In some types of play, children need to understand they have to wait, take turns, share or listen to others. This type of play will require children to:

- take turns at the different roles, which may involve waiting
- listen when others are speaking
- share the resources
- be respectful of the opinions, choices and preferences of other children.

Where children have limited experience of play, they may not have been given opportunities to develop skills such as sharing and turn-taking. They may find it difficult to join in with other children as they may come across as being disruptive or not playing fairly. Figure 3.4 shows some of the rules of play that some children may find difficult to understand.

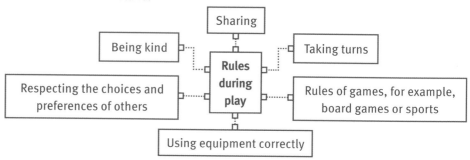

■ Figure 3.4: Children may miss out on play if they do not understand the rules. This can affect their cognitive and intellectual development.

## Communication and language learning and development

### Difficulties communicating preferences and choices

Depending on their age and stage of development, some children find it hard to communicate their preferences and choices. This means they do not have the language to be able to tell people what they want. Where this happens children may use other ways to express themselves.

Children who are not meeting the expected milestones in their language or children who have English as an additional language may also struggle to communicate their preferences and choices. This can impact on their emotional development as it can lead to them feeling frustrated, which can have an effect on their self-esteem.

Some children have communication needs, which means they have difficulties with speaking and listening and with the process of making sense of information.

### Play with others may be limited

If a child is having difficulty communicating, they may not understand what other children are saying to them and may also have problems reading body language. Other children may perceive this as meaning that the child does not want to play. They may stop inviting the child to play, which can lead to feelings of isolation, and poor self-esteem.

### May lack confidence

If children are not invited to play by other children, this can mean that they don't learn the rules of play. Children learn some language from each other, and so not being invited to play, can limit their learning and use of language. Not having the right words can result in children lacking the confidence to communicate and this can lower their self-esteem.

### May not be able to build friendships

When children are not invited to join in a play activity, they may find it difficult to form friendships. Children often become friends through taking part in shared activities, in the same way that adults do. If children are left outside of the group, they can feel frustrated, as they may not understand the reasons why they are isolated. It is important that adults consider why a child is displaying these behaviour patterns and support the child.

---

**DID YOU KNOW?**

Children can display disruptive behaviour if they cannot communicate their needs and preferences.

---

**LINK IT UP**

To remind yourself of children's cognitive and intellectual, and communication and language development across the ages of birth to 5 years, go to learning outcome A of Component 1.
To remind yourself of children who have English as an additional language, go to 'Communication and language needs that may impact on play, learning and development' in this component.
To remind yourself of poor awareness of social norms and values and limited experience of play, go to 'Social and emotional needs that may impact on play, learning and development' in this component.
To remind yourself of development not meeting expected milestones, go to 'How not meeting milestones may impact on an individual's play, learning and development' in this component.

---

**CHECK MY LEARNING**

1 State three things that children who do not understand the rules of play may find difficult.

2 State why a child may find it difficult to communicate their needs and preferences.

3 Explain the possible impact of delayed cognitive and communication development on social and emotional development.

---

**ACTIVITY**

*Gabriel, Ibrahim and Leah, aged 3, are on their way outside to play.*

*'Come on, let's make a den!' says Gabriel.*

*Leah does not know the word 'den' and does not understand what this means; therefore, she stays inside. Also, she would much prefer to do a painting with Gabriel and Ibrahim but does not have the language yet to explain this.*

*'Let's go!' says Gabriel to Ibrahim. 'Leah is not coming.'*

1 What assumption has Gabriel made about Leah?

2 What could be the impact on Leah's social and emotional development?

3 Why might Leah have found it difficult to communicate her needs and preferences?

# How individual needs may impact on social and emotional learning and development (1)

## KEY TERMS

**Isolate** cause a person to be alone/apart from others.

**Emotional resilience** a person's ability to adapt to stressful situations.

**Self-concept** the way people see themselves.

Some children may find co-operative play challenging. This could be because of their stage of development. Children who have had little or no interaction with other children, may try to take the lead during play. This can be difficult for other children to understand and could cause them to **isolate** the child. However, some children may choose isolation if they find it hard to join in group or team activities.

Developing emotional skills can sometimes be challenging for some children. This could be due to their age and stage of development but also a range of other factors.

Think about the things that make you stressed and how you cope with this. What might your reaction be?

## Children may find co-operative play difficult

From 3 to 4 years of age children begin to play well with their peers and learn to share and take turns. They often engage in the same play. This stage of play is called co-operative play. You have already learned about the stages of play in Component 2.

Some children may find co-operative play difficult. This could be because they:

- are unable to take turns
- are unable to recognise the needs and feelings of others
- have not learned to respect the choices and preferences of others
- do not understand the rules of play
- have delayed language or social development
- have not learned to be patient.

Children who find it difficult to play co-operatively:

- will be less confident about interacting with others
- may feel unwanted, which will impact on their self-esteem and their **self-concept**.
- may display inappropriate behaviours because they feel left out
- may miss out on the development of language because playing co-operatively enables children to listen and talk to other children and practise language in their play.

## Children may have poor emotional resilience

Children with poor **emotional resilience** find it difficult to cope with stressful situations. The degree of emotional resilience a child has depends on their age and stage of development. For example, babies and toddlers cannot express their feelings and manage these as well as older children.

Poor emotional resilience can also be affected by many factors:

- transitions
- abuse
- parental depression
- bullying
- family stress, such as divorce/separation.

■ Why might some children find it difficult to play co-operatively?

Stress takes its toll on the brain and the body; therefore, it can have a negative impact on children's learning and development. Stress can instil feelings of fear and make children more dependent on adults.

## Children may isolate themselves or be isolated by others

Some children may isolate themselves from others. This could be because they enjoy their own company and may like to complete activities by themselves or it could be that their social skills are lacking.

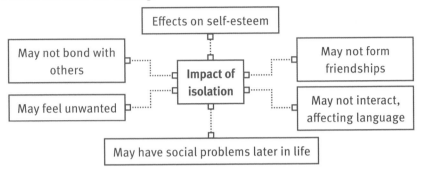

■ Figure 3.5: The possible impact isolation can have on a child's learning and development.

You have already learned that some children may not understand the rules in play. Rather than take the risk of being rejected by others, a child may choose to play alone.

Children may isolate another child because they:
- behave disruptively
- interrupt/spoil the play
- are unable to take turns.

Sometimes, if children are being isolated by others, this could be a sign of bullying.

## Children may refuse or find it difficult to join in team or group activities

Team and group activities such as board games or sport enable children to develop social skills and the confidence to interact with others; however, some children refuse or find it difficult to join in these types of activities. This could be because they do not understand the rules of play or their social skills are not yet developed.

Children who do not like these kinds of activities or find it difficult to join in may need support from an adult to help them to engage. Without this support they may not:
- form bonds and friendships
- learn about differences
- learn to respect others
- learn to negotiate and co-operate with others.

All these skills are important for later life.

**LINK IT UP**

To remind yourself of children's social and emotional development across the age ranges of birth to 5 years, go to learning outcome A of Component 1.
To remind yourself of the stages of children's play, go to learning outcome A of Component 2..
To remind yourself of children who may not understand the rules in play, go to 'How individual needs may impact on cognitive and intellectual, and communication and language learning and development' in this component.

**CHECK MY LEARNING**

1 Explain what is meant by 'co-operative' play?

2 State a reason why a child may:
   a) isolate themselves from others
   b) be isolated by other children.

3 Assess the benefits of team and group activities to children's learning and development.

**ACTIVITY**

Create a poster to be displayed in your classroom to show how individual needs may impact on social and emotional learning and development.

Your poster will need to include information on children:

1 who may find co-operative play difficult

2 with poor emotional resilience

3 who may isolate themselves or be isolated by others

4 who may refuse or find it difficult to join in team or group activities.

# How individual needs may impact on social and emotional learning and development (2)

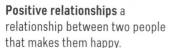
Some children may find it difficult to build **positive relationships** with adults. This can have an impact on children because adults are important in children's play and positive relationships with adults enable children to be confident and explore.

Emotional development refers to the way children develop and control their feelings and how they feel about themselves – their self-esteem. Children express their feelings in their language, facial expressions and behaviour; however, some children have limited **expression** of thoughts and feelings. This can make them feel frustrated and display disruptive behaviour.

**Routines** are very important for children's social and emotional development. Some children find it difficult to cope with changes to their routine. Think about your own routine. How would you feel if this suddenly changed?

## Children who have limited expression of thoughts and feelings

Just like adults, children experience many different feelings, for example:

- fear
- jealousy
- happiness
- anger
- frustration
- sadness.

Some children are able to express their feelings through their language, but some children do not find this easy because they may have limited vocabulary or communication needs. Children can be overwhelmed by their thoughts and feelings which, because they cannot explain what they are thinking or what they want, can result in:

- temper tantrums
- disruptive behaviour
- aggression towards others.

## Children who find it difficult building positive relationships with adults

Children need to make relationships with other adults who may be caring for them. It is important that these adults are approachable as this will make it easier for positive relationships to be built.

Adults can show they are approachable by:

- showing they are interested in children's interests
- having open body language
- making eye contact with children
- being sensitive to children's needs and feelings
- smiling at children
- showing children respect.

If a child finds it difficult to build positive relationships with adults, they may:

- have difficulty developing relationships with others
- be unable to trust people
- be unable to form friendships
- have difficulty understanding the needs and feelings of others
- be unable to control behaviour and emotions
- lack the confidence and independence to explore and try new things.

□ Why do children need positive relationships with adults?

# Children who find it difficult to cope with change, routines and new situations

Change and new situations can be difficult for children to cope with. They get used to having a regular routine and this enables them to feel safe and secure.

Children learn routines from a very young age. For example, a baby soon learns that the sound of a tap running means it is bath time.

Routines make children feel emotionally safe and secure because they enable their lives to have predictability, which means they know what is going to happen next. When routines are changed, children can become confused and unsettled, which can have a significant impact on their emotional development.

## Low self-esteem

Self-esteem is how we feel about ourselves. Some children have low self-esteem, which means they do not feel good about themselves. Low self-esteem can be caused by a range of factors, such as:

- how others react to us
- comparing ourselves to others or being compared to others
- poor relationships with others
- not understanding rules in play
- delayed or restricted development
- not being praised
- not feeling accepted
- feeling of not belonging.

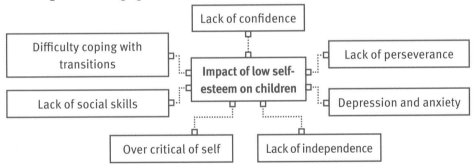

Figure 3.6: Possible impact of low self-esteem on children's social and emotional learning and development.

**LINK IT UP**

To remind yourself of the social and emotional development of children across the ages of birth to 5 years, go to learning outcome A of Component 1..

To remind yourself of transitions children may experience, go to 'Social and emotional needs that may impact on play, learning and behaviour: transitions' in this component.

To remind yourself about children who display disruptive behaviour, go to 'Social and emotional needs that may impact on play, learning and behaviour: disruptive behaviour' in this component.

How do routines, such as regularly reading with a child, help children?

**CHECK MY LEARNING**

1 State one impact on a child's learning and development of being unable to express thoughts and feelings.

2 State two reasons why children may find it difficult to build positive relationships with adults.

3 Explain why routines are important for children's learning and development.

**ACTIVITY**

You have been invited to a job interview at a pre-school. To prepare for the interview, you need to make some notes on the possible impact on learning and development of children:
- who have limited expression of thoughts and feelings
- who find it difficult to build positive relationships with adults
- who find it difficult to cope with change/routines/new situations
- with low self-esteem.

You will need to organise your notes with headings.

Ask a partner to check through your notes. Have you missed anything?

# Create safe environments to support play, learning and development in children aged 0–5 years

Children under 5 years of age need a safe environment in order to support their play, learning and development. It is the role of the adult to ensure all children are safe when engaging in play and learning activities. It is important when choosing resources for children that they are appropriate for the children's age and stage of development so that there are no **risks** to children and no **hazards** that could harm them.

It is important that we are aware of any potential risks and hazards to children and that we ensure these are minimised to keep children safe. How dangerous something is to a child depends on a child's age and stage of development, for example small beads could be dangerous to children aged 6–12 months as children this age put everything in their mouths and could choke, whereas these would be less dangerous to a 5-year-old child as they are less likely to put them in their mouth. How can we ensure that toys and activities are safe for children of different age groups?

## Managing risks and hazards

We can minimise risks and hazards by ensuring that the environment is safe and that toys and activities are not dangerous and are suitable for the age of the child.

**Children 0–18 months** explore by putting everything in their mouths. This is known as 'mouthing'; this means that small items that are suitable for older children to play with, for example, building blocks, can be dangerous for babies and toddlers.

**Children aged 18 months–3 years** often take part in what is known as exploratory play, which can consist of gross motor movements, such as opening and closing doors; this means that adults need to ensure that there is not a risk of accidents, such as trapped fingers.

**Children aged 3–5 years** are becoming more independent in their play and they seek opportunities to play away from adults; therefore, adults need to ensure that any areas where children may be out of sight, such as dens or tents, are safe.

Although it is important to ensure that all children are safe, we must remember there should be a balance between the potential risk of harm and the benefit of children participating in activities. Children need to have experiences in order to help them learn and develop and to support them to manage risks for themselves.

For example, if we stop children 18 months–3 years from climbing, then they may not develop to their full physical potential. We can ensure that children are given age-appropriate climbing frames to climb on and that measures are in place to stop them being hurt.

You can minimise the amount of risk by carrying out **risk assessments** to identify potential hazards that could harm children and what you can do to prevent this from happening. For each activity that children take part in (both indoors and outdoors) adults should list all the things that could be dangerous in the activity and then consider what they can put in place to stop these being a risk to the children's safety.

## Choosing age- and stage-appropriate resources

All toys and resources provided for children must be safe for them to play with and must be appropriate for their age and stage of development. There are a number of symbols that can be found on children's toys to show that they are safe. Adults should look out for these when buying toys for children. It is important to check the safety labels before using equipment or resources to make sure they are up to regulated standards and will not harm or pose a risk to children.

- The Lion Mark was developed by the British Toy & Hobby Association (BTHA) in 1988 to act as a recognisable consumer symbol denoting safety and quality.

- The age advice symbol. This means that the toy is not suitable for children 0–3 years. This could be because it has small parts that very young children could choke on.

- The CE mark is a declaration by the toy manufacturers that a toy is safe. This is a EU standard and prior to Brexit, had to be displayed on all toys entering the UK.

- The BSI Kitemark™ indicates that safety requirements have been met.

RESISTANT

- The fire resistant symbol is attached to items that have passed a scientific control test showing that they are resistant to fire.

- With the UK leaving the EU, the UK now has its own version of the CE mark, the UKCA mark, introduced in January 2021.

## ACTIVITY

Complete the following risk assessment table for the play activities given.

| Activity | What are the hazards? (What could happen to harm the children?) | How can the risks be managed? (What can you do to ensure the children are kept safe?) |
|---|---|---|
| Children under 18 months playing with playdough | | |
| Children 18 months–3 years playing with a play kitchen | | |
| Children aged 3–5 playing in a tent | | |

For each activity write down the benefits of the activity to children's development.

## CHECK MY LEARNING

1 Why is it important to check the symbols on children's toys?

2 State two reasons why it is important to manage risk and hazards when supporting children's play, learning and development.

3 Assess the importance of the balance between the potential risk of harm and the benefit of children participating in activities.

## DID YOU KNOW?

The Lion Mark indicates that the toy has been made by a member of the BTHA and therefore denotes the member's commitment to adhere to the BTHA Code of Practice which includes rules covering ethical and safe manufacture of toys.

## LINK IT UP

To remind yourself of the characteristics of children's development from birth to 5 years, go to learning outcome A of Component 1.

To remind yourself of what children learn from different types of play, go to learning outcome A of Component 2.

# Managing positive risk taking and safety

## GETTING STARTED

Make a list of reasons why playing outside could be risky to children.

How would you encourage children to be safe when playing outside? Consider this for children aged:
- 0–18 months
- 18 months–3 years
- 3–5 years.

Write down your answers.

## KEY TERMS

**Positive risk taking** balancing the potential risk of harm against the benefit of children participating in activities.

**Adult to child ratio** the number of adults to the number of children.

## BEST PRACTICE

Ensure play remains exciting; don't make it boring in order to remove all risks.

## LINK IT UP

To remind yourself of different play structures: adult-led play, adult-initiated play and child-initiated play, go to learning outcome A of Component 2. To remind yourself of the characteristics of children's development from birth to 5 years, go to learning outcome A of Component 1.

## Positive risk taking

You have already learned that a risk is the likelihood of something causing harm.

Taking a risk can be dangerous but there is such a thing as '**positive risk taking**'. This is where we balance the potential risk of harm against the benefit of children taking part in an activity. For example, we may think that children playing outside can be dangerous. However, if they do not do this they will not have access to fresh air and will not get any exercise, which is not good for their development.

Imagine a world where children never experienced the outdoors. What would this be like? Life is full of risk, so the best way to prepare children for life is to ensure that they learn how to judge risk for themselves.

## Age-appropriate personal safety in public areas

It is important to teach children how to be safe in public areas. Children from 2 years of age can be taught simple rules about personal safety. Older children (3–5 years) can be taught to cross roads safely, and be taught their address and parent's/carer's telephone numbers in case of an emergency.

## Teaching children to use resources safely

It is essential that childcare workers teach children to use resources safely. This means explaining how to use and carry scissors (hands clasped around closed blades) so that they don't pose an injury risk to children. Another example could be making children aware that glue and paints and some 'natural resources' can be harmful if ingested.

▪ How can adults teach children to use scissors safely?

## Being aware of choking hazards for under 3-year-olds

Choking hazards for under 3-year-olds include beads, small-world toys and small blocks. Natural resources, such as acorns, could also pose a choking hazard, as could some snacks, such as grapes. It is essential that all snacks are cut into small pieces and water is always offered at snack time.

## Planning adult to child ratios

It is the role of the adult to ensure that all play is suitable for the children's age, stage of development and abilities. There is a legal requirement for there to be enough adults to support children's play and learning. This is called the '**adult to child ratio**'.

The younger children are the more adults are needed. This is because younger children (for example, 0–2 years) are less independent than older children (for example, 3–5 years) and need more adult care to meet their needs.

■ What is the adult to child ratio here?

■ Table 3.11: Current adult to child ratios

| Age of children | Adult to child ratio |
|---|---|
| 0–2 years | 1 adult to 3 children |
| 2 years | 1 adult to 4 children |
| 3–5 years | 1 adult to 13 children |

### ACTIVITY

*You are working with a group of children on a cutting and sticking activity. Francesca, aged 4, is reluctant to join in. She tells you that her daddy told her off at home for picking up the scissors and told her 'Never touch scissors; they are sharp and dangerous!'*

1 Answer the questions, working in pairs, and write down your answers.
   a Why do you think Francesca's dad has said this?
   b How will using scissors support Francesca's development?
   c What are the hazards with this kind of activity?
   d How can the risks be minimised?
2 Role play what you would say to Francesca's dad to explain to him the benefits of risky activities.

### CHECK MY LEARNING

1 Explain what is meant by 'positive risk taking'.

2 If a nursery has 24 children between 0 and 2 years, how many adults will they need?

# Teaching children how to use internet enabled technology (1)

## GETTING STARTED

Make a list of all the different devices children may use when accessing the internet. Put these into categories of those used by children:
- 0–18 months
- 18 months–3 years
- 3–5 years.

Discuss with a partner what devices you used as a child. Can you remember how old you were when you first used the internet? What did you use it for?

The internet is wonderful. It opens up a world of exciting possibilities and enables us to learn, create and connect with people all over the world. Very young children now go online.

Children aged 0–18 months may be given a phone or tablet to watch a cartoon or listen to soothing music.

Children aged 18 months–3 years may be starting to play games and use apps.

Children aged 3–5 years may be chatting online to friends and family.

Children not only have access to technology through devices, such as computers, tablets and mobile phones, but as technology advances there are now many more resources that can enable children to be introduced to technology, such as smart watches (wearable technology), app-enabled toys and toys with voice recognition. **'Smart' devices** can wirelessly connect to other devices or networks that open up endless opportunities for us to interact with others online.

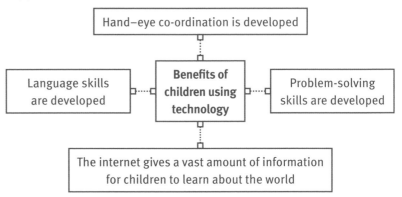

Figure 3.7: Children can benefit from using technology in many ways.

■ Why do adults need to teach children how to use tablets safely?

Using the internet can be beneficial for children if used appropriately, for example, there are lots of apps available that encourage children's learning and creativity. Unfortunately, the internet can also be a risky place for children.

## BEST PRACTICE

Adults should make themselves aware of the risks technology can pose to children and set up parental controls on devices.

■ Table 3.12: Risks associated with older children using the internet

| | |
|---|---|
| Cyberbullying | This is bullying that takes place online and through social networks, games and text messages. |
| Online abuse | This is abuse that happens online. It can include cyberbullying, sexual abuse or exploitation, grooming or emotional abuse. |
| Sharing private information | Children may share personal information online, for example, their home address or photographs/videos of themselves. |
| Phishing | Children may receive messages asking them for personal information such as passwords. The messages might look like they are coming from someone the child knows. |
| Falling for scams | Children may see offers on websites that promise them things, for example, a new game in exchange for their parents' credit card information. |
| Accidentally downloading malware | This is software that is specifically designed to gain access to or damage a computer without the knowledge of the owner. Children may accidentally click on something that downloads a virus. |
| Inappropriate posts | Anything a child posts on the internet cannot be permanently deleted. Children need to be aware that things they post online could be seen for years to come. |

## How to be safe online

Adults can set up **parental controls** on phones, tablets, games consoles, laptops and computers to keep children safe online.

Parental controls will filter what children can see online, such as those shown in Figure 3.8.

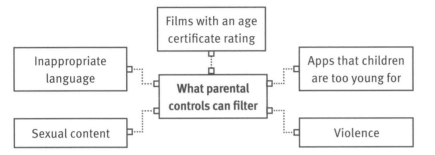

□ Figure 3.8: Adults can set up parental controls to keep children safe online.

They also stop children sharing personal information.

Blocking children from social networking sites will reduce the risk of children talking to people they do not know online or tagging themselves in posts, which will reveal their location to strangers.

## Controls put in place by adults

Parental controls can:

- limit the time of day children can go online, reducing this to day time only so as not to disturb children's sleep
- limit how long a child is online for; it is not healthy for children to spend too long on **internet-enabled** devices because it can limit the amount of exercise they do
- block children from spending money online. For example, some game apps allow players to buy characters or features ('**in-app purchase**'), which can be very expensive. Children aged 18 months–3 years may pay for something accidentally if the parent/carer's credit/debit card details are registered on the device. Older children may deliberately pay for something they want without realising how much it actually costs! Adults can make sure there are no credit/debit cards attached to the app so children will not be able to buy anything and parents/carers' card details will not be available online, which stops the risk of theft and fraud.

**KEY TERMS**

**Smart devices** allow us to connect different devices or networks.

**Parental controls** software and tools that can be installed on internet enabled devices to keep children safe online.

**Internet enabled** the term used for devices that are able to connect to the internet.

**In-app purchases** buying something using an app.

**ACTIVITY**

*Carmel and Gary are parents of two children aged 18 months and 3 years. They are worried about the risks of their children using the internet.*

Design a leaflet to help Carmel and Gary and other parents to understand how to keep their children safe online.

Your leaflet should include:

1  the risks associated with children using the internet
2  how to be safe online
3  controls put in place by adults.

**CHECK MY LEARNING**

1  What is 'internet-enabled technology'?

2  State why each of the following age groups may use the internet:
- 0–18 months
- 18 months–3 years
- 3–5 years.

3  Explain three risks of older children using the internet.

4  Explain what parental controls are.

# Teaching children how to use internet enabled technology (2)

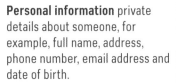

## KEY TERMS

**Personal information** private details about someone, for example, full name, address, phone number, email address and date of birth.

**Age-inappropriate content** information or pictures online that could upset a child, material that is directed at adults that might lead a child into unlawful or dangerous behaviour. This could be pornographic or violent material, or inappropriate language.

How can we talk to children about internet safety and teach them to recognise when something is not appropriate for them to see?

When talking to children about internet safety, adults need to take the child's age and stage of development into consideration. We want to keep children safe but not to frighten them. The conversation could include what apps and games they like, what makes them feel uncomfortable and what to do if they see something that upsets them. Adults should also discourage children from sharing their **personal information** online.

Adults should be aware of what is **age-inappropriate content** for children and should report this using the appropriate channels.

## Talking to children about internet safety

It is important that adults talk to children about how to stay safe online. Adults should be aware of what apps, games or websites children are interested in and should tell children if they are worried about any of these.

Children should be encouraged to tell an adult if they see anything online that scares them or makes them feel uncomfortable. This can include cyberbullying.

Adults should teach children what personal information means and that it is important not to share this information online.

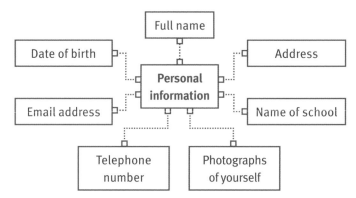

◪ Figure 3.9: Adults should teach children what personal information means.

Explain to children that it is easy for people to disguise themselves online, for example, an adult could pretend to be a child. Children should be aware that if they are talking to someone online who genuinely knows them (such as a family member), they shouldn't need to ask for personal information.

If children are using social media sites, adults should teach them:
- how to block someone
- how to report someone
- not to reveal their location
- not to give their full name.

◻ How could the adult in this picture teach the child to stay safe online?

## Recognising and reporting age-inappropriate content

Some websites can have content that is inappropriate for children. This could include images or comments that could upset a child, or material that is directed at adults, for example, sexual content, violent images or inappropriate language. It is important that children are taught to recognise when something is not appropriate for them to see.

Adults have a duty of care to report age-inappropriate content online. There is a facility for this on social media sites. There may also be times when it is necessary to contact the police.

**BEST PRACTICE**

Adults must follow guidelines for usage and be responsible for recognising and reporting any age-inappropriate content.

**ACTIVITY**

Design a poster aimed at 3–5-year-old children to encourage them to stay safe online.

Consider the age of the children. The poster needs to be simple enough for this age to understand and should not aim to frighten the children. It should include:
- pictures of devices, games and apps that children this age may use
- simple information on how to keep safe online that will not frighten the children.

Compare your poster with the person sitting next to you. Is there anything you have forgotten to include?

**CHECK MY LEARNING**

1 State three types of personal information that children should be discouraged from sharing online.
2 Explain how adults can help children stay safe on social media sites.
3 Explain what an adult can do if they see children looking at something inappropriate online.

# Health and safety considerations for inside environments for children with individual needs

Children's surroundings have a significant impact on their development. Adults should give great care and attention to the room layout, furniture and floor coverings to ensure children are safe when indoors. Think about your childhood memories: What made you feel comfortable as a child? What made you feel safe in a room?

## Width of doorways, aisles and corridors

- Doorways should be wide enough to accommodate prams and pushchairs for children aged 0–18 months and also wheelchairs for children, parents/carers or staff who have a disability.
- Aisles and corridors should be kept clear and should be wide enough to give children and staff easy access to different rooms and areas. There should be enough space to accommodate more than one person at a time, for example, children aged 3–5 years often play in groups and may be moving around together, but children aged 0–18 months will be accompanied by an adult when moving through aisles and corridors, which may involve them being carried or transported in a pram or pushchair.
- In the event of a fire, aisles and corridors need to allow as many people as possible to move out in one go.

## Layout of furniture

- Furniture should be positioned so that there is a clear pathway to enable children to move around easily to access activities and resources.
- Furniture should be positioned so it does not block the children's view. For, example, children aged 18 months–3 years are not as tall as older children so items such as high shelving units could restrict their vision across the room.
- The layout of the furniture should allow enough space for individual and groups of children to move around freely.

### Considering health and safety

When choosing any new resources for children to use, it is important to consider health and safety factors. The health and safety aspects of the type of furniture used may not be obvious to consider, after all, items such as storage units are mainly used by adults. However, storage units can be very heavy and could seriously hurt a child if they were to topple over. Storage units and other heavy furniture should be fixed to the wall so children cannot push them around or knock them over.

Furniture used by children should be child-sized, strong and with rounded edges to prevent accidents because children under 18 months who are crawling or starting to walk can hurt themselves on sharp edges or even pull over lightweight furniture, which can lead to injury.

◘ What are the benefits of this room layout for children?

◘ Table 3.13: Types of furniture suitable for childcare settings

| Types of furniture | Features |
|---|---|
| Chairs | Sturdy<br>Right height so children's feet are on the floor, with arms for children under 18 months<br>Adult chairs stronger for greater weight but same height as children's chairs for interaction |
| Tables | Right height to match chairs to ensure good posture<br>Easily movable so they can be moved around for different purposes<br>Adjustable for children of different heights |

## Types of flooring and floor coverings

- Children spend a lot of time on the floor so this is a very important indoor play surface.
- There should be carpeted areas for babies aged 0–18 months who move around by rolling and crawling and for some activities for older children, such as role play.
- Washable flooring is also required in some areas, particularly toilet and sink areas, eating areas and messy play areas, as it is likely there will be spillages there.
- Hard flooring should be durable and non-slip to ensure children are kept safe.
- Some floor coverings are not suitable for young children, for example, laminate flooring or tiles, as pieces can become dislodged, causing a **trip hazard**.

### ACTIVITY

Design a leaflet to advise a newly opening nursery on the health and safety considerations for inside environments.

The leaflet must cover:
- width of doorways, aisles and corridors
- layout of furniture
- types of flooring and floor coverings.

You must give advice for all the following age groups:
- 0–18 months
- 18 months–3 years
- 3–5 years.

### KEY TERM

**Trip hazard** object(s) on the floor that could cause someone to trip and possibly fall.

### DID YOU KNOW?

There are regulations about the amount of space that is needed per child in a setting and it is a legal requirement to follow these.

### LINK IT UP

To remind yourself of the characteristics of children's development from birth to 5 years, go to learning outcome A of Component 1.

### CHECK MY LEARNING

1 Why is it important to consider the width of doorways, aisles and corridors?

2 State two things that should be considered when planning the indoor environment to ensure children are safe, for each of the age groups:
- 0–18 months
- 18 months–3 years
- 3–5 years.

# How resources can be organised and the use of specific areas

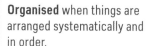

**GETTING STARTED**

With a partner, discuss the benefits of organising things so they can be easily found. Write down your ideas.

Make a list of how you could organise all the items in your bedroom at home.

**KEY TERMS**

**Organised** when things are arranged systematically and in order.

**Specific areas** different areas in a setting that organise the play activities and resources.

**BEST PRACTICE**

It is really important that you plan the use of resources carefully to ensure the best play, learning and development outcomes possible for each child in the setting. To make sure that your professional practice is always best practice, you need to think about all of the following.

- The children who are going to use the resources.
- How resources could best support the play and learning in your plan.
- The interests and preferences of the children in the group.
- Getting the resources approved by your manager.
- Any adults involved and any additional needs they may have e.g. seating.

Resources should be **organised** in a way that enables children to find things easily. Think of a time when you have been unable to find something that you wanted. How did this make you feel?

Childcare settings should be well organised not only so everyone knows where everything is but also to minimise the risk of accidents and to keep children safe.

Many settings are split into **specific areas** separating the different resources and activities. Each area has its own risks and safety considerations depending on the kinds of resources being used there and the types of play taking place. It is the adult's role to ensure that all areas are kept safe and are suitable for the ages of children using them.

## How resources can be organised to enable children to find things easily

- Adults should consider how resources are stored and displayed for the children. It is good practice to store toys and resources in organised sets so that children can find things easily.
- Drawers, shelves and boxes where resources are kept should be at the correct height for children to enable them to find things easily.
- For younger children, aged 0–18 months, drawers, shelves and boxes can be labelled with a picture to show children what is in there. For example, a picture of building blocks on the box where these are kept.
- There should also be the word displayed for children aged 18 months–3 years who can recognise letters and children aged 3–5 years who may be starting to read.
- Having the resources organised in this way makes it easier for children to tidy up, which can prevent trip hazards.

◻ How is this adult helping the children to find things easily?

# Use of specific areas for play activities and routines

A good way to support children's learning through play is to divide the room into activity areas.

◘ **Table 3.14: Common areas and the safety aspects that adults should consider**

| | |
|---|---|
| **Role play area** | This area should have enough space for children to move around, dress up and act out situations and stories.<br>There should be sufficient storage for dressing-up items and props and child-sized light and movable objects as the areas could be turned into anything from a home to a play shop or doctor's surgery! |
| **Book area** | Ideally, the book area will be in the corner of the room, enabling children to relax and have some quiet time. Soft seating should be available to create a homely environment.<br>The book shelves should ideally be heavy and immovable. However, the shelves where the books are stored should be at varied heights, with some low enough for children aged 0–18 months and 18 months–3 years to reach and some slightly higher for the 3–5-year-old children. |
| **Messy area** | This may cover painting as well as gluing and sticking and materials like sand, water, playdough or gloop. It is important that this area is near to the sink to provide handwashing facilities for the children and to enable spillages to be cleaned up quickly. There should be a mop and a sweeping brush available nearby to prevent trip and slip hazards. |
| **Construction and small world area** | This area consists of building materials, such as different types of blocks, and small imaginative play resources, such as toy animals, people, cars and trains. This area needs to be spacious as children will be playing on the floor. There should also be lots of storage to prevent trip hazards.<br>This area is best situated in a corner of the room to stop children using it to gain access to other areas. This will protect children from being bumped into and stood on when they are on the floor. |
| **Mark making area** | Pencils, crayons, felt tip pens and chalks should be organised into separate containers and be easily accessible to the children. There should be enough space for the children to work, for example, children aged 0–18 months or 18 months–3 years may need to work on large pieces of paper and will need plenty of room so they do not knock other children around them or poke them in the eye with a sharp pencil. |
| **Baby and toddler rooms** | Children aged 0–18 months have different needs to older children. They learn by exploring with their senses and through physical movement. Rooms for children of this age should have plenty of space for babies who are rolling, crawling or starting to walk but also quiet secluded areas where babies who cannot yet move by themselves will be protected from older babies who may bump into them.<br>There should be a suitable space for changing babies' nappies with consideration of the height of changing tables to ensure babies do not roll onto the floor. |
| **Safe spaces** | A space where children can rest or take a nap. |

**LINK IT UP**

To remind yourself of the different play opportunities for children, go to learning outcome B of Component 2.

◘ **Why should baby rooms have a carpeted area?**

**DID YOU KNOW?**

Children learn more and feel safe and secure when things are in order and their indoor environment is well designed.

**LINK IT UP**

For Create safe environments to support play, learning and development in children aged 0–5 years, please see page 146 and for Managing positive risk taking and safety, please see page 148 in learning outcome B of Component 3.

**ACTIVITY**

Write an article for a childcare magazine that gives advice on:

1 how resources can be organised to enable children to find things easily

2 the use of specific areas for play activities and routines.

You must give advice for the age groups:

- 0–18 months
- 18 months–3 years
- 3–5 years.

Remember to include some pictures as examples.

**CHECK MY LEARNING**

1 State two benefits of organising resources for children.

2 Explain how well-organised resources can impact on children's learning.

# Health and safety considerations for outside environments for children with individual needs (1)

**GETTING STARTED**

Make a list of all the things that will need to be considered when taking children on an outing in the outdoors. Think about the different age groups:

- 0–18 months
- 18 months–3 years
- 3–5 years.

It is considered good practice for children to have as much access to outdoor environments as they do to indoor ones. Outdoor play can take place in the setting's outdoor area but may also be away from the setting, for example, on an outing. Outdoor play is very beneficial to children's development; however, there are safety considerations that need to be taken into account. Hazards in the outdoors can be very different to those indoors. How can you ensure that the outdoor environment is safe for children to play in?

There are many things that need to be taken into account to ensure children are safe in outside environments. Adults need to consider the different types of weather and how to plan for these. Children's hunger, thirst and **toileting needs** will also need to be taken into consideration.

**KEY TERMS**

**Toileting needs** the need to use the toilet.

**Appropriate clothing** suitable for the weather.

## Appropriate clothing

Children should have access to outside environments all year round and in all weathers. This means that children need to wear **appropriate clothing** in order to stay safe when playing outside.

**BEST PRACTICE**

Check accessibility beforehand when planning an outing for children to ensure the venue, and the toilet facilities, are accessible for all.

▢ **Table 3.15: Clothing for different weathers**

| | |
|---|---|
| Clothing for sunny weather | Sunglasses<br>Sun hats<br>Long-sleeved t-shirts to protect arms from the sun<br>High SPF sun screen should also be applied to protect children (with permission from their parents/carers) |
| Clothing for rainy weather | Rain coats with hoods<br>Waterproof trousers<br>Waterproof all-in-ones for children aged 0–18 months<br>Wellington boots<br>Umbrellas |
| Clothing for cold weather/snow | Warm padded coats<br>Warm padded all-in-ones for children aged 0–18 months<br>Hats<br>Gloves<br>Scarves<br>Warm socks<br>Wellington boots/snow boots<br>Lots of layers, such as fleeces and jumpers, underneath coats |

## Planning ahead

### Clothing changes

The weather in the UK can be very unpredictable! It is good practice when children will be playing outdoors for adults to regularly check the weather forecast and ensure that they are prepared for any sudden changes. This is particularly important if planning an outing for children, for example, rain covers may need to be taken for pushchairs for children aged 0–18 months in case of a sudden downpour. The temperature can get colder later in the day and we get colder the longer we are outside; therefore, coats, gloves and hats will need to be available just in case children start to feel cold.

□ What else may need to be considered when taking children outdoors on a rainy day?

## Toileting needs

When taking children on an outing, adults will need to check there are toilet facilities and nappy changing facilities. Children should be given plenty of opportunities and reminders to go to the toilet and potties should be taken for children aged 18 months–3 years who may still be toilet training. Spare clothing should be available in case of any accidents and also disposable gloves, wipes and plastic bags for soiled clothing.

## Hunger and thirst

When in outdoor environments children should drink plenty of water, particularly on hot days. Adults should monitor how much children are drinking to ensure they do not get dehydrated. There should also be snacks available in case children are hungry.

> ### DID YOU KNOW?
> Outdoor learning is a major part of the curricula in the UK for children aged 0–5 years. Children should play outside every day in all types of weather.

> ### LINK IT UP
> To remind yourself how exercise affects children's growth and development, go to learning outcome B of Component 1.

### ACTIVITY

*You are working at 'The Children's Choice' day nursery and have been asked to plan an outing to the park for a group of children.*

Create a plan that includes the following:
- appropriate clothing
- planning ahead for:
  - clothing changes
  - toileting needs
  - hunger and thirst.

You must show you have considered the age ranges:
- 0–18 months
- 18 months–3 years
- 3–5 years.

### CHECK MY LEARNING

1 State the appropriate clothing for sunny weather, rain and cold weather/snow.

2 Explain two things that need to be considered when planning an outing for children.

3 Explain the importance of planning ahead when taking children outdoors.

# Health and safety considerations for outside environments for children with individual needs (2)

When playing in outdoor environments, adults should consider **accessibility** by ensuring that children can enter and exit buildings and outdoor spaces safely and that the different outdoor surfaces and levels are safe for children to play on. The outside environment should be planned to accommodate both noisy and quiet play.

Outdoor play resources should be suitable for all children, taking into account different ages and stages of development. Remember that many activities that are carried out inside can be adapted to be taken into the outdoor environment.

Look back at 'Health and safety considerations for inside environments for children with individual needs'. How could the different areas be duplicated outdoors?

## Accessibility

It is good practice for children to be allowed to move freely from inside to outside and vice versa to develop their play, and they need to do so safely.

☐ Table 3.16: Accessibility considerations for children in the different age groups

| 0–18 months | There should be **ramps** available where there are stairs. |
| 18 months–3 years | Hand rails should be provided on stairs for children who may still be unsteady on their feet. |
| 3–5 years | Doors should be open so that children can move in and out freely. |

Open doors should be safe to ensure that they cannot slam shut, trapping children's fingers.

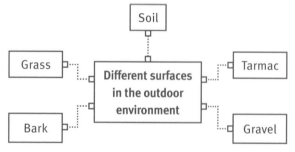

☐ Figure 3.10: It is important to plan the surfaces for outdoor environments.

- It is important to plan the outdoor environment to ensure that the surface closest to the door is smooth, to prevent accidents when children step outside.
- Adults should check the outdoor area is safe and make sure that there is no litter, broken glass or animal faeces.
- Adults should have salt available to put down when it is icy, to prevent children from slipping.
- The outdoor area should be secure with fences and locked gates, so that children cannot escape and also strangers cannot get in.

## Choice of outdoor play resources

The outdoor play resources should cater for children of all ages and stages of development.

- **0–18 months** Children like to explore natural materials like sand, water, gravel and mud.
- **18 months–3 years** Children like items such as magnifying glasses for looking at insects. Plant pots and gardening tools enable them to explore nature.
- **3–5 years** There should be items such as cardboard boxes, plastic crates, tyres, play tents and sheets to enable them to make dens and hideaways.

### Wheeled toys

Wheeled toys should be available and these should be suitable for children's different ages and stages of development.

- **0–18 months** There should be sit-and-ride toys and push-along toys as they are still learning to walk and control their bodies.
- **18 months–3 years** Children will be able to ride a tricycle and push a toy pram.
- **3–5 years** Children are more advanced in their physical development and two-wheeled bicycles could be introduced for those who are ready.

### Physical needs

Adults will need to consider children who have physical needs. Ramps may be required and items such as climbing frames may need to be adapted to cater for children with mobility needs.

## Choosing quiet or noisy play spaces

Outdoor play areas should be split so that there are large areas where children can run around and make noise but also quieter corners for activities like gardening, looking for insects or making a den. There should be areas providing shade from sunshine and rain. The large area needs to be spacious enough for children to move around freely and not too cluttered. Older children should be encouraged to 'park' up their wheeled toys so that these do not become a hazard to children who are running around. There should be space for adults to push children aged 0–18 months around in their prams or pushchairs.

## Different levels

It is good practice when children are outdoors to enable them to experience different **levels** to develop their physical skills of balance and co-ordination. This could include: stairs, climbing frames, low walls and logs. There should be ramps and slopes to enable children to ride wheeled toys both uphill and downhill.

## Signs, symbols and maps

Signs and symbols can be used to support children in the outdoor area. For example, laminated pictures of tricycles to show children aged 18 months–3 years where to park these and words for children aged 3–5 years who are learning to read. Signs and symbols can also be used to point children in the right direction of the different areas, for example, 'Garden' or 'Sand pit'. When taking children on outings, children aged 3–5 years will benefit from being given a simple map of the area and shown where to go if they get lost.

**LINK IT UP**

For Consideration of weather implications see pages 158–159.

**ACTIVITY**

Design an outdoor area that is suitable for children aged:
- 0–18 months
- 18 months–3 years
- 3–5 years.

Draw your design on a large piece of paper and label the different areas and resources. You should show you have considered:
- accessibility
- outdoor play resources, taking into consideration ages and stages of development
- quiet and noisy play spaces.

**CHECK MY LEARNING**

1 State two suitable outdoor resources for each age group:
- 0–18 months
- 18 months–3 years
- 3–5 years.
2 Explain why children need both noisy and quiet play spaces in the outdoor environment.

# Adapting play to promote inclusive learning and development

Consider the following scenarios.
- Only girls can play with the dolls and prams.
- Only older children can play outside.
- Some children cannot access the sand area because they have a disability.
- A child cannot understand the story because he is learning English as an additional language.
- A child is excluded from a Christmas card making activity because she is not a Christian.

**1** Discuss with a partner how these are examples of not being inclusive.

**2** Why is it important that all children can access all activities?

**3** Write down your ideas.

## KEY TERMS

**Inclusive** including everyone.

**Right to learn** a moral or legal entitlement to have an education and learn.

**United Nations Convention on the Rights of the Child** a statement of children's rights that must be followed.

**Adapt** make something suitable for all children.

Adults need to adapt play to promote **inclusive** learning and development. This means make changes to activities for all children to ensure that they can take part and learn. For example, adding a ramp to the outdoor area to ensure that children with a physical disability can access the area. Can you think of any other examples?

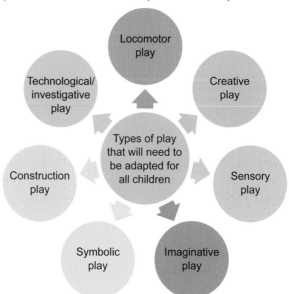

◻ Figure 3.11: Being inclusive means ensuring all types of play are adapted for everyone.

Being inclusive also means ensuring all types of play are adapted for all individual circumstances and for different abilities and age groups:
- 0–18 months
- 18 months–3 years
- 3–5 years.

It is important to recognise that every child has a **right to learn** and within this right is the need to promote all the five areas of development.

Adults will need to understand how to adapt all activities to ensure that all areas of development are promoted to include all children.

## Recognition that every child has a right to learn

Every child has a right to learn. This means they have a moral and legal entitlement to have an education. The United Nations International Children's Emergency Fund (UNICEF) is a charity working in many different countries across the world to defend children's rights.

In 1989, UNICEF produced the **United Nations Convention on the Rights of the Child**. This is a statement of children's rights and it has been approved in many countries around the world.

The United Nations Convention on the Rights of the Child has 54 articles that cover all aspects of a child's life and sets out the rights that all children everywhere are entitled to.

One of these articles states that 'every child has the right to an education'. This means that we have a legal responsibility to ensure that every child learns.

You have already learned in Component 2 that children from birth to 5 years old learn through play. To ensure that every child learns through play, adults need to **adapt** activities for children with individual needs to promote their learning and development. By individual needs we mean:

- physical needs
- cognitive/intellectual needs
- communication and language needs
- social and emotional needs.

## Promoting five areas of development for all children

When considering a child's right to learn adults need to understand that this covers all five areas of development, which are interrelated. You have already learned about these in Component 1.

**BEST PRACTICE**

Demonstrate a recognition of the right of all children to learn, in language that children can understand.

◻ Table 3.17: The five areas of development

| Physical development | Control over the body<br>Development of the senses<br>Gross and fine motor skills |
|---|---|
| Cognitive/intellectual development | Development of information processing<br>Memory<br>Problem-solving skills |
| Communication and language development | Development of speech sounds and language skills<br>Listening and attention skills<br>Social skills<br>Formation of sentences |
| Social development | Development of relationships<br>Building confidence and self-esteem<br>Development of friendships |
| Emotional development | Development of bonds and trust<br>Independence<br>Development of emotional resilience |

All the areas of development are as important as each other; therefore, adults need to ensure that all children are given opportunities to learn and develop in each of the five areas.

The five areas are all interrelated, which means one area of development is dependent on the others. For example, a child cannot learn to write until they have developed their fine motor skills to hold the pencil and their language skills to understand letters and words.

This means that adults need to adapt activities for all children to ensure that all areas of development are covered, and that development is seen as being holistic rather than separated into the different areas.

**LINK IT UP**

To remind yourself of holistic development, go to 'Development' in Component 1.

To remind yourself of the five areas of development across the ages of birth to 5 years old, go to learning outcome A of Component 1.

**ACTIVITY**

*'Butterflies' Day Nursery looks after 60 children.*
- *There are a mixture of boys and girls.*
- *The nursery has rooms for children aged 0–18 months, 18 months–3 years and 3–5 years.*
- *There are children from a range of different ethnicities speaking a range of different languages. Some of the children are learning English as an additional language.*
- *The nursery has several children who have individual needs.*

1  Explain why it is important that the nursery ensures that every child has the opportunity to learn. You must refer to the United Nations Convention on the Rights of the Child.

2  Explain why it is important that the nursery promotes all five areas of development for all children.

**CHECK MY LEARNING** ◼◼◼

1  Explain what is meant by the right to learn.

2  State two examples of how a setting can be inclusive.

# The role of the adult (1)

## Implementing adult-led play, adult-initiated play or child-led play

In learning outcome A of Component 2, you learned about adult-led play, adult-initiated play and child-initiated play.

**Adult-led play** is when adults plan and organise children's play and the adult takes the lead in order to teach children particular concepts or skills. For example, the adult may plan to build train tracks with the children aged 18 months–3 years and count the pieces to teach them to count to ten.

**Adult-initiated play** is when adults plan and organise children's play to allow children to explore. It is the role of the adult here to organise toys and resources in ways that will encourage children to play with them. The adult should allow the children to explore but also they should introduce new materials and concepts to the children. For example, after setting up a painting activity for children aged 3–5 years, the adult may introduce some different sized brushes to the children and may suggest that they mix the colours.

**Child-initiated play** is when children choose what to play and how to play. The role of the adult here is to ensure that the children lead the play and decide what to do. The adult should observe and show that they are interested but should not interfere. For example, if children aged 18 months–3 years are building a tower, the adult should not suggest that they knock it down and build something else.

Children need adults in their play to support them, to ensure that play remains safe. It is the adult's role to model appropriate behaviours and responses and to supervise the children without interrupting or spoiling their play. Think about when you were a child and an adult interrupted your play. How did this make you feel?

However, it is not always possible for adults to stand back. There are times when adult intervention is needed to ensure that children do not hurt themselves or become bored. Adults can offer children new ideas and resources or give alternative suggestions to them in order to maintain the children's **stimulation** and to keep them safe. Overall it is important that all play is suitable for the children's ages, stages and abilities, including levels of confidence and how easily and quickly they get bored.

## Role modelling appropriate behaviours and responses

During play, adults should **role model** sharing, taking turns and helping others. This will encourage children to be caring to others in their play. Adults should teach children to use resources safely and should be a role model for correct use.

## Supporting children's play

It is important that the adult is available to supervise and support the children but they need to judge when it is best to leave children to get on with their play by themselves.

If the adult is **intrusive** and interferes too much this could affect the children's development. For example, if you rush to stop a toddler opening the cupboard in the play kitchen and open it for them because you are afraid they might trap their fingers, this has stopped them from being independent and developing their physical skills.

### Appropriate intervention

Sometimes adults may need to intervene if something is not safe or to help children to be respectful of others.

## Offering new ideas and resources or alternatives

Sometimes adults may need to give children some new ideas or resources to ensure that their play remains safe and to enable accessibility for the encouragement and stimulation of play. For example, an adult might discretely replace a broken toy with another one or add some water to the sand so that it is less likely to get in the children's eyes.

The adult may suggest that children change what they are doing without making it obvious that this is a safety precaution.

## Ensuring that all play is suitable for children's ages, needs and abilities

Play should not only be suitable for the children's ages but adults also need to take the children's needs and abilities into account. Some children may be less confident than others and may need reassurance from an adult to join in. Others may need the play to be made more exciting because they are ahead in their development and are becoming bored.

Adults also need to understand that play activities may need to be adapted in order to meet the needs of children who have additional needs. For example, having larger crayons in the mark making area for a child who has weak fine motor skills.

■ Why would an adult need to intervene in this situation?

■ Adults should model how to carry scissors correctly with the hand clasped around closed blades.

---

**ACTIVITY**

*Paul works in the local day nursery. He is having difficulty keeping the children's interest in the construction area. The children have been throwing the building bricks around and he is worried that the area is becoming unsafe.*

Write down what advice you would give to Paul. Your advice must cover the following points:

1 Role modelling appropriate behaviours and responses.

2 Supporting children's play – being available but not intrusive.

3 Offering new ideas, resources and alternatives.

4 Ensuring the play is suitable for the children's ages, stages and abilities.

Role play with a partner with one of you taking on the role of Paul and one of you the role of the adviser.

---

**LINK IT UP**

To remind yourself of the role of the adult in promoting learning through play, go to learning outcome A of Component 2.

---

**CHECK MY LEARNING**

1 State two examples of when it is appropriate for an adult to intervene in children's play.

2 Assess the role of the adult in keeping children's play safe, giving one example for each age group: 0–18 months, 18 months–3 years and 3–5 years.

3 Explain how an adult can be a good role model to children in their play.

# The role of the adult (2)

It is the role of the adult when working with children to promote inclusion to ensure all children can join in with organised activities. This involves having a positive attitude to difference and coming up with solutions to barriers that can stop children participating, rather than excluding them.

Adults can promote inclusion by role modelling **desired behaviours** when interacting with children who have **additional needs**. It is also the adult's role to cater for children's different interests and preferences. You have already learned in Component 2 about child-initiated play, which is where children choose what to play with and how to play. Imagine being told what to do all the time and not being given a choice. How would this make you feel and how would it affect you?

## Promoting inclusion

Inclusion means to include everyone regardless of their:

- ethnicity
- gender
- age
- religion
- language
- abilities
- additional needs
- disabilities.

To promote inclusion, adults need to ensure that all children can join in organised activities. This will sometimes require adaptations to the environment or new equipment or resources to be brought in for particular children. This will ensure that there are no barriers to children learning and developing.

Some examples include the following:

- special seats on outdoor swings so children with physical disabilities can take part in physical activities
- different sized paintbrushes available for children of different ages and stages of development, so they can all join in with creative activities
- books in different languages, so all children can develop their literacy/reading skills
- counting in different languages, so all children can develop their mathematics/counting skills
- dressing-up clothes and cooking utensils from different cultures, so all children can take part in imaginative play
- soft balls with bells inside for babies with visual problems.

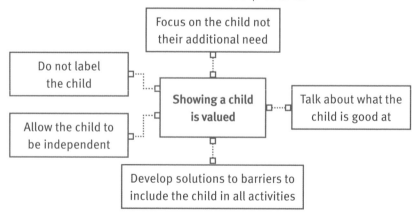

◩ Figure 3.12: Ways in which adults can make sure children with additional needs are valued and included.

### Inclusion and children who have additional needs

In the past, children with additional needs were given negative labels and were separated from other children. Today, things are very different and children with additional needs are included and given the same opportunities as other children.

## Giving children a choice

It is important that children are given a choice when both planning and choosing activities.

Children can plan their own activities if adults spend time with them talking about what they want to do and allowing them to choose their own materials and resources.

To facilitate this type of approach, it is important that resources are organised to enable children to find things easily. You have already learned about this in 'How resources can be organised and the use of specific areas'.

Giving children choices supports their learning and development as it allows them to:
- learn to make decisions for themselves
- develop independence skills.

However, it is important that the degree of choice given is appropriate for the age and stage of development of the children. Table 3.18 shows some examples of how children in different age ranges can be given choices.

**◨ Table 3.18: How children in different age ranges can be given choices**

| | |
|---|---|
| 0–18 months | Children can be given a treasure basket containing different items and they can choose independently which items to explore. |
| 18 months–3 years | Children can be asked to choose a book that they would like to look at with an adult. |
| 3–5 years | Children can be given a choice of what they would like to eat and could serve themselves at the table. |

**DID YOU KNOW?**

It is a legal requirement for settings to be inclusive.

**BEST PRACTICE**

Role model desired behaviour by showing respect for all children.

**LINK IT UP**

To remind yourself of how resources can be organised to enable children to find things easily, go to 'How resources can be organised and the use of specific areas' in this component. To remind yourself of child-initiated play, go to Component 2, 'How play can be organised to promote learning, child-intiated play'.

**ACTIVITY**

*Andreas is starting his first job working with children aged 3 to 5 years. He is unsure of his role in adapting activities for the children who have individual needs.*

Create a help guide for Andreas to support him.

The help guide must include:
- promoting inclusion
- role modelling desired behaviours when interacting with children who have individual needs
- giving children choice.

**CHECK MY LEARNING**

1. State three ways that adults can promote inclusion.
2. State one way that children can be given choices at:
   - 0–18 months
   - 18 months–3 years
   - 3–5 years.
3. Assess the impact on 3–5-year-old-children's emotional and social development of being given choices.

# The role of the adult: responding to children

**GETTING STARTED**

Make two lists on a piece of paper.
- One list of the different ways adults can praise children.
- One list of the different rewards that could be given to children.

What is the difference between praise and rewards? Write down your ideas.

**KEY TERMS**

**Praise** express approval.

**Reward** something given to someone to recognise their efforts or achievements.

**BEST PRACTICE**

Remember to label the behaviour, not the child. Praise specific actions to reinforce positive patterns of behaviour. Giving reasons why you approve of the behaviour can be more effective than using rewards, in certain instances. If using rewards try to avoid over using them.

◘ Figure 3.13: Desirable behaviour is likely to be repeated if children are praised or rewarded for it.

It is the role of the adult to respond positively to children in their play, learning and development. These responses include **praise** and **rewards**.

Children use their behaviour to get the attention of the adults around them. Praise and rewards are needed for children to understand how to get the attention of adults in positive ways.

Can you think of ways in which you were praised or rewarded as a child? Has someone praised you recently? How did it make you feel?

## Responding positively to desired behaviours in children

### Praise

When adults praise children's behaviour they are expressing approval for it. This helps children to understand what desired behaviours are and they are more likely to repeat the behaviours.

If children are not praised for their behaviour, they are less likely to repeat it. This is why praise can be effective in supporting children to behave well. Sometimes it is a good idea for adults to ignore a child's unwanted behaviour because if children realise the behaviour is not getting them any attention they are likely to stop it. Obviously, some behaviours cannot be ignored, for example, a child hurting another child.

Praise can impact children's learning and development by:
- helping children to feel good about themselves, building self-esteem
- building confidence.

### Rewards

Adults sometimes use rewards as a way of responding positively to desired behaviours. Stickers and gestures from adults are two examples.

The rewards given to children will need to be carefully considered to ensure that they are appropriate for the child's age and stage of development. For example, it would not be effective to give a 1-year-old child a sticker as they may not understand what this is. A clap would be a much more effective way of rewarding a child of this age.

Just like praise, rewards can help children to understand what is desired behaviour and they are likely to repeat something if they are rewarded.

Rewards work well if they are used at the time of the desired behaviour. If they are given later, children may forget what they have done. Giving out certificates at the end of the week for good behaviour would not be effective for a group of 18 month–3-year-old children as they may have forgotten what happened earlier in the week.

Rewards can also be ineffective if they are used too much as children may behave in a certain way just to get the reward rather than because it is the 'right thing to do'.

## Recognising when children are becoming bored, losing concentration or finding activities difficult

It is important that adults recognise when children are becoming bored with an activity or are losing concentration. This can be displayed as disruptive behaviour.

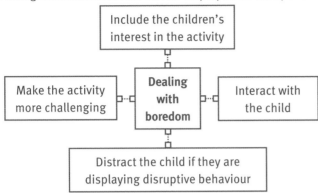

■ Figure 3.14: Adults should recognise when children are becoming bored with activities and deal with the boredom.

Children can become bored because they are losing concentration. Adults can interact with the children to help them focus and avoid distractions, for example, put the activity somewhere quiet, move other children who may be interrupting the activity.

There may be times when children are finding activities difficult. To avoid this it is the role of the adult to:

- ensure activities are appropriate for the children's ages and stages of development, for example, an 18-month-old would not be able to play a board game involving mathematical sums
- divide up big tasks into smaller ones, for example, while gardening, the activity should focus on filling up the plant pot first, before putting in the seed
- allow sufficient time for children to engage in the activity, for example, a child couldn't complete a jigsaw in the same amount of time as an adult
- support children by introducing different resources, for example, in the creative area if a child is struggling to use a paintbrush they could be given some different sized brushes to hold.

**LINK IT UP**

To remind yourself of disruptive behaviour, go to 'Disruptive behaviour' in this component.

**ACTIVITY**

You are going to appear on a radio programme about supporting children's behaviour.

The programme will be covering:
- responding positively to desired behaviours using praise and rewards
- recognising when children are becoming bored, losing concentration or finding activities difficult.

Make some notes of what you will say on the programme. You will need to refer to children of different ages:
- 0–18 months
- 18 months–3 years
- 3–5 years.

Practise with a partner what you are going to say.

**CHECK MY LEARNING**

1 State one reason why praise is important for children.

2 State one reward suitable for a child aged 0–18 months.

3 Assess the possible impact of rewards on the self-esteem of a child aged 3–5 years.

# Benefits to other children of playing with children with additional needs

## GETTING STARTED

What do you think the benefits are to children of being in an inclusive environment?

Write down your ideas.

Compare your ideas with a partner.

In 'Adapting play to promote inclusive learning and development' you learned about how to promote inclusion. This is where adults adapt activities for all children in play, learning and development. Providing an inclusive environment has many benefits to children.

- It supports them to learn how to include others in their games and activities.
- It promotes **positive behaviours**, social skills and sharing of resources.
- Children become more responsive to the needs of others.

Where children are around other children who are different to them, they learn to understand difference, accept people for who they are and be more tolerant of others.

Imagine a world where we were all the same. What would this be like? How would this affect children's play, learning and development?

## KEY TERMS

**Positive behaviours** behaviours that are good and desired.

**Communication methods** the different ways in which we can communicate with each other.

**Tolerance** ability to put up with something without complaining about it, which might otherwise be annoying.

## Children learn how to include others in their games and activities

If the environment that children are exposed to is inclusive, children will learn how to include others in their games and activities. They will recognise that other children learn in different ways and will be able to adapt their play to accommodate others.

Where children are around other children who have different needs, they begin to understand that some children learn at a different pace to themselves or that they have some limitations to what they are able to do. This results in children being sensitive to the needs of others and they start to ensure that other children have equal chances to join in.

Children learn to become:

- adaptable
- patient
- tolerant of others

which supports their social and emotional development.

It is important to remember that children's ability to include others in their games and activities depends on their age and stage of development. For example, children aged 0–18 months do not yet understand the concepts of sharing or waiting. You have learned about development across the ages of birth to 5 years old in Component 1.

■ What do children learn from being in an inclusive environment?

## Promotes positive behaviours

When play and learning activities are adapted for all children this promotes positive behaviours, as children learn to be sensitive to the needs of others. This supports them to be caring and enables them to improve their social skills, for example:

- sharing and turn-taking
- learning from each other
- accepting that everyone is different
- building up a good rapport with others
- making friendships with children from different ethnicities, religions and with different abilities
- socialising with all genders
- less likely to discriminate against others when they are older.

Also, when children's emotional development is supported as being kind and accepting of others it makes children feel better about themselves, which increases their self-esteem.

## DID YOU KNOW?

Many children who have additional needs attend a mainstream setting with other children rather than a 'special' setting.

## Children become more responsive to the needs of others

In an inclusive environment, children will become aware of different **communication methods** and will learn to respond to other children using these in order to meet their needs.

- *Adam, aged 3, speaks Punjabi and is learning English as an additional language. His friend Elliot has learned to say 'Hello' in Punjabi as he has picked this up from Adam.*
- *Claire is 5 years old and has a hearing impairment. Claire's teacher is able to communicate with her because she can use British Sign Language.*
- *The children at 'Oakwell Pre School' have learned to sit still and not shout at the table at snack time as they are aware that any sudden noise or movement could upset Billy, who has a visual impairment.*

These examples show how being in an inclusive environment has supported the children to understand the needs and feelings of others. This is called empathy. Having empathy for others will result in children being more patient and **tolerant** of others.

**LINK IT UP**

To remind yourself of development across the ages of birth to 5 years, go to learning outcome A of Component 1.
To remind yourself of promoting inclusion, go to 'Adapting play to promote inclusive learning and development' in this component.

 How do you think adding bubbles to the water in this picture has supported the children to behave positively?

**ACTIVITY**

*Fatima, aged 3, will soon be starting at the school nursery where you are a student. She is learning English as an additional language.*

1 Research and then create an information sheet to inform Fatima's parents about how activities will be adapted for her at nursery.
2 Explain how adapting activities for Fatima can benefit the other children in the nursery.

**CHECK MY LEARNING**

1 State why adapting activities for all children in play, learning and development supports children to include others in their games and activities.

2 State three social skills that children may develop from activities being adapted for all children.

# Adapting activities and resources to support a child with physical needs (1)

In 'Health and safety considerations for inside environments for children with additional needs' you learned about health and safety considerations, including the layout of furniture and accessibility, and the physical circumstances that may impact on learning and development, such as restricted or delayed gross motor skills. Can you think of any other physical needs that children may have?

Children with physical needs may need **adjustments** to be made to the environment, so they can access activities and resources. Adults should select appropriate resources to support **grasping**, **holding**, **releasing** and **transferring**.

## Making adjustments to the environment

Children with physical needs will need adjustments to their environment to enable them to use resources and take part in activities. For example, adjusting the height of tables or easels so they can be comfortably used.

### Space

Adults should ensure that there is **sufficient space** available for a child with physical needs to carry out activities safely.

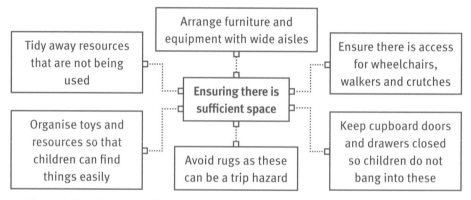

Arrange furniture and equipment with wide aisles

Tidy away resources that are not being used

Ensure there is access for wheelchairs, walkers and crutches

**Ensuring there is sufficient space**

Organise toys and resources so that children can find things easily

Avoid rugs as these can be a trip hazard

Keep cupboard doors and drawers closed so children do not bang into these

◼ Figure 3.15: Adults should ensure that there is sufficient space available.

Most of the advice in Figure 3.15 applies to all children, but it is important to remember that children with physical needs may be more likely to knock into furniture than other children, and they need more support to ensure that they can move around freely and not trip over.

### Lighting

To enable children with physical needs to move around easily, the amount of lighting may need to be adjusted to improve **visibility**.

If children can see where they are going, they are less likely to bump into things or trip. While this is important for all children, it is especially important for children with physical needs as they may require more light than other children to ensure that they keep safe when moving around the activities.

Adults should ensure that activity areas are well lit and should add lamps if needed. Some settings use dimmer switches, so the light can be adjusted easily.

### Adjust the level of activities and resources

It may be necessary to adjust the level of activities and resources to support children with physical or sensory needs.

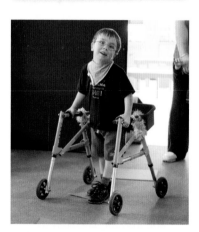

◼ Why is it important for children with physical needs to be given enough space?

- Some children may prefer to have activities on the floor rather than at a table. For example, mats can be put down so creative activities such as painting, sand or playdough can take place on the floor.
- Different children may need tables of different heights, so it is a good idea to have adjustable tables, so the height can be changed quickly and easily.
- Some children may benefit from tables with a slanting top. This can support children aged 3–5 years to read and write more comfortably as they promote good posture and enable children to see more clearly.
- In the outdoor environment there should be climbing frames of different heights and ramps and slopes to enable children to access various parts of the outdoor area easily.

## Choosing appropriate resources for children with fine motor skills delay

When adapting activities and resources to support a child with restricted or delayed fine motor skills, it is important to remember that this does not mean giving children resources that are not appropriate for their ages.

- Rattles are good to support the development of grasping, but you would not give these to a 3–5-year-old child because these are toys that are aimed at babies, so they would not stimulate an older child.
- Picking up buttons and beads supports children's fine motor skills but you would not give these to 0–18-month-old children as they could be a choking hazard.

◘ Table 3.19: Resources to support children to grasp, hold, release and transfer items

| Resources to support grasping | Books with tabs to support the turning of pages. Grippers on pencils and crayons to support children to hold these correctly. Playdough, clay and modelling clay to enable children to practise the movement of grasping. |
|---|---|
| Resources to support holding | Paintbrushes with knobs at the end of them. Cups or bottles covered in fabric making them easier to hold. Large toys such as soft toys or balls that need to be held with two hands. |
| Resources to support releasing | Small objects that children aged 3–5 years can hide in their hands and then open their hands to reveal, for example, buttons or coins. Hand puppets Toys to push, for example, pop-up toys. |
| Resources to support transferring | Items such as spoons or crayons can be placed in a child's non-preferred hand, so they can transfer it to their preferred hand. Putting in and taking out activities such as shape sorters for 0–18-month-old children or putting coins into a money box slot for 3–5-year-old children. |

## Choosing appropriate resources for children with gross motor difficulties

Children who have gross motor difficulties may need adaptions to resources to enable them to take part in activities. For example, creative activities could take place at a table so that children who use walking frames or wheelchairs can take part. This would also support social skills, giving opportunities for conversations with other children.

Pretend play can be adapted so that equipment such as toy cookers are at an accessible height. Suitable outfits for dressing up could be provided so that they did not get caught in wheels or unsteady feet.

Large outdoor equipment including swings could be fitted with special seats so that a child with gross motor difficulties could sit comfortably and safely.

**BEST PRACTICE**

Choose age-appropriate toys and resources that are adapted to support inclusive learning and development.

**ACTIVITY**

A new nursery is being set up. Before it opens the staff need to prepare the environment so it supports children with physical needs. Prepare a presentation to advise staff that must include:

- making adjustments to the environment
- choosing resources that are age and stage appropriate
- selecting appropriate resources that all children can use.

**CHECK MY LEARNING**

1 State two ways that adults can ensure there is sufficient space for children with physical needs.

2 State one suitable resource to support each of the following:
   - grasping
   - holding
   - releasing
   - transferring.

3 Explain the possible adaptations for children aged 3–5 years with a visual impairment, giving two examples.

# Adapting activities and resources to support a child with physical needs (2)

If children have a sensory impairment, which means they require support, this is called having **sensory needs**. It is important that adults provide materials and resources for sensory needs.

It is important that materials and resources provided are appropriate to the age group. Children aged 0–18 months put everything in their mouths; therefore, it is important that the materials and resources provided are safe. How can adults ensure this?

Children with physical or sensory needs may need movable objects to be secured so they remain still. It may also be appropriate to adjust the level of activities and resources to suit children's needs. You have already learned about the use of equipment at different levels in 'Health and safety considerations for outside environments for children with additional needs'.

## Securing movable objects

In order to support children who have physical or sensory needs to use equipment and resources, it may be necessary to secure movable objects to keep them still. If an object is moving when a child is trying to use it, this can frustrate the child and have an impact on a child's ability to engage in the activity, and could even be dangerous.

Some examples of securing movable objects are shown below.

▫ How could the objects in these pictures be 'secured' to stop them moving?

## Adjust the level of difficulty to ensure participation of all children

It is important to ensure that all children can participate in any activity at their own level of development. Several children in a group may be at different levels of development either because they are not meeting the expected milestones in one or more areas, or for other reasons, for example, due to limited experience of play caused by home circumstances, including multiple transitions. Another reason could be that a child has English as their second language.

Some children may need rules of games explaining using smaller words and having access to pictures. Other children may need the support of a specific adult who guides them through the activity. It is important that support and adaptations happen in a way that doesn't make a child feel 'different' or not part of the group.

## Provide materials and resources for sensory needs

Sensory needs may mean that a child has a visual or hearing impairment, for example, they have difficulty seeing or hearing. This can be permanent or temporary. Adults need to provide materials and resources for sensory needs. Resources should always be kept in the same place so a child with a visual impairment knows where to find them. When a child has a hearing or visual impairment it is important that adults maximise their other senses to enable children to access activities.

◩ **Table 3.20: Materials and resources for sensory needs**

| Sight | • **Contrasting colour schemes,** for example, bright colours alongside softer, paler colours or different colours alongside each other<br>• Mirrors<br>• Pictures<br>• Brightly coloured and shiny objects |
|---|---|
| Sound | • Objects that make sounds<br>• Balls with bells inside<br>• Rattles<br>• Squeaky toys<br>• Toys that play music |
| Smell | • Scented playdough<br>• Bags containing herbs or dried flowers, for example, lavender<br>• Scented toys<br>• Flowers and plants |
| Taste | • Different foods<br>• Playing with food items such as mashed potato, cooked cold pasta, baked beans |
| Touch | • Sand<br>• Water<br>• Dough, clay and modelling play<br>• Gloop<br>• Soil<br>• Gravel<br>• Treasure baskets (basket of items that are not plastic, for example, wood, metal, shell, fabric, stone, cork and cardboard)<br>• 3D art materials such as sculptures, canvas and wood |

When providing materials and resources for sensory needs it is important to ensure that they are appropriate for the age group. For example:

- playing with gravel may be a choking hazard to children aged 0–18 months
- squeaky toys may not be stimulating enough for a child aged 3–5 years.

## Adapting activities for hearing impaired children

To help children with hearing impairments access activities childcare workers can use gestures to communicate, or picture/visual clues. It is important to make sure you have the child's full attention before communicating so the child should be looking directly at you. You are an important resource yourself, so you must remember to speak clearly and use age-appropriate language.

## Adapting technological/digital resources to suit the child's needs

Adjusting the screen brightness and sound level on electronic devices is one way of ensuring you meet the needs of sensory-impaired children.

### ACTIVITY

Create three mind maps, one for each of the following:
- securing movable objects
- adjusting the level of activities and resources
- providing materials and resources for sensory needs.

Ensure you consider the different age groups:
- 0–18 months
- 18 months–3 years
- 3–5 years.

### LINK IT UP

To remind yourself of sensory activities, go to learning outcome A of Component 2.
To remind yourself of sensory impairment and how this can impact on learning and development, go to 'Physical needs that may impact on play, learning and development' in this component.
To learn about the use of equipment at different levels, go to 'How individual needs may impact on physical learning and development' and 'Health and safety considerations for outside environments for children with additional needs' in this component.

### CHECK MY LEARNING

1 State one example of a movable object that could be secured to make an activity easier for a child with physical or sensory needs.

2 State one example of how the level of activities and resources could be adjusted.

3 Assess the importance of making adjustments for children with physical needs.

# Adapting activities to support a child with cognitive and intellectual needs (1)

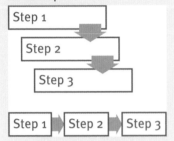

■ **How are these children learning from each other?**

Children with cognitive and intellectual needs may have learning difficulties. This means they may have difficulty acquiring knowledge and skills.

Children with cognitive and intellectual needs will benefit from adults providing opportunities for them to learn and play near to other children doing the same activity to encourage the sharing of ideas. Encouraging children to play where there are adults and other children present will create opportunities for the modelling of activities.

Some children with cognitive and intellectual needs have a short **concentration span**, which means they cannot focus their attention for a long period of time. It is the adult's role to support these children by shortening activities. Adults may also need to break activities down into short steps. You may have heard the term 'practice makes perfect' – what does this mean?

It is important to remember, that some children have learning and memory needs. You can increase the quality of a child's play and learning experience by using the following approaches:

1   repeating activities
2   keeping resources in the same place to provide consistency and develop memory skills.

## Providing opportunities to learn and play near to other children

It is important to support children with cognitive and intellectual needs by ensuring that the environment is arranged both physically and socially in a way that enables children to play near to other children, so they can see them and learn from them. For example, in the creative activities, placing painting easels facing each other rather than in a row.

There should be enough space for more than one child to take part in an activity at a time. This will encourage sharing of ideas, and children who are unsure how to use equipment or engage in an activity will be able to copy their **peers**.

## Shortening activities

There are times when activities will need to be shortened to suit concentration spans because some children cannot concentrate for a long time. This can mean that if activities take a long time, they will lose interest and not learn.
- Rotate toys for 0–18-month-old children so they do not get bored. For example, move the treasure basket elsewhere so they can access something different.
- When counting with a group of 18-month-olds concentrate on counting to five or ten rather than beyond this.
- Choose shorter reading books with fewer pages and words for children aged 18 months–3 years who find it hard to listen for a long time.
- When baking with children aged 3–5 years make something that is quick such as chocolate crispy cakes that do not need to be cooked, rather than something like bread, which takes a long time as you need to wait for it to rise.
- During a card matching game with 3–5-year-olds use only half the sets of cards so the game does not take too long.

## Using peers or other adults to demonstrate activities

Children learn by observing others and copying. This can be their peers or adults. Children or adults may show children how something works.

To ensure demonstrations can take place, adults need to ensure that children can see adults and other children and that the furniture and equipment are arranged appropriately.

## Breaking activities down into short steps

Some children need activities to be broken down into steps to make them more manageable.

Children learn through exploring and through trial and error. This means learning from their mistakes. Breaking activities into steps supports children to practise their skills.

Figure 3.16 shows how putting on a coat for outdoor play can be broken down into steps for a 2-year-old child.

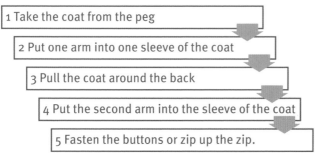

1 Take the coat from the peg

2 Put one arm into one sleeve of the coat

3 Pull the coat around the back

4 Put the second arm into the sleeve of the coat

5 Fasten the buttons or zip up the zip.

▣ **Figure 3.16: Putting on a coat for outdoor play can be broken down into steps.**

Breaking this down into steps enables the child to understand the task of putting on a coat, one step at a time. The child will be able to process each step separately, which makes the task much more manageable than if the adult said, 'Put on your coat' and expected the child to do this in one go. Some of the steps may need to be repeated in order for the child to grasp what they need to do next. When breaking down activities into steps it is important that adults give simple, clear instructions to children, so they can concentrate and process the different steps.

---

**ACTIVITY**

Create a list of 'top tips' on how to adapt activities to support children with cognitive and intellectual needs to be displayed in a day nursery staff room.

You should include:

- providing opportunities to learn and play near to other children doing the same activity
- shortening activities
- using peers or other adults to model activities
- breaking down activities into short steps.

---

**LINK IT UP**

To remind yourself of children's cognitive and intellectual development across the ages of birth to 5 years old, go to learning outcome A of Component 1. To remind yourself of cognitive/ intellectual play and learning, go to learning outcome B of Component 2. To remind yourself of role models, go to 'Social and emotional needs that may impact on learning and development' and 'Supporting children's play' in this component.

▣ **How could an adult support this child to put on his coat?**

---

**CHECK MY LEARNING** ▪▪▪

1 State one way that adults can provide opportunities for children to learn and play near to other children doing the same activity.

2 Explain why some children need activities to be shortened.

# Adapting activities to support a child with cognitive and intellectual needs (2)

It is sometimes necessary for adults to **modify** toys and equipment to support a child with cognitive and intellectual needs. During activities, it may also be necessary to **limit** the number of materials available to avoid **overwhelming** the child. Have you heard the term 'less is more'? Sometimes using fewer or 'less' materials can have more benefit to the child because when there are 'more' this is too much for them to deal with.

Some children can benefit from the use of **technological** or **digital resources**. This term refers to computers and digital equipment that can be adapted through apps and programmes to allow children with particular needs to be more independent.

## Modifying toys and equipment to suit individual needs

In order to support the individual needs of children it may be appropriate to modify toys and equipment so that they are able to use them.

Materials for children with individual needs do not have to come from special shops or websites and cost a lot of money. Regular toys and equipment can be modified to make them more suitable:

▣ Table 3.21: How regular toys and equipment can be modified to make them more suitable

| | |
|---|---|
| Reducing the number of parts | Remove some items from a treasure basket leaving just a few items |
| Removing items that are too small | Remove the small blocks from the building blocks |
| Using specific colours | Have only two or three colours of paint in the creative area |

Not all children with individual needs will need the same changes to be made. Remember the changes that are needed can also depend on the age of the child.

▣ Why might this area be overwhelming for a child?

## Limiting the number of materials available

Some children with cognitive needs are very rigid in their thinking, which means they may have limited ideas. If there are too many resources in an area, this can be overwhelming for a child as they may not know where to start and what to do.

Adults may need to limit the number of materials available in order to meet the child's needs.

For example, in the literacy/reading area, just having a few books for the 18-month-old–3-year-old children to choose from rather than a shelf full of different ones, which may be too much for some of the children. More books can be introduced at a later stage when the children are ready.

## The use of technological/digital resources

Some children can benefit from the use of technological or digital resources in order to meet their individual needs.

- Digital devices, such as computers and tablets, can be adapted. There are apps and programmes that use screen reading technology. These can help children aged 3–5 years who are struggling to recognise their name. The device will read the name on the screen out to the child, so they can hear it being said.
- There are also apps and programmes that enable children with speech and language needs to be able to communicate more effectively, which can also help with cognitive/intellectual development. For example, children click or press on a picture of what they want, and the computer/tablet speaks this out to the adult or other children. This can be used to help children communicate what activity they want to play or what colour they would like to use when painting.
- For younger children (0–18 months) there are battery operated digital toys, for example, toys that have animals on them and buttons to press that make the animal sounds.

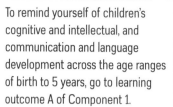

**LINK IT UP**

To remind yourself of children's cognitive and intellectual, and communication and language development across the age ranges of birth to 5 years, go to learning outcome A of Component 1.

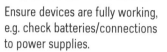

**BEST PRACTICE**

Ensure devices are fully working, e.g. check batteries/connections to power supplies.

**ACTIVITY**

You are planning a painting activity for children who are all 3 years old. Two of the children in the group have a cognitive and intellectual impairment.

Produce a plan to show how you will:
- modify the material to meet individual needs
- limit the number of materials available.

Present your planning sheets to each other and copy down other people's ideas to add to your knowledge.

**CHECK MY LEARNING**

1. State one example of how technological/digital resources can support children aged 3–5 who have cognitive and intellectual needs.
2. Explain why adults may need to limit the number of materials available to children aged 18 months–3 years.

# Adapting activities to support a child with communication or language needs (1)

Adults may need to adapt activities to support a child with communication and language needs. Adults can use group and/or team activities to promote **social inclusion**, encourage friendships with other children and build bonds and trust with adults.

It is important that where a child has communication and language needs they are supported to build confidence in their own skills. One way this can be achieved is through the use of **alternative communication**. This enables children to 'communicate' alongside speech that is not clear.

Alternative communication methods such as **Picture Exchange Communication System® (PECS)** and **Makaton** relieve a child's frustration if they are unable to speak and give them the confidence to initiate their own conversation and be independent. Do you know of any other alternative methods of communication?

## Using group and/or team activities to promote social inclusion

Some children who have additional needs are not very interested in other people and can have difficulty making friendships. Using group and/or team activities can promote social inclusion and give children a reason to need to interact with others.

Taking part in an activity in a group or a team:
- extends a child's speech, language and communication development
- can allow some children to overcome the difficulties they have communicating with others
- enables them to build friendships, build bonds and trust with adults and learn to accept other people around them.

It is important to recognise which group and team activities are appropriate for different age ranges. For example, a circle time activity would not be suitable for children 0–18 months or 18 months–3 years because they are not at the stage where they are interacting with others. You have already learned about the stages of children's play in Component 2.

## Use alternative communication

Alternative communication refers to different forms of communication that can be used instead of or along with talking.

### Picture Exchange Communication System® (PECS)

PECS is a system that enables children to initiate their own conversation through the use of picture cards. The child hands a picture card to an adult to tell them that they want something. Just like verbal communication PECS will start with children aged 18 months–3 years learning simple words before moving on to building sentence structures with children aged 3–5 years. This is done by using sentence strips. A sentence strip enables the child to arrange pictures together in a line to make up a sentence.

### Makaton

Makaton is a form of communication where children use signs and symbols to support speech or instead of speech. Drawn symbols are used alongside signs made using hands and facial expressions.

tap twice

□ **Figure 3.17:** Makaton symbol for 'mummy'.

□ **Figure 3.18:** Makaton symbol for 'hello'.

■ What do you think these PECS cards are saying?

**LINK IT UP**

To remind yourself of children's communication and language development across the ages of birth to 5 years, go to learning outcome A of Component 1.

To remind yourself of the stages of children's play, go to learning outcome A of Component 2.

To remind yourself of communication and language and social play and learning, go to learning outcome B of Component 2.

To remind yourself of how social and emotional development needs may impact on learning and development, go to 'How individual needs may impact on social and emotional learning and development' in this component.

## Build children's confidence in their own skills

Children with communication and language skills may lack confidence. Adults can build children's confidence in their own skills in the following ways.

- Reduce the complexity of their own language and emphasise key words in a sentence when speaking to children.
- Give short and clear instructions that children can follow. These may sometimes be non-verbal. For example, when asking a child to put a cup on the table, the adult can give them the cup and point to the table.
- Model correct use of language rather than correcting a child's mistake. For example, if a child said, "I goed to my Grandma's" the adult can say back, "Yes, you went to your Grandma's" rather than telling the child they should have said 'went' instead of 'goed'.
- Use alternative communication, which can enable children who are non-verbal to initiate their own conversations and be independent.
- Demonstrate activities, so children learn without needing language.
- Praise children when they attempt to communicate.
- Repeat activities so children become familiar with the vocabulary used in them.

Building up confidence in children's own skills will increase their self-esteem and this will support their language and communication development.

**ACTIVITY**

Plan a group activity for children aged 3–5 years that will promote social inclusion.

Your plan must include:

- ways to build children's confidence in their own skills
- ways to include children who use alternative communication.

Share your plan in a group and compare your different ideas.

**CHECK MY LEARNING**

1 Discuss how children may benefit from the use of group and/or team activities.
2 Explain the differences between PECS and Makaton.

# Adapting activities to support a child with communication or language needs (2)

## KEY TERMS

**Identification of words** to establish what words mean.

## BEST PRACTICE

Exaggerate the actions when singing nursery rhymes so all children can see and link the action to the word. Use lots of expression in face and vocal tone.

You learned in Component 2 about communication and language play and learning, including nursery rhymes. Nursery rhymes and songs encourage children's listening skills. The use of these, particularly when they have actions and words that are repeated, can support children with the **identification of words**.

Labelling also supports the identification of words. Labelling is a form of communication and, if children see pictures, they begin to associate the written word with the object. Labels also encourage independence and choice as they enable children to understand where things are and where to find them.

Labels can also be used to display routines and activities. Children often need help in learning routines. Why do you think it is important that children understand their routine and what is going to happen next?

## Using nursery rhymes with actions to promote the identification of words

Children love to join in with singing led by an adult. Nursery rhymes with actions can be used to promote the identification of words.

For example, in the song 'Head, Shoulders, Knees and Toes' children are encouraged to point to their head, shoulders, knees and toes when saying the words. This helps them to identify what the words 'head', 'shoulders', 'knees' and 'toes' mean.

The use of nursery rhymes with actions will vary according to the child's age and stage of development. Table 3.22 shows some examples of rhymes that are appropriate at each age range.

◘ **Table 3.22: Nursery rhymes that are appropriate at each age range**

| 0–18 months | Simple finger rhymes where the adult makes actions on a child's hands or feet, for example, *'Round and round the garden, like a teddy bear...'* |
|---|---|
| 18 months–3 years | Action songs can be introduced including songs where actions and words are repeated, for example, *'Five little ducks went swimming one day....'* (the rhyme is repeated, with the number of ducks reducing in every verse until there are none left). Children begin to anticipate movements while hearing and singing the words, for example, the action for *'swimming'*. |
| 3–5 years | Children this age begin to notice patterns in songs, for example, words that rhyme, such as, 'Miss Polly Had a Dolly who was **sick**, so we phoned for the doctor to be **quick**...' Children also notice the repetition of initial sounds. This is called alliteration, for example, '**P**eter **P**iper **p**icked a **p**eck of **p**ickled **p**eppers'. |

## Labelling equipment

It is good practice for adults to label equipment. This encourages independence and choice as children will know where things are. Common items such as the clock, sink and table can be labelled, as well as activity areas and boxes/drawers containing equipment.

For younger children, pictures can be used.

The benefits of labelling equipment are that it:
- assists with tidying up
- helps children learn the words for what is on the picture

◘ Which area could this picture be used to label? Which words could you add to the picture?

- supports children with the development of reading
- enables children to know where things are
- keeps things organised for the adults
- helps children learn that words have meaning.

## Displaying routines and activities as pictures

You have already learned about the use of labels for equipment. In order to support children with communication and language needs, it is a good idea to display the routine of the setting using pictures and simple words.

This will enable children to understand the order in which the activities happen, so they know what will be coming next.

Pictures can also be used to give children step-by-step instructions for an activity or part of their routine.

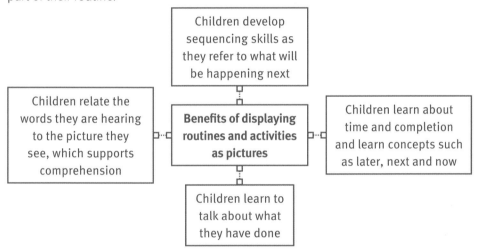

■ Figure 3.19: Reasons to display the routine of a setting using pictures and simple words.

**LINK IT UP**

To remind yourself of children's communication and language development across the ages of birth to 5 years, go to learning outcome A of Component 1.
To remind yourself of communication and language play and learning including nursery rhymes, go to learning outcome B of Component 2.
To remind yourself of how resources can be organised to enable children to find things easily, go to 'How resources can be organised and the use of specific areas' in this component.

**DID YOU KNOW?**

It is common practice in childcare settings for adults to put photographs of children alongside their names on their coat pegs and drawers.

**ACTIVITY**

1 Design a set of labels, one for each of the following:
- physical activities, for example, outdoor area
- creative activities
- imaginative play activities
- literacy/reading area
- mathematics/counting area

Your labels will need to include pictures and simple words.

2 Design a set of pictures with words to show step-by-step instructions for one of the following:
- putting on a coat
- snack time
- painting.

**CHECK MY LEARNING**

1 Explain how the use of nursery rhymes with actions can support children with communication and language needs.

2 State two benefits of labelling equipment for children.

3 State two benefits of displaying routines and activities as pictures.

# Adapting activities to support a child experiencing social and emotional needs (1)

Some children have specific social and emotional needs, which may mean that activities need to be adapted in order to support the development of their **self-resilience**. Self-resilience can be promoted by providing activities that will help the child feel capable and help them feel they 'can do it'.

Self-resilience can also be promoted by giving children choices. However, sometimes it is necessary to limit the choices of activity, so a child does not feel overwhelmed.

Can you remember what 'transitions' are and how they can affect children? One way in which adults can support children experiencing transitions is to plan tasks for them to reduce their worry. This is called providing a **structured approach**.

## Promoting self-resilience

In order to support children experiencing social and emotional needs it is important that adults promote self-resilience.

Self-resilience is made up of the following skills:

- being independent – being able to do things for yourself and think for yourself
- being able to look after yourself – feed, dress and clean yourself
- feeling confident about your own capabilities
- being able to persevere with activities and not 'giving up easily'.

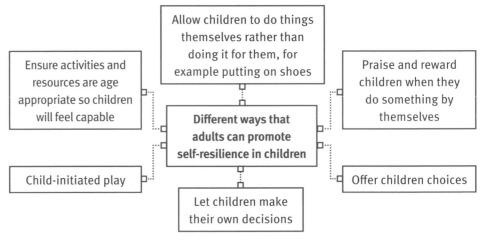

- Figure 3.20: Adults should promote self-resilience in children.

### Allowing children to do things by themselves

To promote children's emotional development, adults need to let children do things like getting dressed or brushing their teeth by themselves, even if this takes a long time. However, it is important that activities are age appropriate. For example, we would not expect a 0–18-month-old to pour their own drink, but this would be appropriate for a 3–5-year-old child.

### Limiting the choices of activity

Although it is important to offer children choices, sometimes adults may need to limit these to avoid stress.

# Providing a structured approach

To support children during transitions adults can provide a structured approach, which means planning and organising specific tasks to be assigned to the child to reduce their worry. Table 3.23 shows some examples.

◘ **Table 3.23: Supporting children during transitions**

| Starting or moving care/educational providers | Ask children aged 3–5 years starting school or nursery to choose their own items of uniform and pack their own bag or lunchbox. |
| --- | --- |
| Birth of a new sibling | Give a child of 18 months–3 years a job to do to support the new baby, for example, bring the nappy at changing time. |
| Moving house | Ask a child aged 3–5 years to be in charge of packing and unpacking their toys. |

Giving children a task to do during the transition will give them something to focus on and make them feel helpful, which will increase their self-esteem and reduce their worry, and will support their emotional development.

# Maintaining engagement

It is important that adults maintain the **engagement** of children. This means being able to keep children involved. This is important during tidying up periods as some children do want to tidy up and become upset if they find themselves with nothing to do, which can be unsettling and distressing.

Adults can fill tidying up periods with short activities, for example:

- a tidying up game of putting all the animals to bed/putting all the cars in the garage
- counting resources as they are put away into containers
- having child-sized sweeping brushes and dustpans and brushes for clearing away materials, such as sand
- matching games, for example, matching different equipment to different containers – all the red bricks in the red box, all the yellow bricks in the yellow box
- singing a song about tidying up.

Having short activities in tidying up periods enables children to feel important. It allows them to deal with the tidying up but keeps them engaged. This supports the development of their self-resilience.

**LINK IT UP**

To remind yourself of children's social and emotional development across the ages of birth to 5 years, go to learning outcome A of Component 1.

To remind yourself of child-initiated play, go to Component 2, 'How play can be organised to promote learning, child-intiated play'.

To remind yourself of a child experiencing a transition, go to 'A Child experiencing a transition' in this component.

To remind yourself of adapting activities to support a child with cognitive and intellectual or communication and language needs go to 'Adapting activities to support individual needs' in this component.

◘ **How could adults support this child who is worried about moving house?**

**ACTIVITY**

1 Create a factsheet to explain to a group of child development learners what self-resilience is and how to promote it.

2 Create a list of ways that children experiencing transitions can be supported by the provision of a structured approach.

3 Write a paragraph to explain how adults can maintain children's engagement by filling tidying-up periods with short activities.

**CHECK MY LEARNING**

1 Explain why adults may need to limit children's choices of activity.

2 State why a structured approach supports children experiencing transitions.

# Adapting activities to support a child experiencing social and emotional needs (2)

In order to support a child experiencing social and emotional needs it is important that adults set out activities that focus on a child's areas of interest.

It is important that children are given opportunities to express themselves. They need to feel confident that it is ok to have different feelings, which will make them more likely to talk about how they feel. Children use play to work out their emotions and adults can encourage expression of thoughts, feelings and ideas by providing appropriate resources.

Adults should encourage group activities because these build confidence in participating with other children and encourage sharing and turn-taking. However, it is important that the group activities planned are different for the different age groups. How do you think group activities differ across the age ranges?

## Setting out activities that focus on a child's areas of interest

Setting out activities that focus on a child's areas of interest can support children who are experiencing social and emotional needs as their confidence and self-esteem will be raised because they will feel valued.

There are times when activities can support a child who is experiencing a particular issue. Adults can choose books and games to support a child to help them come to terms with the issue that is worrying them. They could set up different role play areas such as:
- a dentist surgery for a child who is going to the dentist for the first time
- an airport/pretend plane for a child who is anxious about flying.

This kind of play gives the child an idea of what is going to happen, which can reduce their anxiety and give them confidence when the time comes.

There are also a number of books and stories available that can support children going through transitions, for example, stories about families who have separated, books about the first day at school, stories where a child experiences the death of a significant adult. These books help to reassure children, show them that other people have experienced the same thing and can support them in expressing their feelings.

## Promoting choice and control over the environment

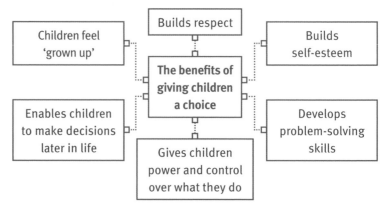

Figure 3.21: Reasons to allow children to have choices.

To support their emotional and social needs children need to be provided with choice and control over their environment.

This can be achieved by providing a range of materials and resources that can be used to complete an activity. For example, in the creative play area having different coloured paper and card, glue, paint and collage materials so that children can choose what they would like to use.

## Encouraging expression of thoughts, feelings and ideas

It is important that children are given plenty of opportunities to express their thoughts, feelings and ideas. Pretend play gives these opportunities to children.

Pretend play enables children to develop their imaginations. They can be things that are not possible in real life and can imagine what it feels like to become someone else.

 **How can using puppets support children?**

◘ **Table 3.24: How pretend play can enable children to develop their imaginations**

| | |
|---|---|
| Dressing-up clothes | Children may dress up as a superhero to experience what it is like to be 'good' or a pirate to pretend to be 'bad'. |
| Role play | While in 'character' children can pretend to be angry, sad or to cry. They can comfort distressed peers who are also in character. |
| Cooking materials | Banging a spoon on a bowl or banging pan lids together can support children to express their anger. |
| Puppets and dolls | Puppets and dolls can be put into character by both adults and children. A child may be more likely to talk to a puppet or a doll than an adult. |

## Social norms and role modelling

Adults can use different types of play to promote social norms and values and prepare children for fitting into the adult world. For example, using pretend play to include turn-taking or sharing resources.

Modelling respect by praising children when they complete an activity and thanking children when they have helped to tidy up at the end of a session helps children's social and emotional development.

## Encouraging small group activities

Group activities build children's confidence in participating with other children and encourage sharing and turn-taking. They enable children to form relationships, which is an important aspect of social development. When encouraging group activities, it is important to ensure that these are appropriate for the ages and stages of development.

◘ **Table 3.25: Examples of suitable group activities for different age ranges**

| | |
|---|---|
| 0–18 months old | Provide opportunities for children to sit together. Put them facing each other so they can see and touch each other. |
| 18 months–3 years | Provide opportunities for children to play alongside each other, for example, dancing to action songs together. |
| 3–5 years | Plan circle time activities that enable children to talk in a group and also develop their listening skills. |

**ACTIVITY**

At 'Toytown Nursery', the 18 month–3 year-old children will be making daffodils. They will be using cut up egg boxes for the middles, which they will paint yellow. They will stick yellow paper leaves around the egg box middle and use a green pipe cleaner for the stem.

1 Explain how the children are not being given a choice during this activity.

2 How could this affect them? Write down your answers.

**CHECK MY LEARNING**

1 State two ways that adults can set out activities that focus on a child's areas of interest.

2 Assess the benefits of giving children with additional needs choices.

# Learning outcome C: assessment practice

## How you will be assessed

You will be assessed with a written examination under supervised conditions. This will allow you to demonstrate your knowledge and understanding of how children's learning and development can be affected by their individual circumstances. You will also demonstrate your understanding of the importance of inclusion and the role of an adult in keeping children safe when engaging in play activities and how the environment and play activities can be adapted to support the learning and development of all children. It is worth 40% of the overall grade for the qualification.

The first questions use words such as complete, give, identify or state, to test your recall of facts. Further into the examination questions become longer, based on some facts about various individuals and asking you to assess, describe or explain those facts.

### CHECKPOINT

**Strengths**
- What are learning and development needs and the factors that affect them?
- What is inclusion and what is the role of adults in keeping children safe?
- How can play activities be adapted to support learning? How do play activities help in the development of a child?

**Challenge**
- Can you recall facts and explain them clearly and accurately when asked to?
- Do your answers demonstrate accurate knowledge and understanding and contain points relevant to the scenario given?
- Are your answers well-developed and logical, showing you have considered a range of different inter-relating aspects?

## PRACTICE ASSESSMENT ACTIVITY

1 Which **one** of the following is a potential example of delayed gross motor skills?

   a A child is confident in outdoor play

   b A child finds it difficult to use a crayon

   c A child has poor concentration skills

   d A child finds it hard to explore

   (1 mark)

2 State **one** possible effect of poor concentration skills that could affect a child's learning and development.

   (1 mark)

3 Rosa is 4 years old and has a cognitive development delay. Her teacher Mrs Shah has organised a project for the children to celebrate the school being 100 years old. The children will be working on the project for the full morning. Rosa also has a communication and language delay.

   a Explain one way in which Mrs Shah could adapt the project to support Rosa's cognitive and intellectual development. (2 marks)

   b Explain how keeping resources and equipment in the same place would support Rosa. (2 marks)

   c Discuss how Mrs Shah could support Rosa's communication and language development. (6 marks)

### TIPS

This component builds on what you have already learned in Components 1 and 2, so it is worth looking through your notes on those units before you start your revision.

### TIPS

Read each part of the question carefully. Check carefully whether you have to write one, two or even three points in your answer.

### TAKE IT FURTHER

Read through your answer. Have you explained one way in which Mrs Shah could adapt the project for Rosa? Has your answer included information on how Mrs Shah could support Rosa? Does your answer show that you have taken into account Rosa's needs?

# Glossary

**Accessibility** how easy it is for an area to be reached or entered.

**Accurate** free from mistakes.

**Adapt** make something suitable for all children.

**Additional needs** a term used to indicate that a child requires extra support or services to enable them to participate fully in activities.

**Adjustments** alterations or movements made to achieve a desired fit, appearance or result.

**Adult to child ratio** the number of adults to the number of children.

**Adult-initiated** where adults provide resources for an activity but let children play with them in a way they choose.

**Adult-led** where an activity for children is chosen and led by adults.

**Age-inappropriate content** information or pictures online that could upset a child, material that is directed at adults that might lead a child into unlawful or dangerous behaviour. This could be pornographic or violent material, or inappropriate language.

**All areas of development** physical, cognitive/intellectual, communication and language, social and emotional.

**Alternative communication** forms of communication used instead of or along with talking.

**Appropriate clothing** suitable for the weather.

**Areas of deprivation** areas where there are potential health risks due to poverty, unemployment and lack of financial investment.

**Associative play** sharing resources but playing alone.

**Attention skills** noticing and concentrating on something.

**Average** a number showing the typical value in a set of data, in particular the mode, median or most commonly the mean.

**Babbling** the stream of sounds babies make before they can say actual words.

**Bodily co-ordination** movement of different areas of the body.

**Body management** skills used to control the body.

**Bond** an emotional tie between two people.

**Caesarean section** birth through an incision made in the abdomen.

**Care or educational providers** settings that provide formal care or education for children. For example, a school.

**Child-initiated play** where children organise their own play activities without the support of adults.

**Chronic** long lasting (used about a health condition)

**Circle time** a time when children sit together with an adult to take part in an activity or a discussion.

**Circumference** the distance around something, in this case, the baby's head.

**Co-operative play** when children are playing with each other.

**Cognitive development** improving your information processing, memory and problem solving.

**Communication methods** the different ways in which we can communicate with each other.

**Concentration span** the amount of time a person can concentrate.

**Conflict** a serious or violent argument

**Congenital** a condition that a child is born with.

**Consistent** remaining the same over time.

**Construction** building or creating something new.

**Constructive** intending to have a use or purpose.

**Contrasting colour schemes** the change in the appearance of a colour surrounded by another colour.

**Delayed fine motor skills** the small movements of a child's hands and fingers are not progressing as quickly as other children of the same age.

**Delayed gross motor skills** the large movements of a child's body are not progressing as quickly as other children of the same age.

**Delayed literacy skills** when a child's reading and writing skills are not progressing to expected milestones of their age and stage of development.

**Desired behaviours** the way in which we want children to behave.

**Development** the gaining of skills and knowledge over time.

**Disruptive behaviour** unwanted behaviour that disturbs and interrupts activities.

**Down's syndrome** a biological disorder, which occurs during embryo development when the cells are dividing and an error occurs causing developmental delays.

**Early years settings** Childcare provided by a childminder, nursery, pre-school or creche.

**Egocentric** Thinking only of yourself and not the feelings or wishes of others.

**Embryo** the stage of pre-birth when the egg has been fertilised and development begins.

**Emotion face** showing different emotions on your face. This can be done by a child or adult, or shown through images or video.

**Emotional bonds** having a connection with a person.

**Emotional resilience** a person's ability to adapt to stressful situations.

**Empathy** being able to understand the feelings of others.

**Engagement** taking part in an activity.

**English as an additional language** when English is not the first language of a child and the first language is the language that the child has been exposed to from birth.

**Enhance** increase or improve something.

**Expected milestones** development that is expected at a particular age.

**Expression** the action of making known one's thoughts or feelings.

**Family structure** the way in which a family is organised.

**Foetus** means offspring and is what a human baby in the womb is called after 8 weeks.

**Food bank** a charity that provides food for free to people in need.

**Friendships** relationships between friends.

**Full term** a baby that is born at or around 40 weeks of pregnancy.

**General anaesthetic** a state of being unconscious controlled by a medical professional

**Gestation** the period of time during which the baby develops in the womb.

**Grasping** the movement of grabbing something by closing the fingers around it.

**Growth** an increase in size and mass.

**Hand–eye co-ordination** co-ordinated control of eye movements with hand movements.

**Hazard** potential for an environment, activity and/or resource to cause harm.

**Holding** to have a grip of something.

**Holistic** made up of parts that are interconnected.

**Housing needs** when families do not have suitable housing, for example living in temporary accommodation or overcrowded housing.

**Identification of words** to establish what words mean.

**Illegal drugs** drugs that are not prescribed and have no benefit for health.

**Imagination** using your mind to be creative.

**In-app purchases** buying something using an app.

**Inclusive** including everyone.

**Independent learning skills** being able to think, problem solve and act without an adult helping.

**Initiate play** to start play.

**Innate** something that is natural, that we are born with.

**Interaction** involvement with others.

**Internet enabled** the term used for devices that are able to connect to the internet.

**Intrusive** causing disruption or annoyance through being unwelcome or uninvited.

**Investigative** finding new information or facts.

**Isolate** cause a person to be alone/apart from others.

**Isolated** being alone and away from others for too much of the time

**Lack of responsiveness** not responding to people.

**Levels** surfaces at different heights.

**Lift-the-flap books** books with liftable flaps showing images underneath.

**Limit** to restrict the amount.

**Limited interaction with adults** not much communication and contact with adults.

**Listening walk** being silent whilst walking in order to hear what is going on around you.

**Locomotor** relating to physical movement.

**Makaton** a language programme using signs and symbols to help children to communicate.

**Manipulating** handling or control over objects.

**Mean** an average worked out by adding all the numbers up and dividing by the number of numbers.

**Milestone** a stage or event in a process.

**Modify** to make changes to something.

**Motivate** to give someone a reason to do something.

**Navigate** move with planned direction.

**Neglect** the failure to care for a child properly.

**Ofsted** a shortened version of the Office for Standards in Education. Ofsted inspects and regulates early years provision, schools, and further education colleges and providers.

**Organised** when things are arranged systematically and in order.

**Overwhelming** very intense and hard to deal with.

**Parallel play** playing alongside others but not playing with them.

**Parental controls** software and tools that can be installed on internet enabled devices to keep children safe online.

**Peers** children of the same age.

**Perceived** interpreting something in a particular way.

**Perseverance** continued effort and determination, despite difficulty.

**Personal information** private details about someone, for example, full name, address, phone number, email address and date of birth.

**Personal interests** topics that children are interested in or things they like to do.

**Picture Exchange Communication System® (PECS)** a form of alternative communication, which allows children with little or no communication abilities to communicate using pictures.

**Placenta** a circular organ in the uterus of a pregnant woman that nourishes and maintains the foetus through the umbilical cord.

**Poor concentration levels** when children find it difficult to focus on what they are doing and/or focus for long.

**Positive behaviours** behaviours that are good and desired.

**Positive relationships** a relationship between two people that makes them happy.

**Positive risk taking** balancing the potential risk of harm against the benefit of children participating in activities.

**Positive role model** someone who sets a good example.

**Praise** express approval.

**Preferences** things that children prefer to do.

**Premature** born before the expected date of arrival. Medically, this is before 37 weeks of pregnancy.

**Prescription drugs** medication that is prescribed for a person by a medical professional.

**Primitive** belonging to an earlier stage of historical development. Primitive reflexes are possibly left-over skills needed before humans evolved.

**Proportion** the extent of something considered in comparison to something else.

**Psychologists** professionals who study the human mind and why people think and act the way they do.

**Ramp** a sloping surface joining two different levels.

**Refine** make changes to improve.

**Regress** return to an earlier state or stage of development.

**Releasing** the movement of letting go of an object that has been grasped.

**Repetition** doing something more than once.

**Resilience** the ability to recover quickly.

**Reward** something given to someone to recognise their efforts or achievements.

**Right to learn** a moral or legal entitlement to have an education and learn.

**Risk assessment** a process of evaluating what might cause harm to people (the potential risks) and making sure things are in place to manage the risk and prevent harm.

**Risk** likelihood of an environment, activity and/or resource causing harm.

**Rivalry** competitiveness over the same objective or over someone's attention.

**Role model** a person looked to by others as an example to be imitated.

**Role-play** acting out the role of someone else or pretending to be a specific person or character

**Routine** a sequence of actions that is regularly followed.

**Self-concept** the way people see themselves.

**Self-resilience** the ability to be independent and prepare for life's stresses and challenges.

**Sensory needs** difficulty seeing or hearing.

**Sensory** relating to one or more of the senses.

**Sibling** a brother or sister.

**Significant family member** a close family member, such as a parent, sibling or grandparent.

**Smart devices** allow us to connect different devices or networks.

**Social bonds** attachment to other people.

**Social inclusion** the process of joining in with others.

**Social norms and values** attitudes and behaviours that are considered normal in society.

**Social skills** used when interacting with others.

**Solitary play** playing alone.

**Spatial awareness** understanding where you are in relation to the objects in your environment.

**Specific areas** different areas in a setting that organise the play activities and resources.

**Spectator/onlooker play** watching others play but not joining in.

**Spina bifida** is caused when the spine and spinal cord of a baby in the womb fail to develop properly.

**Stable** secure, even and well balanced.

**Stimulation** giving something interest, enthusiasm or excitement.

**Story sack** a sack or box that contains a storybook and resources that are linked to the story.

**Structured approach** a planned and organised way of dealing with a situation.

**Sufficient space** enough/adequate space.

**Sustain involvement** being involved for an extended period without interruption.

**Symbolise** (of an object) to represent something else.

**Technological/digital resources** computerised resources.

**Textured stories** these use materials to suggest what something feels like, e.g. fur to represent a bear.

**Textures** the feel, appearance or consistency of surfaces or substances.

**Toileting needs** the need to use the toilet.

**Tolerance** ability to put up with something without complaining about it, which might otherwise be annoying.

**Transferring** moving something from one hand to another.

**Transitions** changes in children's lives.

**Trip hazard** object(s) on the floor that could cause someone to trip and possibly fall.

**Ultrasound scan** a high-frequency sound wave that creates an image on a screen of inside the body.

**United Nations Convention on the Rights of the Child** a statement of children's rights that must be followed.

**Unoccupied play** an early form of play, where a baby does not interact with others and makes movements with their body.

**Varying levels** surfaces at different heights.

**Visibility** the state of being able to see or be seen.

**Vocabulary** The range of words a person knows.

**Weaning** moving on from milk to solid foods.

**Welfare state** the system for protecting health and wellbeing in the United Kingdom. This includes financial and social support, for example through pensions and benefits.

**Wipe board** plastic-backed board that can be wiped clean. They are used with wipe board pens.

# Answers

## Component 1

### p5, Activity

1 *Learner's own answer.*

### Activity

2 Head circumference, height, length, weight.

### p5, Check my learning

Reasons for measuring growth: to identify children who might be unwell, to review and advise on healthy eating, to advise on exercise, to identify children who are at risk of abuse.

### p7, Activity

1. The health visitor might expect to see the dots on the chart dip downwards as the child loses weight.

2. The GP may be concerned that Arun might be losing weight because he has a medical condition or is seriously unwell.

Arun might not be putting on weight because he is not drinking enough milk. He might have had a recent case of sickness and diarrhoea. Arun might be neglected by parents who are not giving him regular feeds. Arun might have a serious illness.

### p7, Check my learning

1. Health visitor – They might weigh the child and measure the circumference of their head and length. This is to check that the child is growing well.

2. Social workers – Social workers might use scales to measure weight. This might be because they are worried that the child is not getting enough food, or because they feel the child is being neglected or is not getting the medical attention that they need.

3. Early years educators – They might observe that a child has lost or gained weight. They would have a responsibility to provide a curriculum that helps children to be active to reduce weight, and to provide healthy snacks and meals. If the child is losing weight, they need to discuss this with the parent and might need to inform child protection professionals.

4. Parents – This will be informal, such as by making marks on the wall as the child grows or because the child need a larger car seat. This is for their own reassurance and to make sure that they can keep their children safe and secure, such as with the car seat.

### p8, Activity 1

*Learner's own description.*

### p9, Activity 2

Ella is 8 months old, so her next milestones might include: moving on to all fours and then crawling, and starting to stand with support, such as holding hands or using furniture. She will pass objects between her hands, shake them and put them in her mouth. She will start babbling more tunefully. Ella might become shy around new people and want comfort from her parent or carer. She will probably enjoy rhymes and songs.

### p9, Check my learning

*Learner's own answer.*

### p11, Activity

1. Suggestions for fine motor skills might include playing with stacking rings or bricks or eating finger foods.

2. Suggestions for gross motor skills might include sit-and-ride toys, balance bikes, playing with a football.

### p11, Check my learning

*Learner's own answer* – this should be based on the content in Table 1.5, page 11.

### p13, Activity

- Evana – Smile at her. Make eye contact and talk quietly.

- Taneeshiya – Play peek-a-boo. Copy the noises the child makes and use individual words to name things and repeat them.

- Hubert – Start to name each toy. Play 'who is this?' so the child names the toy. Introduce the child to new words.

### p13, Check my learning

*Learner's own answer* – key information in the timeline should include: birth – crying, 6–8 weeks – smiling, 3 months – less crying and range of sounds increases, 6 months – babbling, 12 months – words, 15 months – vocabulary expanding.

### p15, Activity

1. Maisie would want to reach for the mobile because it looks appealing. Because it makes a noise when she touches it, she would want it to make a noise again.

2. They could place the toys just out of her reach. They could use toys that make a noise or move so that they capture her interest. They could call her name as they hold the toy.

### p15, Check my learning

- Newborn – By watching and hearing.

- 3 months – Still mainly by watching and by adults interacting with her.

- 6 months – By trying things for themselves, such as reaching for items and touching them. By copying adults.

- 9 months – By crawling towards things, picking them up, putting them in their mouth. By copying adults.

- 12–18 months – By opening things, shaking them, touching them and tasting them. By using single words and by adults talking to them.

### p17, Activity

*Learner's own answers could include:*

**Positives:**

- Children can learn about things that they might not encounter elsewhere, for example, images of wild animals.

- Children can learn through repetition, for example, nursery rhymes.

- Technology can be used to connect families that are apart, such as through video calling.

**Negatives:**

- Children might be exposed to content that is unsuitable.

- Using technology can be addictive, which affects concentration and behaviour.

- Having too much screen time can limit children's real-life interactions, which could have a negative impact on their social development.

### p17, Check my learning

*Learner's own answer* – key information on the web page should include: birth to 3 months only concerned by having needs met; 3 months more aware of who is around them and is an important stage to encourage socialising; at 6 months they will know the difference between people they know and strangers; 9–12 months they will start to enjoy playing but at around 15 months will want to play with other children.

### p19, Activity

- Dorota could bring a familiar toy from home or a comfort item to help her to settle. The key person could find out what she likes to play with at home and provide this for her, such as her favourite story book to read with her.

- Dorota will be sad because she misses her family, and she might be scared of the new environment. She might be confused by what is happening. She might cry, sit by the door or want to look out of the window. She might call for her mother.

**p19, Check my learning**

*Learner's own response.*

**p21, Activity**

*Learner's own response.*

**p21, Check my learning**

Answers could include any of the following or others:

- Putting on their shoes (but not doing up the laces).
- Putting on their jacket or coat (but not necessarily doing up the buttons).
- Starting to brush their teeth.
- Feeding themselves using a fork and spoon.
- Washing their hands.
- Using the potty or toilet.

**p22, Activity 1**

- Precious could provide the children with a mirror to look at themselves and each other. She might also give them hats and sunglasses to try on so they can see what they look like.
- Precious could hide things around the playroom for children to find. For example, she could hide a teddy bear for them to find. Precious could make a role-play area where children can dress up and play, such as hospitals and vets.

**p23, Activity 2**

1  Amira's next milestones in talking could be:
   - making the sounds of the animals she enjoys playing with. Then she will start to name the animals.
   - As she likes music, Amira might start to repeat songs and familiar rhymes.
   - Soon, Amira will start to put two and three words together to make a sentence, such as 'Daddy more milk'.

2  To encourage her development:
   - Her carers can start to introduce Amira to a wider range of words – for example, naming the toy animals.
   - They can start to sing nursery rhymes, such as 'Incy Wincy Spider'.
   - The carers can talk to Amira in a commentary on what they are doing, such as 'now we need to put your socks on', so that Amira can hear words in a sentence.

**p23, Check my learning**

- Curiosity – When you read to children they will want to know what happens next and want to turn over the page. They will study pictures of things that they do not know about, such as characters.

- Make-believe and imaginative play – Children might act out some of what they see in books. With some things – dragons, for example – they will not know what they are, what they look like and what noise they might make unless they see them in a book. Books can help children to use their imagination in their play, such as being a superhero or going to look for a character in the woods.
- Naming of objects and people – The images in a book never change, so children can go back to them repeatedly. This helps their memory for naming people and objects.

**p24, Activity 1**

- Provide games where children need to take turns, such as throwing a ball and catching with an adult.
- Encourage children to work together, such as making a cake, taking turns stirring and adding ingredients.
- Provide puppets for children to use to talk to each other.
- Give children small tasks, such as helping with tidying up, where they need to work together.

**p25, Activity 2**

- 18-month-old child – The child is starting to want to become independent, which is normal for her age. However, she has a short attention span and realises that she cannot do certain things for herself and needs an adult to help, but might be upset that she cannot do it herself.
- 2-year-old – The son is having temper tantrums because he is experiencing emotions he does not understand and cannot control. This leads him to feel overwhelmed. This is normal and although this feels embarrassing, most people know this is a phase that passes. Try to stay calm.

**p25, Check my learning**

Children might show:

- Frustration – Give the child the chance to do things for themselves and ask if they want help.
- Jealousy – Try to make the child feel loved and included.
- Anger – Let the child calm down and show them affection.
- Sadness – Children need to understand that they can feel sad. The adult should comfort them.

**p27, Activity**

*Learner's own research.*

**p27, Check my learning**

- Locomotion – This means movement.
- Balance – The ability to stay upright and perform tasks without stumbling or falling
- Hand–eye co-ordination – This is when children use their eyes and hands together, for example, looking at a circle while tracing over the top of it.
- Dynamic tripod grip – This is the agreed correct way to hold a pen or pencil – between the thumb and forefinger with a stabilising third finger.

**p28, Activity 1**

Examples could include the following:

- Counting – Rhymes, such as 'Five Little Ducks'. Counting pieces of fruit at snack time.
- Memory – Card games, such as pairs. Shopping list game.
- Concentration – Playdough or construction toys.
- Ordering or sequencing – Puzzles and stacking games.

**p29, Activity 2**

*Learner's own answer.*

**p29, Check my learning**

Children could:

- introduce themselves and say their name and learn the names of others
- share jokes and ask questions
- talk about ideas for things to play.

**p30, Activity**

The teacher could encourage Silvie to join in with group games involving other children, such as catching a ball or hide-and-seek. She could encourage Silvie to bring something in from home to talk about so she can tell the children something about herself.

**p31, Activity**

*Learner's own research and design.*

**p31, Check my learning**

- Children aged 3 years might be able to take turns, amuse themselves and have some independence.
- Children gain emotional resilience by having different experiences and learning from them. They should have chances to try things, not always get them right and have another go, such as pouring water into a cup from a jug or making a tunnel to push a car through. The more they try and fail and try again, the more they learn they can recover from things when they go wrong.

- Bounce-back ability means being able to recover from disappointment and setbacks and still be enthusiastic and positive.

**p36, Activity**

*Learner's own investigation and research.*

**p37, Check my learning**

*Learner discussion.*

**p39, Activity**

*Learners' own research.*

**p39, Check my learning**

- Chronic illness is long term and might last for a person's whole life.
- Short–term illness might be severe but it does not last long.

How each can have a negative impact on children's emotional and social development:

- Children might spend time in hospital, which affects their ability to make friends at school.
- Having an illness might mean others treat the child differently or do not invite them to parties.
- Being unwell might mean children are too ill to play or cannot join in with all games.

**p40 Activity**

For a balanced diet, learners should make sure their meals include each of the food groups: proteins, carbohydrates, fats, dairy, and vitamins and minerals.

1 *Learner's own answers.*

2 *Learner's own answers.*

**p41, Check my learning**

*Learner's own answers.*

**p43, Activity**

- Case study 1 – Inka might become quiet and withdrawn, her muscles might be underdeveloped, inability to concentrate if tired.
- Case study 2 – David might be underdeveloped, he might feel stressed and become tired and withdrawn, he might feel isolated in temporary housing.
- Case study 3 – Tomas might be underdeveloped. He might become stressed, tired and unhappy.

**p43, Check my learning**

Effects on children's growth and development from living in poor housing conditions could include the following:

- 0–18 months: restless, tearful, more at risk of accidents, underdeveloped muscles
- 18 months–3 years: difficult to settle, stress, lack of space to learn about their identity and belongings

- 3–5 years: slow to form friendships, which can affect learning, underdeveloped muscles, tired, irritable and not able to focus and learn.
- *Learner's own answers.*

**p45, Activity**

Medical professionals might be concerned about Belinda's baby after it is born because:

- Belinda has not been looking after herself. Her physical appearance is dishevelled, and she has cuts on her arms. This shows that Belinda might be having mental health problems. When someone has mental health problems it can affect their ability to make good decisions.
- If Belinda is depressed, she might be sleeping more and might not wake to feed her baby. Babies' immune systems are still developing, and if Belinda is not keeping herself and her home clean it could mean that the baby encounters germs that could make them very ill. Therefore, Belinda might not be able to keep her baby safe and meet its needs.
- Belinda is underweight, suggesting she is not eating properly. This might mean that she does not provide enough milk and regular feeds for her baby.
- Belinda has not attended her appointments. This might mean that she does not accept any help that is offered to her. Babies need monitoring in their early weeks to ensure that they are putting on enough weight and making good progress. If Belinda does not attend these appointments, her baby could become seriously unwell.

**p45, Check my learning**

*Learner's own answers.*

**p47, Activity**

1 *Learner's own answers.*

2 *Learner's own answers.*

**p47, Check my learning**

*Learner's own answers.*

**p49, Activity**

*Learner's own answers.*

**p49, Check my learning**

- Discrimination means to judge a person or group of people unfairly, for a variety of reasons, such as gender, race, age, social background or ability.
- It can make it difficult for children to make friends and form relationships because they may feel isolated and shy and become withdrawn, which leaves them open to bullying, which affects their confidence and wellbeing.

- An early years setting should make sure to have culturally appropriate toys and food available for all ethnicities, story books that feature many different types of family such as families with two parents of the same gender, suitable space for disability aids to make sure all children feel welcome and included.

**p50, Activity**

*Learner's own answers.*

**p51, Check my learning**

*Learner's own description.*

**p53, Activity**

Positives of different types of family:

- Only child – Doesn't have to compete for parents' attention, share toys or belongings, happy to play alone.
- Large family – Always someone to talk to, quick to learn how to negotiate and resolve conflict, good social skills at school.
- Step-family – Children can enjoy step-siblings, especially if they are close in age.
- Extended family – Children learn to share with trusted adults, separate easily from parents, for close bonds, independence.

Disadvantages of different types of family:

- Only child – Might be upset when a new baby arrives, might find it hard to share or experience difficulties being with other children at school.
- Large family – Arguments and rivalry.
- Step-family – With a new step-parent or step-sibling the child might feel pushed out, parenting styles may differ and this could cause conflict.
- Extended family – Different rules and expectations.

**p53, Check my learning**

Factors that might change a child's family structure:

- Family breakdown – This might make the child feel confused, upset and angry.
- Remarriage – The child might be happy and excited by the marriage or feel pushed out.
- Death of parent – This will make the child anxious, distressed, sad and confused.

**p55, Activity**

*Learner's own answer.*

**p55, Check my learning**

Disadvantages for children growing up in low-income families could include:

- Less money for activities, such as day trips and holidays.

- Fewer resources, such as toys, clothing and equipment.
- Family might be stressed, leading to less quality time with parents.

Advantages for children born into high-income families could be:

- Better health due to better living conditions.
- More equipment to help with learning.
- Access to education from a younger age.

### p57, Activity

*Learner's own answer.*

### p57, Check my learning

*Learner's own answer.*

### Component 2

### p63, Activity

*Learner's own answer.*

### p63, Check my learning

1. Unoccupied play: birth–3 months. Children play alone and will move their arms and kick their legs. Solitary play: birth–2 years. Not interested in other children and will often repeat actions.

2. Solitary play can give a child the chance to use their imaginative skills as they think of new ways to play with objects they have not seen before. Playing alone allows children to explore what they want without the distraction of other people.

### p65, Activity

*Learner's own answer.*

### p65, Check my learning

1. Examples of parallel play include children playing with blocks or painting alongside each other. Examples of spectator play include painting or mark making.

2. Some social skills that may be used during parallel play are sharing and trust.

3. Parallel play can help a child to learn new skills as they watch other children play alongside them. They will copy the other child's behaviour and actions and begin to understand how to interact with others.

### p67, Activity

*Learner's own answer.*

### p67, Check my learning

1. In associative play, a child might look as though they are playing in a group, but they are actually playing on their own. They may share resources and ask other children questions or talk to them. In co-operative play, children work together to reach an end goal.

An example of associative play is building with blocks separately; an example of co-operative play would be building a rocket together.

2. Language skills are important during associative play as children will often want to talk to others around them. By doing this they can pick up on new vocabulary and understand how to interact with others. If they do not have the language skills, then they will play on their own and may not easily communicate or develop those skills.

3. Children need to be able to share and take turns if they are taking part in co-operative play because they have to work with other children.

### p69, Activity

1. *Learner's own answers.*

2. *Learner's own answers.*

3. *Learner's own answers.*

### p69, Check my learning

1. Locomotor play is when a child physically moves around using their gross motor skills. They might do this for an activity given to them or just because they like it.

2. Children under the age of 18 months are unable to take part in symbolic play because they haven't developed the skills to understand how an object can represent something else.

### p71, Activity

1. *Learner's own answers.*

2. *Learner's own answers.*

### p71, Check my learning

1. Activities used in technological/investigative play include drawing with an electronic pen, water play using beakers and apps that link letters to sounds.

2. Skills developed in construction play are spatial awareness, fine motor skills and problem-solving skills.

### p75, Activity

1. *Learner's own answer.*

2. *Learner's own answer.*

3. *Learner's own answer.*

4. *Learner's own answer.*

### p75, Check my learning

1. If a child is nervous about leaving their parents, they will prefer to learn in a home environment because it is more familiar to them. They are used to it and are able to see their parents. They can also go to community groups as their parents would be with them and they also get to see other children, which they may not have access to at home.

2. Community groups are beneficial for new parents as they allow the parents to meet other adults and professionals and get advice. They can share their experiences and learn from others.

3. Play in a reception class is different from a community group because in reception, children have to follow the EYFS framework in order to learn and develop. In a community group they don't have to follow the EYFS framework because development is not monitored. Community groups also don't have as much money so may have a limited range of toys and resources.

### p77, Activity

1. Learners may use answers from within the topic (see table below). They may also use knowledge from their own experiences or supplied by the teacher in the classroom setting.

| Non-mobile | Mobile |
|---|---|
| Touch/push a ball | Catching/kicking a ball |
| Sound toys | Obstacle course |
| Prop pillows | Building blocks |
| | Ride-on toys |
| | Push and pull along toys |
| | Painting |
| | Playdough and other creative crafts |

2. Practising routines through song and dance helps children learn routine tasks.

3. *Learner's own answers.*

### p77, Check my learning

1. Examples of physical activities to encourage walking at 10 months: using a baby walker, using push toys, holding on to carer's hands as they try to walk.

2. Promoting fine and gross motor skills under 18 months can help children learn to take care of themselves as they get more control over their movements and can develop manipulation and accuracy. This means that as they get older, they will be able to grip a toothbrush or put their own coat on.

3. Examples of gross motor skills to stay healthy: ride-on toys, outdoor play, dancing. Example of fine motor skills to stay healthy: grasping activities, e.g., holding pencils, jigsaws to improve hand–eye co-ordination. All of these would be important for a child's cognitive development as each skill helps improve information processing, memory and problem solving.

**p79, Activity**

1. Gross motor skills promoted by riding a tricycle include: balancing, steering, bodily co-ordination, swerving and manoeuvring.

2. *Learner's own answer.*

**p79, Check my learning**

1. To encourage Jacob to eat vegetables the adults at his nursery could have a 'talk time' about food to encourage talking about why vegetables are healthy and good. They could also plan activities where all children can try different vegetables and play with them. This will encourage Jacob because he will see other children taking part and he will be able to feel the different textures. The adults could also ask Jacob and other children to help prepare the vegetables at snack time, so he feels part of the experience and will be more likely to try them.

2. To improve Bella's fine motor skills she could thread beads, starting with larger beads first. This will help with her dexterity, manipulation and her hand–eye co-ordination. As she improves, she can use smaller beads. She can also use crayons, play with jigsaws and play with sand and water. She could also use books to improve her fine motor skills because turning the pages will help her with her grasp and strength.

**p81, Activity**

*Learner's own answer.*

**p81, Check my learning**

1. Role play can promote development across all areas in the following ways:

   - Physical: using fine motor skills to dress and use props.
   - Cognitive/intellectual: using imagination and symbolism in play.
   - Communication/language: practising communication skills when acting, learning new vocabulary from others and adults, practising pronunciation.
   - Emotional: understanding the emotions of others and their own.
   - Social: learning how to share and take turns with props and to compromise.

2. When a child is colouring or painting, the fine motor skills are being developed. These activities improve hand–eye co-ordination as older children try to colour inside the lines. Colouring and painting also allow children to strengthen their hand muscles and dexterity when using different grip methods.

**p83, Activity**

*Learner's own answer.*

**p83, Check my learning**

1. 'This little piggy went to market' has words that are repeated, so it is easier for a child to listen to and try to practise. It also has actions: the child is more likely to pay attention and listen as they follow the actions.

2. 'Goldilocks and the three bears' can help to promote numeracy skills because the story contains numbers and sizes.

**p85, Activity**

*Learner's own answer.*

**p85, Check my learning**

1. Cognitive/intellectual activities can promote emotional development because a child can build their resilience as they keep trying to complete the activity. This will mean that they are less likely to get frustrated when older.

2. Technology can be used to teach children about colours by using paint software that allows children to mix colours together. Certain apps name the colours, so the child can hear and repeat them.

**p87, Activity**

*Learner's own answer.*

**p87, Check my learning**

1. Taking Caleb to the zoo can improve his attention and listening skills because he will be listening to the noises that the animals make and watching what they are doing. The adults can start discussions about this to encourage Caleb to pay more attention to what is going on around him. He will also learn to know that he has to pay attention when an adult is talking, as he has to do this to stay safe while they are on a trip.

2. The development of listening skills is important for children's cognitive and social development because it allows them to take in what is said to them. They are able to learn vocabulary and new concepts and understand rules. Socially, listening helps them to develop friendships, as they need to be able to listen to other children around them.

**p89, Activity**

*Learner's own answer.*

**p89, Check my learning**

1. Listening skills are important in the communication process because children are able to pick up new words and meaning. This will lead to good communication and language skills in the future.

2. Improving the listening skills of young children can improve their speech because as they listen, they pick up on new words and how to pronounce them. Improving listening skills using the repetition in nursery rhymes can also help to improve speech as children learn to recognise patterns and sequences, which will help them to refine their speech as they get older.

3. Differences between children 6 months and 18 months expressing emotion: see Table 2.4, page 89.

**p91, Activity**

*Learner's own answers.*

**p91, Check my learning**

1. Sharing stories with each other can promote communication and intellectual development as it allows children to use their imagination. They are also able to use vocabulary that they may have just learned as they talk about the book.

2. To get a 2-year-old to calm down and try to express their emotions in an appropriate way, you can use books to help them build their knowledge of different emotions. This will help them to see and understand what different emotions are. You could also use role play or puppet shows to teach the child about emotions and how to tell others how they feel.

**p93, Activity**

1. *Learner's own answer.*

2. Supporting speech can help to promote a child's intellectual development as they learn the meaning of new words and start to become more inquisitive about things around them. Emotionally, they are then able to use more complex words to describe their own feelings, which reduces the likelihood of tantrums. Socially, supporting a child's speech can lead them to make friends as they are more open and inquisitive about others. Being able to talk to other children and make friends means that they are starting to understand more about other people's experiences.

**p93, Check my learning**

1. It is important that children listen carefully when playing a game like 'Simon says' because it can help them refine their speech sounds. As they get older, they will have a bigger vocabulary but will often not pronounce words properly, so a listening game can help them with new words and how to say them.

2. Puppets can help a child who may find it difficult to control their emotions as it is a way to help them show their emotions in a safe space. They can hide behind the screen and act out their own emotions in the way they use the puppets, which can make them feel more comfortable and give them confidence in expressing how they feel.

## p95, Activity

1. *Learner's own answers.*

2. *Learner's own answers.*

## p95, Check my learning

1. An adult can involve a 10-month-old child in a sharing activity by passing toys between themselves.

2. Sharing activities can promote the development of children aged 18 months by helping them begin to understand how they can interact with other children as they get older. They will also be able to build their compromise and negotiation skills.

## p97, Activity

1. Jariyah's behaviour has changed because her brother has now started nursery. She is likely to be experiencing jealousy but does not understand this feeling. Because of this she acts in an inappropriate way, such as having tantrums and being argumentative.

2. Emotion faces could help Jariyah as they can help her to understand her emotions by linking facial expressions to specific emotions.

3. Emotion faces can promote Jariyah's emotional development as they will give her a better understanding of her own emotions and the emotions of others around her. Her communication and language development may improve by using them as she learns how to pronounce the words for specific emotions and to describe why she feels a particular way.

## p97, Check my learning

1. Group activities can promote compromise as they allow the child to be able to consider what other children are doing and what they want. For example, using a sharing bin, children can use any prop that is in it but they cannot take from other children. They have to compromise and wait their turn.

2. Activities that promote compromise can also promote social development because the children will be developing an understanding of others' needs and learning about sharing and turn-taking. This will mean that they are able to make friends as they get older, as these skills are needed for building friendships.

3. The nursery could plan for Olivia to take part in a puppet show where adults teach about emotions. This might encourage Olivia to express her emotions so they can understand why she is so shy. The puppets could also be used to show different situations so that Olivia and other children can learn how to react to them. This will make Olivia more self-aware and will improve her confidence.

## p99, Activity

1. *Learner's own answer.*

2. *Learner's own answer.*

3. Friendship benefits the following:

- Physical development: having friends means that children will want to play together. This can lead to them further developing their fine and gross motor skills and keeping healthy.

- Intellectual development: they will learn about other children and cultures and are more likely to participate in learning activities if they are doing them with their friends.

- Emotional development: builds trust and co-operation between each other and a greater understanding of each other's emotions.

- Social development: improves social skills such as sharing, turn-taking, compromise and negotiation skills as they play in different ways. Having a friend makes them feel good about themselves, as they are cared for, and this increases their self-confidence.

- Communication and language development: children will actively participate in conversations with other children, which will improve their sentence structure and pronunciation of words. It will also help them to identify new vocabulary.

## p99, Check my learning

1. Circle time could help Rory with her emotions because it allows her to listen to other children express themselves. During circle time, the adult might ask children to share one thing they like doing and why. The adult will encourage them to do this in a calm way, so this shows Rory how to express herself to other children. It would also improve her self-esteem and confidence.

2. To help Rory make friends though play, the adults could set up games and activities that allow children to work together. This would help her to develop trust in others. Activities such as show-and-tell that allow children to express themselves with others could also help Rory, as she would get to know other children and might have something in common with them.

## p103, Activity

1. The benefits of Mark leading this activity are that he can help the children to use the scissors safely, introduce them to new vocabulary, such as names of shapes or colours they may not know.

2. The disadvantages are that the children might all end up cutting out the same shapes, using the same colours and not have enough time to do it if they are less dextrous.

## p103, Check my learning

1. Adult-led play is play where an adult leads and gives instruction to children. The adult will have planned carefully and made sure that children have access to the right resources. They will also supervise them closely.

2. Potential benefits of adult-led play:

- High risk activities: some activities could be dangerous for children to do on their own, so the adult will supervise them. This is a benefit as it means that the children are not put in any danger when playing.

- New vocabulary: as the adult is playing with the children and leading them, they can prompt the children to answer questions or express their feelings. This is a benefit because it means that children can increase their vocabulary and learn to express their emotions.

Potential disadvantages of adult-led play:

- Learning is limited: children may want to learn about something else or ask questions linked to learning something different from what the adult has planned. As the adult has planned a specific focus for the activity already, they might not let children explore or ask about something else, which would limit their learning.

- Learning limited by time: when the activity has been planned, the adult will have allocated a set amount of time to complete it before moving on to something new. This may rush the children, and they might not have enough time to think about what they have done and develop their own understanding of it.

- Limited repetition: if the adult has not given enough time to the activity, children might not be able to practise the skills they are meant to be learning. This is a disadvantage because they have limited time to repeat something, such as learning to write their name.

## p105, Activity

1. *Learner's own answers.*

## p105, Check my learning

1. Adult-initiated play can encourage new skills and concepts because the children have to work out what to do in their own way. The children will develop new skills, such as sorting items on their own.

2. Some potential disadvantages of adult-initiated play are:

   Children may not learn the expected skill/concept: the adult will leave out the resources for the children to use but won't explain what they have to do, as they want the children to work it out their own. This can lead to children not learning the skills that the adult wants because they have not been told how. This is a disadvantage because the activity has been planned specifically to improve a particular skill, e.g., pencil grip, and if the child uses the resources in a different way, it means that they are not developing the intended skill.

3. Adult-led play means that the adult will be with the children and will guide them through the activity; in adult-initiated play, the adult plans the activity and leaves the resources out for the children to work out on their own what they need to do.

### p107, Activity

*Learner's own answers.*

### p107, Check my learning

1. Child-initiated play is when a child can make or choose their own play activities without needing an adult.

2. Some children may not achieve learning goals because they may only focus on one area of learning that they like, which means that they are not developing other skills. They might also ignore other children and prefer to play on their own, which would mean they are not learning social skills and communication with others.

3. Child-initiated play can help to develop social skills because children are more likely to play for longer when they have chosen the activity. This means that they will be around other children for longer and will start to understand more about sharing and turn-taking. If they are playing in the same areas, they may make new friends and help others.

### p109, Activity

1. *Learner's own answers.*

2. *Learner's own answers.*

### p109, Check my learning

1. It is important that adults plan some activities to take place outdoors as there is more space for children to move around and practise their gross motor skills. It also gives them the opportunity to make noise and use their imagination as they explore what is around them.

2. Sensory play is any activity that uses one or more of the five senses.

3. In adult-initiated sensory play, the role of the adult is to make sure that children have access to suitable materials that will encourage them to use their senses.

### p111, Activity

1. *Learner's own answers.*

2. *Learner's own answers.*

### p111, Check my learning

1. Adults need to explain activities to children so that they know how to use equipment safely and know the rules. This will give them confidence in what they are doing.

2. Demonstrating an activity can help children to understand it because the adult has taken the time to show them how to use something or what they have to do.

3. If an adult takes a child's personal interests into account when planning an activity, the child will feel valued and be more motivated to take part. This will promote their learning and they will become more engaged in the activity.

### p113, Activity

1. Akram might not engage with the equipment and resources he is given because if they weren't chosen correctly, he might not be motivated to use them, they might not promote exploring or encourage him to ask questions because he didn't get to choose.

2. If Akram is given equipment that doesn't challenge him, he might get bored and lose interest and this might affect him learning new problem-solving skills.

3. *Learner's own answers.*

### p113, Check my learning

1. Examples of outdoor equipment/resources:

   • Coloured chalk: children can use chalk to make drawings on the floor or walls and this helps them to explore and develop an understanding of different textures.

   • Magnifying glass: children can use a magnifying glass to see objects up close. They can explore animals and insects, such as ants and other aspects of nature.

   • Mud kitchen: children are able to use their senses while playing in a mud kitchen. They can explore the differences between mud, soil and sand. Leaves and sticks can also be added.

2. The disadvantages of not giving enough time for children to use resources is that they may miss out on learning, as they have not had enough time to practise their skills or develop new ones. It can also demotivate a child if they have to stop their play too soon.

### p115, Activity

*Learner's own answers.*

### p115, Check my learning

1. Adults should join in play with young children so they can explain and demonstrate the play activity, because younger children might not understand what they have to do.

2. Adults can join in play by sharing resources with the children to show them this skill so that the children can then try sharing and turn-taking for themselves.

3. Adults can encourage sharing in activities by showing the children how to do it. Examples of turn-taking:

   • 0–18 months: peek-a-boo, rolling a ball back and forth.

   • 18 months–3 years: hand printing, sharing ride-on toys.

   • 3–5 years: simple dice games, playing on a slide.

### p117, Activity

*Learner's own answers.*

### p117, Check my learning

1. It is important to consider whether the activity is age appropriate as it could be dangerous to allow a small child to use equipment or resources that are for an older child.

2. A lack of resources during a painting activity could mean that some children are not able to take part properly. They might not be able to mix paints and learn about new colours or improve their grip if there are not enough paintbrushes for everyone.

## Component 3

### p123, Activity

1. *Learner's own answer.*

2. *Learner's own answer.*

### p123, Check my learning

1. Different physical needs that can affect a child's play, learning and development:

   • Delayed fine motor skills.

   • Delayed gross motor skills.

   • Visual impairment.

   • Hearing impairment.

2. Sensory impairment is visual or hearing impairment. Either of these can affect a child's play, learning and development in all areas.

3. The differences between delayed gross motor skills and delayed fine motor skills:

- Delayed gross motor skills: the large movements made by their bodies are not progressing to expected milestones of their age and stage of development. For example, a child with delayed gross motor skills may not be able to explore their environment, which can affect their other development, such as communication and language (can't talk about experiences), social (not making friends) and emotional (low self-esteem).

- Delayed fine motor skills: the movements of their hands and fingers are not progressing to expected milestones of their age and stage of development. For example, a child with delayed fine motor skills may find it hard to explore new materials using their hands. Children can usually hold a crayon and draw simple shapes by the age of 3. A child who has delayed fine motor skills may not be able to do this at 3, which can make them feel frustrated and delay them starting to form letters and write.

### p124, Activity

There are a number of ways 4-year-old Adeel's poor concentration could affect his learning and development, including:

- His communication and language skills and his social skills because he may not learn how to take turns in a conversation.

- His listening skills, so he may not learn all the information he needs to and could make mistakes, for example, with regard to health and safety rules.

- Because Adeel finds listening difficult, he may not make friends because other children may think that he is not interested in them.

- Because Adeel feels restless, he may not be able to take the time to learn a new physical skill such as riding a bicycle.

### p 125, Check my learning

1. Poor concentration levels are when children have a short attention span and cannot focus on what they are doing.

2. Poor concentration levels can affect all areas of a child's development.

3. Global developmental delay is when a child takes longer to reach some development milestones than other children of the same age.

4. Factors that could cause a child to have memory issues can include:
   - developmental and cognitive/intellectual disabilities

- concussion and traumatic brain injuries
- physical and mental health illness
- childhood trauma.

### p127, Activity

*Learner's own answer.*

### p127, Check my learning

A child's preferred language normally becomes the one they spend most time hearing and speaking. For example, if the language they hear and speak in pre-school is English, then English could become their preferred language.

### p129, Activity

Three benefits to Willow's learning and development in using the large play equipment could be:

- an increase in her confidence in her own abilities

- to support the development of her gross motor skills

- to encourage interaction with other children to support her social and emotional development.

### p129, Check my learning

1. Social norms and values are attitudes and behaviours that are considered normal in society.

2. The reasons why some children have difficulties forming strong bonds with adults could be due to the following:
   - Premature birth
   - Postnatal depression
   - Child's health
   - Parents' health
   - Abuse

3. With limited play opportunities children may be impacted in the following ways:
   - not be given opportunities to find out what they like and are interested in
   - find it difficult to control their emotions
   - be unable to make friends and learn to get along with others
   - not learn how to use resources and equipment
   - not progress in all areas of development
   - find it difficult to adapt to different situations
   - lead to anxiety and depression.

### p131, Activity

Answers could include:

1. Other children might not want to play with Ruby because she does not know how to share and take turns, and she lacks social skills.

2. Ruby's behaviour might put other children off because they might feel unsafe and worry she will hurt them.

3. It will be even harder for Ruby to learn the social skills she needs to learn to play with other children.

### p131, Check my learning

1. Reasons for the importance of forming friendships.
   - Enables children to have positive interaction with others.
   - Provides acceptance and gives confidence.
   - Enhances learning and development because children learn from other children.

2. Reasons why children may have difficulties forming friendships. Any two of the following:
   - Delayed social skills
   - No strong bonds with adults
   - Delayed language skills
   - Personality traits in children that mean that they like to lead everything.

### p133, Activity

1. Challenging the authority of adults, defiant behaviour.

2. The children may copy Kieran because they may also not have many social skills yet and they look to each other for social cues.

3. Kieran's learning and development might be affected because other children might not want to play with him because of his disruptive behaviour. Also the disruptive behaviour may hinder his learning and concentration.

### p133, Check my learning

1. Examples of disruptive behaviour: hurting others, temper tantrums and emotional outbursts, defiance, interrupting others, breaking toys or other items, interrupting others.

2. Possible reasons for disruptive behaviour.
   - Delayed language development.
   - Sensory impairment.
   - Poor concentration skills, which could impair cognitive development and academic performance at school.

3. Examples of how disruptive behaviour by one child can affect the learning and development of others:

- It can distract children from learning because they are concentrating on the incident, even if they are not involved.

- It can make other children feel unsafe in the setting because they feel threatened by the disruptive child.

### p135, Activity

*Learner's own answer.*

### p135, Check my learning

1. Examples of transitions a child may go through:
   - Starting care or educational providers.
   - Birth of a new sibling.
   - Change in family structure.
   - Moving house.

2. Effects of starting care or educational providers on children of different ages:
   - 0–18 months – children may cry or become clingy.
   - Older children may ask lots of questions to reassure themselves that all of their needs will be met. For example, where the toilets are, people's names or whether their favourite activities will be available.

3. Similarities between the impact of a change of family structure and the birth of a sibling:

   Additional siblings, either step siblings or a new baby, can cause jealousy at any perceived extra attention, or attention being shared out between more children. This can cause a child to resent what they may see as an intrusion into their stable life. With the birth of a new sibling, a child may be cared for by grandparents or other relatives, to enable a new mother to recover, which can also cause feelings of insecurity.

### p137, Activity

*Learner's own answer.*

### p137, Check my learning

1. Definition of 'expected milestones':

   Milestones are aspects of children's development that are expected at certain ages. Milestones are used to measure children's development to see if they are developing at an expected rate.

2. Reasons why a child may not be meeting expected milestones:

   A child may have a delay either in one area of development, or several. If a child has a delay in all areas of development, it is called global development delay.

3. Being unable to initiate play may impact on a child's ability to socialise because they may not develop language and social skills.

### p139, Activity

*Learner's own answer.*

### p139, Check my learning

1. For outdoor play equipment 'varying levels' means the difference in height between a slide, a swing, stepping stones, etc. Indoors this relates to the heights of tables and chairs.

2. Children who struggle with fine motor skills may struggle with grasping small objects, manipulating materials such as playdough and using scissors or fastening buttons.

3. Children who tire easily may be going through a transition or not getting enough sleep.

### p141, Activity

1. Gabriel thinks Leah does not want to play with him; he does not realise that she did not understand him.

2. Leah may feel that the other children do not wish to play with her, and she may have lower self-esteem because she feels unwanted.

3. Leah may have limited experience of play or a delay in language development.

### p141, Check my learning

1. Difficulties for children who do not understand the rules of play could include the following:
   - not understanding turn-taking
   - having to wait
   - using equipment correctly
   - coming across as disruptive.

2. Difficulties in the communication of needs and preferences due to:
   - limited opportunities to play
   - delayed milestones due to communication and language skills
   - learning English as an additional language
   - difficulties with speaking, listening and processing information.

3. Impact of delayed cognitive and communication development on social and emotional development.
   - This can impact on their emotional development as it can lead to them feeling frustrated, which can impact negatively on their self-esteem.

### p143, Activity

*Learner's own answer.*

### p143, Check my learning

1. Co-operative play: from 3 to 4 years of age children begin to play well with their peers and learn to share and take turns. They often engage in the same play. This stage of play is called 'co-operative play'.

2. a) A child may isolate themselves because they:
   - prefer their own company
   - may lack sufficient social skills
   - feel unwanted due to family or other circumstances
   - may not understand the rules of play.

   b) May be isolated by other children because they:
   - behave disruptively
   - interrupt/spoil the play
   - unable to take turns.

   Isolation could be being used as a form of bullying by the other children.

3. Team and group activities enable children to develop social skills, such as bonds and friendships, respecting others, learning about differences, negotiating and co-operating skills and confidence to interact with others.

### p145, Activity

*Learner's own answer.*

### p145, Check my learning

1. The impact on a child's learning and development of being unable to express their thoughts and feelings:
   - May result in temper tantrums, disruptive behaviour or aggression towards others.

2. Reasons for difficulties with forming relationships with adults:
   - Previous experience of adults, e.g., abuse, neglect, trauma involving adults, limited experience of adults outside of the family circle.

3. The importance of routines for learning and development:
   - Routines make children feel emotionally safe and secure because they enable their lives to have predictability, which means they know what is going to happen next. When routines are changed, children become confused and unsettled, which can have a significant impact on their emotional development.

**p147, Activity**

| Activity | What are the hazards? (What could happen to harm the children?) | How can the risks be managed? (What can you do to ensure the children are kept safe?) |
|---|---|---|
| **Children under 18 months playing with playdough** | Children at this age put everything in their mouths. A child could choke. | An adult should be present at all times; non-toxic materials should always be used. |
| **Children 18 months–3 years playing with a play kitchen** | Children could trap their fingers in a cupboard or oven door. | An adult should supervise at all times. |
| **Children aged 3–5 playing in a tent** | The tent could collapse on the children. A child could pull it over. | All play equipment should be regularly monitored. An adult should be within seeing distance at all times. |

**p147, Check my learning**

1. It is important to check the symbols on children's toys to ensure that the toys are safe for children and will not harm them in any way.

2. It is important to manage risks and hazards when supporting children's play, learning and development because:

   • Children need experiences to help them to learn and develop and they need to be supported to manage risks for themselves.

   • Not allowing children to take part in activities due to risks can delay their development. E.g., preventing the use of an age-appropriate climbing frame could delay physical development.

3. When assessing the balance between the potential risk of harm and the benefit of children participating in activities you can minimise the amount of risk by carrying out **risk assessments** to identify potential hazards that could harm children and what you can do to prevent this from happening. For each activity that children take part in, adults should list all the things that could be dangerous in the activity and then consider what they can put in place to stop these being a risk to the children's safety.

**p149, Activity**

1. a) Francesca's father is concerned for her safety.

   b) They will support development of her fine motor skills and increase her confidence.

   c) Francesca could cut herself or another child who came too close.

   d) Providing safety scissors, explaining the correct use to Francesca, teaching her simple safety rules.

2. In the role play you should demonstrate the correct use of scissors.

**p149, Check my learning**

1. Positive risk taking is balancing the risk of harm against the benefits of children participating in activities.

2. 8 adults.

**p151, Activity**

*Learner's own answer.*

**p151, Check my learning**

1. Internet-enabled technology includes smart watches, app-enabled toys, voice-recognition toys and SMART devices that allow connection to different devices or networks.

2. Reasons for each of the following groups to use the internet:

| 0–18 months | 18 months–3 years | 3–5 years |
|---|---|---|
| To watch a cartoon or listen to soothing music | Play games and use apps | Chat online to friends and family |

3. Risks of older children using the internet

| Cyberbullying | This is bullying that takes place online and through social networks, games and text messages. |
|---|---|
| Online abuse | This is abuse that happens online. It can include cyberbullying, sexual abuse or exploitation, grooming or emotional abuse. |
| Sharing private information | Children may share personal information online, for example their home address or photographs/videos of themselves. |
| Phishing | Children may receive messages asking them for personal information such as passwords. The messages might look like they are coming from someone the child knows. |
| Falling for scams | Children may see offers on websites that promise them things, for example a new game in exchange for their parents' credit card information |
| Accidently downloading malware | This is software that is specifically designed to gain access to or damage a computer without the knowledge of the owner. Children may accidentally click on something that downloads a virus. |
| Inappropriate posts | Anything a child posts on the internet cannot be permanently deleted. Children need to be aware that things they post online could be seen for years. |

4. Parental controls are software tools that can be installed on internet-enabled devices to keep children safe online.

**p153, Activity**

*Learner's own answer.*

**p153, Check my learning**

1. Children should not reveal their full name, location, or family information.

2. Adults should explain what personal information means, how to block someone and how to report someone.

3. Adults can report age-inappropriate content online using the facility on social media sites, report this to supervisors/managers or, if appropriate, report it to the police.

**p155, Activity**

*Learner's own answer.*

**p155, Check my learning**

1. You should consider the width of doorways, aisles and corridors to ensure access for prams, pushchairs and wheelchairs.

2. Safe indoor environments for children:

| Safety considerations | 0–18 months | 18 months–3 years | 3–5 years |
|---|---|---|---|
| Doorways, aisles and corridors | Should be accompanied by adults or be carried to keep safe and reduce risk of injury to themselves or adults/older children | Must be kept clear due to trip hazards | Must be kept clear due to trip hazards |
| Furniture | Could block access to resources/play areas. Rounded corners to prevent injury | Could block view e.g. tall shelves. Could be a risk of falling if chairs over-balance. Rounded corners to prevent injury | Needs to be at the right height for children to use them. Rounded corners to prevent injury |
| Types of floor and floor coverings | Need carpeted area for safe rolling and crawling. Spillages, loose tiles could cause slips and trips | Loose tiles and spillages could cause slips and trips | Loose tiles and spillages could cause trips and slips |

### p157, Activity
Learner's own response.

### p157, Check my learning
1. Two benefits of organising resources for children are that it ensures everyone knows where everything is, and it minimises the risk of accidents and keeps children safe.
2. Well-organised resources mean that children will be better able to use the resources correctly.

### p159, Activity
Learner's own response.

### p159, Check my learning
1. Appropriate clothing:
- **Sunny weather:**
  Sunglasses
  Sun hats
  Long-sleeved t-shirts to protect arms from the sun
  High SPF sun screen should also be applied to protect children (with permission from their parents/carers)
- **Rain:**
  Rain coats with hoods
  Waterproof trousers
  Waterproof all-in-ones for children aged 0–18 months
  Wellington boots
  Umbrellas

- **Cold weather/snow:**
  Warm padded coats
  Warm padded all-in-ones for children aged 0–18 months
  Hats
  Gloves
  Scarves
  Warm socks
  Wellington boots/snow boots
  Lots of layers, such as fleeces and jumpers, underneath coats
2. When planning an outing you should consider potential weather changes and additional equipment for specific needs.
3. It is important to plan ahead for outings so that risks are minimised, children's needs are met holistically and parental permission has been obtained.

### p161, Activity
Learner's own response.

### p161, Check my learning
1. Suitable outdoor resources:

**0–18 months:** natural materials, sand, water, gravel, mud; wheeled toys, sit-and-ride toys, push-along toys

**18 months–3 years:** magnifying glasses to look for insects, plant pots and gardening tools to enable them to explore nature; wheeled toys, tricycles and toy prams

**3–5 years:** cardboard boxes, plastic crates, play tents to enable them to make dens and hideaways, bicycles. Children with mobility needs may need adapted equipment to support their play, learning and development.
2. Children need access to different outdoor spaces to develop interests and develop different areas. For example, spaces to play and be noisy and quiet places to read or chat in small groups. Children may feel intimidated by noisy play or may not feel sociable that day and need a quiet space to retreat to.

### p163, Activity
1. The United Nations Convention on the Rights of the Child states that every child has the right to an education. In order to do this, adults must ensure that all five areas of development are addressed when providing play and learning opportunities. These should be age appropriate and adapted where required for children with additional needs.
2. It is important to promote all five areas of development because a delay in one area of development may affect another. For example, if a child has a delay in physical development and cannot move around to participate in group activities, their social, emotional and language skills could also be delayed.

### p163, Check my learning
1. The right to learn means that adults have a legal duty to make sure that children are provided with an education from birth, in order to develop as fully as possible in all five areas.
2. A setting can be made inclusive by providing resources and toys that are adapted to meet individual needs of children, for example, books in larger print sizes for children with a visual impairment; or setting up home corners to reflect different cultures and by training staff in British Sign Language (BSL) to support children with hearing impairments.

### p165, Activity
1. During play, adults should role model sharing, taking turns and helping others. This will encourage children to be caring to others in their play. Adults should teach children to use resources safely and should be a role model for correct use.
2. It is important that the adult is available to supervise and support the children but they need to judge when it is best to leave children to get on with their play by themselves. If the adult is **intrusive** and interferes too much this could affect the children's development. For example, if you rush to stop a toddler opening the cupboard in the play kitchen and open it for him because you are afraid he might trap his fingers. This has stopped him from being independent and developing his physical skills.

3. Sometimes adults may need to give children some new ideas or resources to ensure that their play remains safe and to enable accessibility for the encouragement and stimulation of play. For example, an adult might discretely replace a broken toy with another one or add some water to the sand so that it is less likely to get in the children's eyes. The adult may suggest that children change what they are doing without making it obvious that this is a safety precaution.

4. Adults must take the children's needs and abilities into account as well as making sure play is suitable for all ages. Some children may be less confident and may need reassurance from an adult to join in. Others may need play to be made more exciting because they are ahead in their development and become easily bored. Adults also need to understand that play activities may need to be adapted to meet the needs of children who have additional needs. For example, having larger crayons in the mark making area for a child who has less developed fine motor skills.

## p165, Check my learning

1. Adults should intervene in children's play if something is not safe, or to help children to be respectful of others.

2. Keeping children safe:

| 0–18 months | 18 months–3 years | 3–5 years |
|---|---|---|
| Making sure that there are no small objects, which could cause a child to choke | Preventing the risk of accidents, such as anything that could trap small fingers | Ensuring that play areas out of sight, e.g., dens or tents are safe to use |

3. *Learner's own answer.*

## p167, Activity

*Learner's own answer.*

## p167, Check my learning

1. Adults can promote inclusion by not labelling a child, allowing a child to be independent, developing solutions to barriers to include the child in all activities, showing the child that they are valued and talking about what the child is good at.

2. Giving children choices:

| 0–18 months | Children can be given a treasure basket containing different items and they can choose independently which items to explore. |
|---|---|
| 18 months–3 years | Children could be asked which book they would like to look at with an adult. |
| 3–5 years | Children could be given a choice of what they would like to eat and could serve themselves at the table. |

3. The impact on the social and emotional development of 3–5-year-olds of being given choices:

- It supports children's development as it allows them to make decisions for themselves.
- It supports independence skills.

## p169, Activity

*Learner's own answer.*

## p169, Check my learning

1. Praise helps children to feel good about themselves. It builds self-esteem and confidence.

2. A suitable reward for a child of 0–18 months would be a clap and a smile.

3. Rewards can raise self-esteem and confidence.

## p171, Activity

*Learner's own answer.*

## p171, Check my learning

1. Adapting activities for all children allows them to become more tolerant of others, more patient and more adaptable. This supports their social and emotional development.

2. Social skills children may develop from adapted activities:

- Sharing and turn-taking
- Building up a good rapport with others
- Making friendships with children from different ethnicities and with different abilities
- Socialising with all genders.

## p173, Activity

*Learner's own answer.*

## p173, Check my learning

1. Ensuring sufficient space for children with physical needs:

- Tidy away resources that are not being used
- Organise toys and resources so that children can find them easily
- Arrange furniture and equipment with wide aisles
- Avoid rugs to prevent trip hazards
- Ensure there is access for wheelchairs, walkers and crutches

- Keep cupboard doors and draws closed so that children don't bang into these.

2. Suitable resources for support of the following:

- Grasping – books with tabs to support the turning of pages
- Holding – paintbrushes with knobs at the end of them
- Releasing – hand puppets, toys to push, e.g., pop-up toys
- Transferring – 0–18 months: shape sorters, 3–5 years: putting coins into a money-box.

3. Adaptations for children with visual impairments aged 3–5 years. For example:

- Providing books in large print for children with a visual impairment can support their cognitive/intellectual development and also build confidence and self-acceptance.
- Providing keyboards with brightly coloured or illuminated, larger keys can increase a child's sense of belonging to the group.

## p175, Activity

*Learner's own answer.*

## p175, Check my learning

The answers could include the following:

1. Support art activities by securing paper to tables with tape or reusable adhesive.

2. Mats could be placed on the floor to adapt the level during creative activities.

3. To enable full participation in activities and appropriate use of resources, comply with the United Nations Convention on the Rights of the Child.

## p177, Activity

*Learner's own answer.*

## p177, Check my learning

1. Adults can encourage children to learn and play near other children by placing painting easels facing each other rather than in a row during creative activities.

2. Some children may need activities shortening to make them more manageable. For example, for a two-year-old, putting on a coat can be broken down into small steps.

## p179, Activity

Your plan should state that you will:

- explain the activity to the children
- use one method, e.g., finger painting or rollers or brushes – as too many ideas could confuse the children
- use a limited number of colours – some children with cognitive needs may be overwhelmed by being offered too many choices

- make sure that each child can access materials easily
- keep the activity short – decide how long it should last
- give guidance if children need this, but allow them to work independently to support confidence and self-reliance
- arrange the activity so that children can see each other and talk to support social skills
- warn the children before you end the session, so that they can begin to finish their work.

**p179, Check my learning**

1. Apps and programmes can support children aged 3–5 who have cognitive and intellectual needs; children can press or click on a picture of what they want, and the computer/tablet speaks the word to the adult or other children.

2. Reasons for limiting the number of materials available for children 18 months–3 years:
   - some children with cognitive needs may be very rigid in their thinking
   - too many resources in one area could leave the child wondering what to do and what to choose. This could also be age related.

**p181, Activity**

*Learner's own answer.*

**p181, Check my learning**

1. How children may benefit from group and/or team activities:
   - Extends a child's speech and language and communication development.
   - Can allow some children to overcome the difficulties they have communicating with others.
   - Enables them to build friendships, build bonds and trust with adults and to learn to accept people around them.

2. The differences between PECS and Makaton:
   - Picture Exchange Communication System®(PECS) is a system that enables children to initiate their own conversation using picture cards.
   - Makaton is a form of communication where children use signs and symbols to support speech or instead of speech. Drawn symbols are used alongside signs made using hands and facial expressions.

**p183, Activity**

*Learner's own answer.*

**p183, Check my learning**

1. Nursery rhymes can be used to support children with communication and language needs because songs with actions can promote the identification of words.

2. The benefits of labelling equipment for children could include the following:
   - assists with tidying up
   - helps children learn the words for what is on the picture
   - supports children with the development of reading
   - enables children to know where things are
   - keeps things organised for the adults
   - helps children learn that words have meaning.

3. The benefits of displaying routines and activities as pictures:
   - enables children to understand the order in which the activities happen, so they know what will be coming next
   - pictures can also be used to give children step-by-step instructions for an activity or part of their routine.

**p185, Activity**

1. *Learner's own answers.*

**p185, Check my learning**

1. Adults may need to limit children's choice of activity to prevent stress.

2. Using a structured approach supports children experiencing transitions because: giving children a task to do during the transition will give them something to focus on and make them feel helpful, which will increase their self-esteem and reduce their worry, and will support their emotional development.

**p187, Activity**

1. The adult is not giving the children a choice as they have planned the activity and selected the materials to be used. The children are being directed to follow the adult's plan.

2. The children could find this frustrating because they are unable to express themselves in this activity. As the plan is prescriptive, children may be concerned that they are 'getting it wrong', which will not support their emotional development. Children may appreciate the structure, if they have stresses or worries, e.g., because they are going through a transition or are new to the setting.

**p187, Check my learning**

1. How adults can set out activities that focus on a child's area of interest:
   - set up different types of role play
   - use books that relate to issues a child is experiencing.

2. The benefits of giving children with additional needs choices:
   - builds self-esteem
   - children feel 'grown-up'
   - builds respect
   - develops problem-solving skills
   - gives children power and control over what they do
   - helps with decision-making later in life.

**p189, C3: Assessment practice**

1. **d.** A child finds it hard to explore

2. Possible answers:
   - They may not persevere with learning.
   - They may find it difficult to take turns in conversations.
   - They may lose interest very quickly.

3. a) Mrs Shah could shorten the project into smaller activities, breaking these down into smaller steps. This would support Rosa's concentration and memory skills, which could be affected by her cognitive delay.

   b) This would support Rosa's memory skills by seeing the same items in the same place every time she needed them. This would help Rosa to develop her long-term memory so that she can keep using this memory while she is working on the project.

   c) Mrs Shah could make her instructions to Rosa short and clear so that she can understand the words. This would raise Rosa's confidence so that she will use the words and increase her vocabulary. It would help Rosa and the other children if Mrs Shah used less complex language when she speaks in the class, so that Rosa feels included as part of the group. Mrs Shah should praise Rosa and all of the children when they communicate, so that they gain confidence. Repeating instructions to the children will help them remember and become familiar with the vocabulary used.

# Index